The Cycle of Juvenile Justice

The Cycle of Juvenile Justice

SECOND EDITION

Thomas J. Bernard and
Megan C. Kurlychek

OXFORD
UNIVERSITY PRESS
2010

OXFORD
UNIVERSITY PRESS

Oxford University Press, Inc., publishes works that further
Oxford University's objective of excellence
in research, scholarship, and education.

Oxford   New York
Auckland   Cape Town   Dar es Salaam   Hong Kong   Karachi
Kuala Lumpur   Madrid   Melbourne   Mexico City   Nairobi
New Delhi   Shanghai   Taipei   Toronto

With offices in
Argentina   Austria   Brazil   Chile   Czech Republic   France   Greece
Guatemala   Hungary   Italy   Japan   Poland   Portugal   Singapore
South Korea   Switzerland   Thailand   Turkey   Ukraine   Vietnam

Published by Oxford University Press, Inc.
198 Madison Avenue, New York, New York 10016

www.oup.com

Oxford is a registered trademark of Oxford University Press

Library of Congress Cataloging-in-Publication Data
Bernard, Thomas J.
The cycle of juvenile justice / Thomas J. Bernard and
Megan C. Kurlychek.—2nd. ed.
    p. cm.
Includes bibliographical references and index.
ISBN 978-0-19-537036-2 (pbk.)
1. Juvenile justice, Administration of—History.
2. Juvenile justice, Administration of—United States—History.
I. Kurlychek, Megan Clouser. II. Title.
HV9065.B47   2010
364.3609—dc22   2009036133

Printed in the United States of America
on acid-free paper

Acknowledgments

Thomas J. Bernard
July 23, 1945–July 28, 2009

I feel blessed to have had the pleasure of knowing Tom as a teacher, mentor, and eventually coauthor and friend. His illness and ultimate loss of life during the completion of this, what would turn out to be his final project, was not only a personal loss, but also a significant loss to the field.

Thomas Bernard was a great theorist, scholar, and mentor of others. Through his teaching and writing, he influenced many people in the field both personally and professionally. His works have helped others to organize and think about policy, use theory, and conduct research in a grounded, systematic, and scientific way. While Tom's contributions are far too lengthy to note, some highlights include such notable manuscripts as *Vold's Theoretical Criminology, Consensus Conflict Debate: Form and Content in Social Theories, Behind a Convict's Eyes: Doing Time in a Modern Prison, Life for a Life: Life Imprisonment, America's Other Death Penalty*, and, of course, the publication of the first edition of *The Cycle of Juvenile Justice* in 1991. Throughout all his work, Tom maintained the highest ethics and integrity and was wholeheartedly focused on truly improving the lives of those less fortunate.

Beyond the profession, Tom was truly a gift to his family and friends. Tom knew how to lead a balanced life. He grounded his professional career with a deep love of his family and friends; service to his field and community; and a sincere commitment to caring for others. Although Tom can no longer be with us in person, his spirit lives on through his work, and through those of us who had the unique experience of being mentored by this wonderful man.

Contents

1. Ideas and the Cycle of Juvenile Justice,   3

2. What Stays the Same in History?   10

3. The Origin of Juvenile Delinquency,   33

4. The Origin of Juvenile Justice: Juvenile Institutions,   48

5. The Origin of Juvenile Justice: The Juvenile Court,   71

6. The Supreme Court and Due Process,   95

7. Due Process and Adjudication Hearings:
   An Idea That Didn't Sell,   122

8. Disposition Hearings Today: The "Get Tough" Movement,   139

9. Youths in the Adult System,   163

10. Juvenile Justice in the Twenty-first Century,   187

11. The Lessons of History Applied Today,   206

12. The End of Juvenile Delinquency?   232

Index   237

The Cycle of Juvenile Justice

1

Ideas and the Cycle of Juvenile Justice

There is a cyclical pattern in juvenile justice, in which the same sequence of policies has been repeated over three times in the last two hundred years.[1] Present juvenile justice policies can be explained by this cycle, and future changes in these policies can be predicted by it. The specific sequence of policies in the cycle is described in figure 1.1.

The cycle begins at a time when justice officials and the general public are convinced that juvenile crime is at an exceptionally high level and that there are many harsh punishments but few lenient treatments for juvenile offenders. In this situation, justice officials often are forced to choose between harshly punishing juvenile offenders and doing nothing at all. As a consequence, many minor offenders are let off scot-free because lenient treatments are not available and because justice officials believe that the harsh punishments will make the minor offenders worse.

Further along in the cycle, justice officials and the general public eventually conclude that the "forced choice" between harsh punishments and doing nothing is part of the problem. That is, they come to believe that harsh punishment actually increases juvenile crime but that doing nothing at all increases it, too. The solution is to introduce lenient treatments for juvenile offenders. A major reform of juvenile justice policies accomplishes this task, and everyone is optimistic that juvenile crime rates will soon decline.

Juvenile crime is thought to be unusually high. There are many harsh punishments and few lenient treatments. Officials often are forced to choose between harshly punishing the juvenile offenders and doing nothing at all. ⇒	Juvenile crime is thought to be unusually high and is blamed on the "forced choice." That is, both harshly punishing and doing nothing at all are thought to increase juvenile crime.
⇑	⇓
Juvenile crime is thought to be unusually high and is blamed on the lenient treatment. Harsh punishments gradually expand and lenient treatments gradually contract. ⇒	A major reform introduces lenient treatments for juvenile offenders. This creates a middle ground between harshly punishing and doing nothing at all.

Figure 1.1. The Sequence of Policies in the Cycle of Juvenile Justice

But then both justice officials and the general public remain convinced that juvenile crime is at an exceptionally high level. After some time, they begin to blame the lenient treatments for the high crime rates. Initially, the responses to serious juvenile offenders are "toughened up," so that those offenders receive harsh punishments rather than lenient treatments. The responses for average or typical juvenile offenders are then also "toughened up" so that they, too, begin to receive harsh punishments. This process continues until there are again many harsh punishments available for responding to juvenile offenders and few lenient treatments. At that point, justice officials again are often forced to choose between harshly punishing juvenile offenders and doing nothing at all. Still, justice officials and the general public remain convinced that juvenile crime is at an all-time high. The cycle has returned to where it started.

Ideas That Drive the Cycle

There are three primary ideas that perpetuate this cycle. That is, at every stage of the cycle, justice officials and the general public believe: (1) that juvenile crime is at an exceptionally high level, (2) that present juvenile justice policies make the problem worse, and (3) that changing those policies will reduce juvenile crime. These people usually believe that their ideas are new and different, but in fact they have been continuously believed for at least two hundred years. These ideas drive us from one policy to the next as we pursue a lower level of juvenile crime.

Two other perceptions also change as the cycle moves from policy to policy: the idea of juvenile delinquency and the idea of juvenile justice. The idea of juvenile delinquency is a general overview of what delinquency is and how it originates. The idea does not have to be very specific and it does not have to explain all delinquency. For example, one person might think that delinquency in general is criminal behavior committed by juveniles who care only about themselves, not about the rights of other people. Another person might regard delinquency as a cry for help from juveniles who come from neglectful or abusive home environments. Closely related to this idea of delinquency is the idea of the delinquent him or herself. That is, in the first instance, the delinquent is viewed as more like a hardened criminal than like a child; in the second instance, the delinquent is seen as more of a child victim than a hardened criminal.

The ideas of delinquency and of the delinquent are of paramount importance because people have an idea of juvenile justice that is associated with their ideas of juvenile delinquency and the juvenile delinquent. In the example above, the person viewing the juvenile as a hardened criminal would probably favor policies that punish that juvenile in proportion to the offense committed, similar to the philosophy of the adult criminal justice system. The person viewing the juvenile as a victim probably would favor policies that respond to that juvenile's cry for help, either by aiding the juvenile directly or by addressing the neglectful and abusive social environment in which the child lives.

Reforms of the juvenile justice system can, then, be phrased in terms of these two types of ideas. The idea of juvenile justice is the reform itself: it provides a brief and readily understandable image of the policies that the reformer wants to implement. The idea of juvenile delinquency explains why the reformer thinks the new policy will work by proposing a simple image of the kind of people delinquents are. That is, if delinquents really are the way the reformer describes, then the proposed policy will work when it is put into practice. If, however, delinquents are quite different, then the new policy will not work and may even make the problem of delinquency worse.

For example, those who favor punishment and deterrence policies (an idea of juvenile justice) typically describe delinquents as in the first example above (i.e., criminals who care only for their own well-being and do not care about the rights of others). If this image of the juvenile delinquent is correct, then punishment and deterrence policies probably will reduce delinquency, but reform and rehabilitation policies probably will have no effect and might even make the problem worse. If, however, delinquency is a cry for help from victims of neglectful and abusive environments, as proposed in the alternative example, then punishment and deterrence policies probably will have no effect and might even make the problem worse, while reform and rehabilitation policies probably will reduce delinquency. Thus, to understand juvenile justice policy and practice, we must begin with an understanding of the reformers' ideas about juvenile delinquency and the juvenile delinquent.

Ideas in History, Philosophy, and Law

Our ideas about the world, and how it works, are inevitably shaped by the time period in which we live. For example, at the time of Galileo, it was presumed that the earth was the center of the universe. Galileo's proposal that it was not that way earned him one of the first documented sentences of "house arrest" for his criminal ideas. On the contrary, today if someone suggested that the earth was the center of the universe, he would be subject to ridicule. Our ideas about juvenile delinquents and juvenile justice are no different. These ideas emerge at certain points in history, and they reflect the historical conditions of the time.

Ideas are elaborated into philosophies, in the sense of their being rational, coherent, and organized ways of understanding and interpreting the world. The philosophies then form the basis for laws that define juvenile delinquency, direct the juvenile justice system, and determine juvenile justice policies. We propose, therefore, that what we define as juvenile delinquency and juvenile justice can be understood only by studying the ideas in the context of history, philosophy, and law; that is the approach taken in this book. In addition, we propose that the main reason for studying the past is to better understand how we arrived at our present state of being and where we might be headed in the future. This is true for all aspects of social life, but it is especially the purpose of this examination of the history of juvenile delinquency and juvenile justice.

Purpose and Organization

In this book, we will be making the primary argument that a stable and reasonable juvenile justice policy can be established only by breaking the cycle of juvenile justice. We need to open our eyes to the historical forces that have driven this cycle, so that we can learn from the past instead of blindly repeating it. More than anything else, this requires that we change our ideas about juvenile delinquency and juvenile justice.[2] Here, we challenge the reader to rethink his or her ideas about who is a delinquent, what constitutes delinquency, and what the proper response (or lack of response) to delinquency might be.

In chapter 1, we argue that a cycle of juvenile justice exists and that ideas drive that cycle. In chapter 2, we begin to elaborate on this argument, identifying aspects of juvenile delinquency and juvenile justice that have remained the same for at least two hundred years. For example, we discuss how young people, and young males in particular, have always committed more than their share of crime. People tend to believe that this situation is a recent phenomenon and that young people were not like this back in "the good old days." But this misconception keeps us stuck in that cyclical search for new juvenile justice policies that can return us to this imagined utopian past.

Chapter 3 takes a closer look at what we define as juvenile delinquency. Here, we make the controversial argument that juvenile delinquency itself changed greatly about two hundred years ago, and that the behaviors we typically describe as juvenile delinquency today first appeared in the United States and Western Europe around the year 1800. We argue that this "modern phenomenon of juvenile delinquency" arose because of urbanization, industrialization, and the breakdown of traditional social controls. This same modern phenomenon later appeared in other places in the world as those locations underwent similar processes of modernization.

Chapters 4 and 5 then examine how American society responded to this new phenomenon of delinquency, with the development of the first juvenile institution and the first juvenile court. Examples from court cases are used to demonstrate how our evolving definition of delinquency and the delinquent have directly impacted our view of what should constitute juvenile justice.

In chapter 6 we begin to explore some more recent developments in juvenile justice, beginning with the due process movement of the 1960s and early 1970s that represented the first U.S. Supreme Court intervention in the internal workings and processes of juvenile justice. Chapter 7 then provides a realistic look at the aftermath of the due process movement, documenting in detail which proposed changes did and did not occur to the adjudicatory stage of juvenile justice processing. That is, while the Court had lofty intentions of introducing due process rights into the adjudicatory stage, we find that the actual practice has fallen short of this ideal.

Chapter 8 then takes a closer look at the effects of the due process movement on the dispositional stage of juvenile justice processing. While the Supreme Court had introduced due process rights at the adjudicatory hearing, so as to focus on accurate fact-finding, it maintained a traditional child-centered focus in the dispositional stage to sustain what it saw as the best feature of the juvenile court. Similar to chapter 7, chapter 8 compares the Court's intentions with actual practice. Indeed, in this chapter we find that not only were the Court's intentions not implemented but, in actuality, almost the polar opposite was true, as the nation was swept by what is now referred to as the "get tough" movement.

One of the greatest impacts of the "get tough" movement was not on the process of juvenile justice but, rather, on its jurisdiction, with many new and creative ways emerging for youths to be tried as adults in the adult criminal justice system. Chapter 9 takes a look at some of these mechanisms, as well as their impact on the actual outcomes for youths processed as adults.

Chapter 10 then brings us up to the close of the twenty-first century, examining the implementation of those "get tough" approaches, as well as other new, and sometimes not-so-new, ideas and policies emerging today on the juvenile justice scene. We look at the changes that have occurred to see how they fit within the juvenile justice cycle and what directions they might predict or prescribe for the future.

Chapters 11 and 12 end the book, offering our vision and hopes for the future of juvenile justice. In our concluding remarks we take the liberty of stepping outside the confines of our lessons from history and exploring what the future might look like if we learned from, instead of merely repeated, the past.

NOTES

1. A similar analysis of cycles in juvenile justice can be found in Theodore N. Ferdinand, "Juvenile Delinquency or Juvenile Justice: Which Came First?" *Criminology* 27, no. 1 (February 1989): 79–106. Ferdinand argued, as do we, that there were increases in the rates and seriousness of delinquency at the time of the origin of juvenile justice, but Ferdinand attributes those increases to the juvenile justice system itself, while we attribute them to urbanization, industrialization, and the breakdown of traditional social controls. We agree with Ferdinand that reforms initially were directed toward minor offenders and were gradually applied to more serious offenders. We also agree that the impetus for reform comes when officials face the choice between harsh punishments and doing nothing at all. Ferdinand, however, argues that each successive reform widens the net by "embracing ever more normal populations," whereas we depict a cycle in which minor offenders are brought into the system with the reform, gradually excluded from it as the system turns its attention to serious

offenders, and then brought back into it with the next reform. For an analysis of cycles in this century, see J. Lawrence, Schultz, "The Cycle of Juvenile Court History," *Crime and Delinquency* 19 (October 1973): 457–476. Analyses that are consistent with a cyclical pattern can also be found in James O. Finkenauer, *The Panacea Solution* (Englewood Cliffs, N.J.: Prentice-Hall, 1981); and John R. Sutton, *Stubborn Children* (Berkeley: University of California Press, 1988). For a more general argument about cycles related to juvenile justice and focused on more recent times, see James Gilbert, *A Cycle of Outrage* (New York: Oxford University Press, 1986).

2. While we argue that juvenile justice policy is the product of cultural or ideological factors, we also argue that juvenile delinquency is the produce of structural factors, including urbanization, industrialization, and the breakdown of the traditional structural controls associated with peasant and feudal societies. See our discussion of the origin of juvenile delinquency in chapter 3 and the end of juvenile delinquency in chapter 10.

2

What Stays the Same in History?

Students often view history as a large and uninteresting pile of information about what happened in the past that they are expected to memorize and repeat on a test. In fact, the main reason for studying the past is to better understand how we arrived at our present situation and where we might be headed in the future. This is true for all aspects of social life and is the purpose of this examination of the history of juvenile delinquency and juvenile justice.

Studying history allows us to see ourselves in a way that otherwise is not possible. Imagine, for example, a fish swimming in water. There is a sense in which the fish does not see the water; rather, the water is its whole world. Now, imagine yourself standing on a dock looking down at that fish. Because you are outside of the water, you see both the fish and the water in which it swims. There is a sense in which you understand the fish's world better than the fish because you can look at it from the outside.

We are like the fish, in that we are immersed in our historical context just as the fish is immersed in the water. Someone standing outside our historical context can observe us, just as we could see the fish in the water. But we normally have no sense of our own context—to us, it is the whole world.

Studying history is one way to get "outside" our historical context and thus gain a perspective on it. Looked at in that way, studying history does not mean memorizing information about some distant time and place. Instead, it means becoming immersed in a different historical context, just as if the fish suddenly jumped out of the water and stood on the dock with you. Once you have "swum" in a different context, you can go back to your own context and view it through a broader lens. You acquire a new understanding of the world in which you live.

What Stays the Same and What Changes?

We start this book by asking a question about juvenile delinquency and juvenile justice: "What has stayed the same in the past and what has changed?" As in most studies of the past, our goal really is to better understand the present and to get an idea of what the future might hold. This question serves that purpose because whatever has changed in the past has at least a pretty good chance of changing again in the future, and whatever has not changed at all in the past will, in all likelihood, stay the same in the foreseeable future (although not necessarily). Thus, the question is intended to establish a baseline for what we can and cannot expect from juvenile delinquency and juvenile justice policy in the present and future.

In this chapter, the precise question we ask is: "What aspects of juvenile delinquency and juvenile justice have stayed the same for at least two hundred years (i.e., since around the year 1800)?" If there are aspects of juvenile delinquency and juvenile justice that have not changed for at least two hundred years, then we will infer that those aspects are not likely to change in the near future in response to new and different policies that we might implement, even if those policies seem to make a great deal of sense to us.

There are at least five aspects of juvenile delinquency and juvenile justice that we believe have, indeed, stayed the same for at least the past two hundred years.

1. Juveniles, especially young males, commit more crime than members of other groups.
2. There are special laws that only juveniles are required to obey.
3. Juveniles are typically punished less severely than adults who commit the same offenses.
4. Many people believe that the current group of juveniles commits more frequent and more serious crimes than juveniles in the past (that is, there is a "juvenile crime wave" at the present time).
5. Many people blame juvenile justice policies for the supposed juvenile crime wave, arguing that they are too lenient (serious offenders laugh at "kiddie court") or that they are too harsh (minor offenders are embittered and channeled into a life of crime).

Although these five aspects have stayed the same for at least two hundred years, at each point in time people have generally believed that things were different only thirty or forty years ago. Thus, these five unchanging aspects are often associated with the "myth of the good old days" and with the optimistic view that juvenile crime could and would end if only we would implement the juvenile justice policies we had back then. In all likelihood, this is a false view. Let us take a closer look at each aspect to further understand this phenomenon.

The Behavior of Youth, Especially Young Males

Regardless of whether crime is high or low at a particular time or place, young people (and especially young males) commit a greater proportion of crimes than would be expected from their representation in the population.[1] For example, juveniles between the ages of 14 and 17 constitute about 3 percent of the U.S. population, according to 2006 estimates from the U.S. Census.[2] If they were arrested at the same rate as everyone else, they would account for about 3 percent of all arrests. Instead, they account for almost twice as many arrests as adults, including twice as many arrests for serious, violent crimes and almost four times as many arrests for serious property crimes. Moreover, of those juveniles arrested, more than 70 percent were male, and when considering violent offenders, over 80 percent were male.[3] Thus, at present, we see that young males do, indeed, appear to commit more than their fair share of crimes. This is not, however, as we noted, a recent phenomenon and can be traced historically through time.

Juvenile Crime in Earlier Times

Even when juvenile arrest rates were what we now consider low, people were concerned about how much crime juveniles committed. For example, in 1938, England was alarmed by a report that found that convictions of males peaked at age 13 and that the probability of conviction was greater from ages 11 to 17 than at any other age.[4] In the United States, a report in 1940 pointed out that "young people between 15 and 21 constitute only 13% of the population, but their share in the total volume of serious crime committed far exceeds their proportionate representation."[5] Extensive publicity about the juvenile crime wave followed in 1941 and 1942.[6] The FBI supported this publicity with statistics that showed large increases in delinquency, but the Children's Bureau, a government agency that also monitored delinquency, said that the increases were due to changes in reporting practices by police and court agencies.

These concerns are not confined to our century. In the middle of the 1800s, many young men roamed the Wild West with guns strapped to their hips, looking for trouble. Although stories about people like Billy the Kid were greatly exaggerated into legends, this was still an exceptionally violent period.[7] For example, in the early 1800s, there were a large number of stories in the press about the extensive criminality of youth.[8]

A commentator on the problem of crime in London during the 1800s was alarmed by the volume of juvenile crime: "It is a most extraordinary fact, that half the number of persons convicted of crime have not attained the age of discretion."[9] About that time, there were 3,000 prisoners in London under the age of 20, half of whom were under 17 and some of whom were as young as 6.[10] These convictions were not merely for minor offenses or youthful misbehaviors. In 1785, the solicitor-general of England stated in the House of Commons that eighteen out of twenty offenders executed in London the previous year were under the age of 21.

Gang fights are often viewed as a modern phenomenon, but Shakespeare's play *Romeo and Juliet*, set in fifteenth-century Italy, involves what we would now call a gang fight. The young men of the Montague family, which includes Romeo, have been in a running battle with the young men of the Capulet family, which includes Juliet. On a hot summer day with "the mad blood stirring," the two groups happen to run into each other on the street. In the initial exchange, a polite greeting ("Gentlemen, good day: a word with one of you") is answered by a challenge to fight ("And but one word with one of us? Couple it with something; make it a word and a blow"). After a few more exchanges, the fight begins and two youths, both about 16 years old, are killed. The events in this story were placed in fifteenth-century Italy, but they could have been situated in the United States in modern times. In fact, the musical, and later movie, *West Side Story* was based on *Romeo and Juliet* but set in New York City in the 1950s. If the play were written today, it might take place on the streets of Los Angeles.

We could extend this tale back to the first crime recorded in the Bible, in which Cain (the eldest son of Adam and Eve) killed his younger brother, Abel. Ever since then, young people in general, and young men in particular, have been committing crimes at a greater rate than other people.

Recent Changes in Juvenile Crime in the United States

Although the main point here is to highlight the consistent overrepresentation of young males in offender populations, we would be amiss if we did not note the changes and trends in juvenile arrest patterns over time, as well as give due consideration to their various interpretations.

Prior to 1952, juvenile arrest rates in the United States were fairly low and fairly stable. In 1951, for example, juveniles accounted for 4.5 percent of all arrests, including 3.7 percent of arrests for serious violent crimes and 14.6 percent of arrests for serious property crimes. With some minor fluctuations, such as a temporary increase during World War II, these figures had been stable at least back to the beginning of the twentieth century.[11]

While low by today's standards, juvenile crime was considered a serious problem at the time. A textbook published in 1954 included the following statement:

> Nowhere does the failure of crime control show up more clearly than among our youth. Even before World War II, according to one study, national statistics indicated that some two million of forty-three million boys and girls in the United States below the age of eighteen years came to the attention of the police annually. Youth play a top-heavy part in the traditional crimes that feed the headlines and for which arrests are made. They frequently commit the familiar crimes against property, often with attendant violence, and their inexperience and lack of judgment make them relatively easy to apprehend.[12]

Juvenile arrests began to rise in 1952, and continued to increase until they peaked in 1974.[13] In that year, juveniles accounted for 45 percent of all arrests, including 22.6 percent of those for serious violent crimes and 50.7 percent of arrests for serious property crimes. That was also the year in which the total juvenile population (i.e., everyone in the country between the ages of 10 and 17 years old) peaked at about 34 million. The juvenile population then declined to approximately 28 million, a decrease of about 20 percent, but by 2006 it had returned almost back to its earlier level.[14]

The decline in the juvenile population was accompanied by a decline in juvenile arrests from 1974 through the late 1980s. Then, juvenile arrests began to increase again, until they again peaked in 1993 and 1994. Not surprisingly, the juvenile population hit a low in 1984 and then began increasing simultaneously with the rise in juvenile delinquency. However, while the juvenile population has continued to increase since that time, juvenile arrests have decreased by about 48 percent from their peak in 1994 through 2004.[15] This pattern primarily mimics trends in adult arrests during this latter time period. These reported trends in juvenile arrests are subject to several interpretations, and they suffer from the same biases found in all official arrest statistics. First and foremost, since many crimes go unreported to police, these data most likely greatly underestimate the overall frequency of delinquency. Second, while the trends in arrests may represent changes in actual behavior, it also likely that, to some extent, they represent changes in the behavior of justice officials, as well as changes in the social tolerance for certain types of behaviors. For example, as previously noted, the FBI had reported great increases in juvenile delinquency in the early 1940s, while the Children's Bureau interpreted these statistics as changes in police and court behavior.[16] Despite these limitations, we believe that what can be ascertained in general from the data is that overall trends in juvenile crime can, to at least some extent, be linked to fluctuations in the overall population of young males in the country. That is, the more young males there are, the more juvenile delinquency there is.

The Behavior of Young Males as an Aspect that Remains the Same

These examples illustrate that stories about the criminality of young people, and of young males in particular, are not unique to a particular time or place. We are always aware of this phenomenon, but we tend to lose track of the fact that it has always been this way. Thus, we should expect that this will continue into the future. While the overall incidence and rate of crime may change, what remains constant is that young people, especially young males, are disproportionately involved in these activities. Some people may argue that if only we would implement a particular policy (e.g., death penalty, psychoanalysis, lengthy prison sentences, education, or employment training), then juveniles will stop committing more than their share of crime. The lessons of history suggest that these people are wrong.

Special Laws for Juveniles

A second aspect that has stayed the same for at least two hundred years (and seems to have remained constant over recorded history) is that certain offenses apply only to youth and not to adults. At present, these are called "status offenses," since they apply only to people with the status of being a juvenile. The most common laws covering these offenses today are those that make it illegal for youth under a given age to run away from home, to refuse to attend school (truancy), and to refuse to obey parents (incorrigibility). Other common status offenses involve drinking alcoholic beverages, violating curfews, and engaging in consensual sexual activities.

Adults are allowed to do all these things, but juveniles who do are committing a punishable offense. Adults who do not like their families can move out, but a juvenile who moves out may be arrested by the police. Adults can quit school or quit their jobs, but a juvenile who quits school may be taken to juvenile court and placed on probation. Adults are free to engage in most consensual sexual activities, but juveniles who engage in the same activities may be sent to a juvenile institution.

Status Offenses in Earlier Times

Originally, offenses that applied solely to youth were focused on the duties that people held for their parents. In the code of Moses in the Bible, for example, there were severe penalties, including death, for striking or cursing your parents,[17] although these severe punishments were rarely carried out.

The Puritans made these biblical passages the basis for a "stubborn child" law in 1646. That law "served as a direct or indirect model for legislation enacted by every American state making children's misbehavior a punishable offense."[18] It was substantially modified through the years, but the law remained in force in Massachusetts until 1973. Since the days of the Puritans, there has been a continued expansion of attempts through legal means to control the noncriminal but "offensive" behavior of children.

Decriminalization? Deinstitutionalization?

Today, there is considerable debate about how to handle these status offenses. Some people argue that the laws against these activities should be repealed; this implies decriminalization of status offenses. People who favor decriminalization argue that status offenses are harmful to the youths who engage in them, but that handling these offenses in juvenile court makes a bad situation worse. They argue that voluntary social service agencies, not the juvenile court, should intervene in these cases.

Other people argue that juveniles who commit status offenses should be handled in juvenile courts, but they should never be locked up for such offenses. These people favor deinstitutionalization of status offenses. This is generally considered a more moderate response, since the offenses remain subject to the juvenile court.

In theory, both deinstitutionalizing and decriminalizing status offenses mean that the juvenile court has little to no power over these offenders. However, in practice we find that the system has found ways to exert considerable power over these juveniles whether or not the laws claim to have decriminalized or deinstitutionalized the offenders.

For instance, in states that have decriminalized status offenses, such as Washington, there has been a tendency to "redefine" status offenders as criminal offenders so that they can still be processed through the juvenile courts.[19] The bottom line is that, for the purpose of sending the juvenile to an institution, almost every status offender does *something* that can be defined as a criminal event. For example, before the law was changed, a youth who refused to obey his parents could have been brought into court on a charge of incorrigibility (a status offense), but he would have been sent to an institution only if court officials thought it was in his "best interests." After the law was changed, that youth could not be sent to an institution at all, but if court officials thought it was in the youth's "best interests" to be sent to an institution, then they could charge the youth with some criminal offense. For example, if he threatened a parent or teacher (but did not harm them in any way), he could be charged with simple assault. The youth then could be sent to an institution (since it was in his "best interests"), but he would now be labeled a delinquent offender rather than a status offender.

The more modest effort to deinstitutionalize status offenses has also resulted in redefining those status offenders as delinquent offenders. This idea was originally embodied in a federal policy that guided the provision of federal funds for juvenile justice to the states. Early figures suggested that almost all status offenders were redefined as delinquent offenders, so that they could be institutionalized.[20] Despite this tendency, many judges opposed the deinstitutionalization policy because they felt that they needed the direct power to institutionalize status offenders.[21]

In response to their concerns, then, federal policy was modified so that a violation of a condition of probation would be considered a criminal offense. Thereafter, a youth charged with a status offense could be brought into court and placed on probation. One of the conditions of probation would be that the youth not commit the status offense again. A youth who committed additional status offenses would then be considered to have violated probation. Because violation of probation is a delinquent offense, this same youth could then be sent to an institution. For example, in 2003, while only 5 percent of all juvenile offenders in residential placement nationally were officially there for status offenses, an additional 15 percent were committed for a technical violation of probation. This figure varied dramatically by state, from a low of 1 percent in Rhode Island to a high of 37 percent in Hawaii. Overall, in at least eight states (Alabama, Alaska, Hawaii, Illinois, New Jersey, South Carolina, Utah, and Wyoming), over one-fourth of all juveniles in placement were there for a technical violation of a condition of probation or court order.[22]

Status Offenses as an Aspect that Stays the Same

The lessons of history suggest that neither decriminalization nor deinstitutionalization will work in the long run. Status offenses go back to the beginning of recorded history. Because this is something that has stayed the same over this long span, it seems unlikely to change in the future.

To some extent, these changes have made the institutionalization of status offenders invisible.[23] Kids are still institutionalized for truancy, but they are no longer defined as status offenders. That is, they either are charged with some minor criminal offense and institutionalized for that offense or school attendance is made a condition of probation so that further truancy is defined as a criminal offense.

It may seem to be a good idea to remove jurisdiction for status offenses from the juvenile court, but the lessons of history also suggest that this will never occur. There have been separate laws for juveniles for as far back as history records, and attempts to change these laws have only resulted in new laws or new approaches to further control these types of behavior.

Mitigation of Punishments for Juveniles

A third aspect that has stayed the same for at least two hundred years (and, indeed, over history) is that juveniles are treated more leniently than adults when they commit the same offenses. That is, when a juvenile is adjudicated for a crime, the punishment is not as severe as when an adult is convicted of the same crime.

Mitigation in Earlier Times

The Code of Hammurabi, written over 4,000 years ago, indicated that juveniles were to be treated more leniently than adults. In ancient Jewish law, the Talmud specified the conditions under which immaturity was to be considered for more lenient punishment. Under these provisions, there was no corporal punishment before the age of puberty, which was set at 12 for females and 13 for males, and no capital punishment before the age of 20. Similar leniency was found among the Muslims, where children under the age of 17 were generally exempt from retaliation and the death penalty, although they could be corrected.

Roman law also included a lengthy history of mitigated punishments for children. As early as the Twelve Tables (about 450 BC), there was absolute immunity from punishment for children below a certain age.

Originally, immunity applied only to children who were incapable of speech, but eventually it was applied to all children below the age of 7. In addition, children below puberty have been given reduced punishment under Roman law since around AD 500. Justinian, for example, established puberty at 14 for boys and 12 for girls. In between age 7 and puberty, criminal responsibility was made dependent on age, nature of offense, and mental capacity.

Under ancient Saxon law, a child below the age of 12 could not be found guilty of any felony, and a child between 12 and 14 might be acquitted or convicted on the basis of natural capacity. After 14, there was no mitigation.

English common law had acquired its modern form by about the middle of the 1300s, and it was summarized by Sir William Blackstone in 1769.[24] In general, the law at that time was based on the following framework for mitigating punishments:

Below the age of 7, juveniles have no responsibility for their actions and therefore cannot be punished for any crimes they commit.

From 7 to 14, juveniles are presumed to lack responsibility for their actions, but the prosecution can argue that they should be punished in spite of their youth.

From 14 to 21, juveniles are presumed to be responsible for their actions, but the defense can argue that they should not be punished, despite their age.

After the age of 21, everyone is responsible for his or her actions and therefore is punished to the full extent of the law.

Mitigation in the Juvenile Court

Today, the juvenile court embodies the concept of less responsibility, and therefore less punishment, for juveniles. In most states, juveniles below the age of 18 are sent to juvenile court when they commit offenses, and the punishments given there are generally more lenient than those given in adult courts for similar offenses. A few states have lower ages for juvenile court jurisdiction. For example, in North Carolina and New York State, only juveniles 15 and younger are sent to juvenile court, while those who are 16 and older are tried in adult court.

Juveniles normally sent to juvenile court may instead be tried in adult courts when they commit serious or frequent offenses. Such procedures go by a variety of names, including *waiver, transfer, certification,* and *direct filing.*[25] Under these provisions, which will be discussed further in chapter 9, juveniles may be treated in the same way as youth ages 7 to 14 were treated under English common law—that is, presumed that they are not fully responsible for their actions—but the prosecutor can argue that there are special reasons they should be tried in adult court.

In addition, in some states, certain offenses are not considered to be within the jurisdiction of the juvenile court at all or only under certain circumstances (dependent on the juvenile's age and prior record). For example, in Pennsylvania, jurisdiction for all homicides lies in criminal courts. Youths charged with this offense are taken directly to criminal court, even if they are only 10 years old. There, the defense lawyer can argue that, because of immaturity, the youth should be handled in juvenile court. If the judge agrees, the youth can be transferred back to juvenile court. These youths are treated the way youths age 14 to 21 were treated under English common law—that is, they are presumed responsible for their actions but the defense may attempt to prove otherwise.

Mitigation as an Aspect that Stays the Same

The specific rules for mitigating punishments for juveniles have changed over time. At some times and in some places, mitigation has extended all the way to age 21, while at other times and places it has applied only to ages 12 or 14. At some times and places, punishments for juveniles have been greatly reduced or even eliminated, and at others they have been only slightly reduced. In the future, we can expect that the specific rules for mitigating punishments of juveniles will continue to change, but the mitigation of punishment itself will remain. Whether we provide greater reductions in punishments or lesser, to more juveniles or to fewer, the mitigation of punishment will remain a feature of any system for processing juvenile offenders.

Views of Adults About the Behavior of Youth

According to Frank R. Donovan, "every generation since the dawn of time has denounced the rising generation as being inferior in terms of manners and morals, ethics and honesty."[26] The view that adults hold of juveniles is different from how juveniles actually behave. This perception goes as far back as historical records, so the situation probably will remain the same into the future. For purposes of this book, we refer to this phenomenon as the "myth of the good old days."

Many adults today complain about how rotten kids are, but this feeling was expressed in colonial America as well. Harvey Green has observed:

One of the most consistent and common themes in the history of relations between American parents and their children is criticism of the younger generation. From almost the moment the settlers of Jamestown and Plymouth stepped off their boats in the early seventeenth century, there arose the cry that children were disobeying their parents as never before.[27]

This phenomenon is not confined to America, either. Over two thousand years before the Pilgrims arrived on American shores, Socrates had his own complaints about youth:

Children now love luxury. They have bad manners, contempt for authority, they show disrespect for elders and love chatter in place of exercise. They no longer rise when their elders enter the room. They contradict their parents, chatter before company, gobble up dainties at the table, and tyrannize over their teachers.[28]

We can go back even further than that. Fourteen hundred years before Socrates, a Summarian father wrote to his son:

Because my heart had been sated with weariness of you, I kept away from you and heeded not your fears and grumblings. Because of your clamorings, I was angry with you. Because you do not look to humanity, my heart was carried off as if by an evil wind. Your grumblings have put an end to me; you have brought me to the point of death. . . . Others like you support their parents by working. . . . They multiply barley for their father, maintain him in barley, oil, and wool. You're a man when it comes to perverseness, but compared to them you are not a man at all. You certainly don't labor like them—they are the sons of fathers who make their sons labor, but me, I didn't make you work like them.[29]

Juveniles as Serious Criminals

Most of the above quotes apply to what we now call status offenses. Perhaps kids today are engaged in serious violent crimes instead of just the delinquencies of the past? Perhaps today many kids are the worst kind of criminals? As Dr. Don Boyes of Cornerstone Communications argues, "Juveniles used to be considered young, athletic, students with ruddy complexion, squeaky voice and acne, but now they are often vindictive, vicious and violent criminals."[30]

Certainly, headlines in newspapers today often support that view. For example, the following headlines are from newspapers in October 2007:[31]

Covington Tennessee Boy, 13, Found With Gun In School

Norristown, Pennsylvania, Boy, 14, Charged With School Shooting Plot

Saginaw, Michigan, Boy, 15, Opens Fire At Football Game, Injures 4

Scranton, Penn., Boy, 16, Charged In Columbine-Style Plot

Cleveland 14-Year-Old Shoots Two Teachers, Two Students At High School And Then Kills Himself

Many people believe that the problem is that juveniles today are being raised without morals. For example, John W. Whitehead argues:

Religion and moral values were once the glue that held our communities and families together. They taught us that there must be internal limits in each of us—lines that must not be crossed. Throughout our history, churches, synagogues, families and schools worked together to teach children right and wrong. And for the most part, we lived within those limits. Today, our children are stuck in a moral vacuum of our own making. Our religious institutions have lost the moral high ground and, thus, no longer speak with authority. And teachers refuse to mention the word "morality" in the classroom out of fear of a lawsuit. Worst of all, the traditional family is in a shambles. The picture of the American family shows a broken home, shattered by divorce, infidelity and distrust. America's divorce rate hovers around 50%, and not even religious leaders are immune.[32]

Others believe the problem is compounded by the increasing prevalence of gangs. California's attorney general issued a report on gangs in 2003, which began with the following statements:

Gangs have spread from major urban areas in California to the suburbs, and even to our rural communities. Today, the gang life style draws young people from all walks of life, socio-economic backgrounds and races and ethnic groups. Gangs are a problem not only for law enforcement but also for the community. Drive-by shootings, carjackings, home invasions and the loss of innocent life have become too frequent throughout California, destroying lives and ripping apart the fabric of communities.[33]

The gang problem is exacerbated by easy access to guns, especially sophisticated assault weapons. For example, a sergeant in the Los Angeles Sheriff's Department stated: "The sophistication of the weapons utilized by gang members is constantly increasing. . . . Assault weapons like the UZI are becoming more and more common. . . . These assault weapons are being used not only in gang versus gang confrontations, but also against law enforcement officers."[34]

In a 1995 *Newsweek* article entitled "The Lull Before the Storm," criminologist James Fox of Northeastern University is quoted as warning that this deadly combination of amoral teens and high-powered weapons would produce a "bloodbath of teenaged violence that will make 1995 look like the good old days."[35] However, such a blood bath never happened after 1995. Indeed, juvenile crime, including serious and violent crime, decreased throughout the latter half of the 1990s and into the twenty-first century. Why, then, do we hear the current outcry and see the fear of violent, amoral juvenile superpredators? As we show in the following section, this outcry is not new, and it appears to be a constant that is immune to actual increases or decreases in juvenile crime.

Adult Views of Juveniles in Earlier Times

In 1989, *Time* magazine described "the beast that has broken loose in some of America's young people." The following give a sense of the article while omitting the numerous examples presented to illustrate each point:

> More and more teenagers, acting individually or in gangs, are running amuck. . . . [T]o be sure, teenagers have never been angels. Adolescence is often a troubled time of rebellion and rage . . . but juvenile crime appears to be more widespread and vicious than ever before. . . . Adolescents have always been violence prone, but there are horrendous crimes being committed by even younger children. . . . The teen crime wave flows across all races, classes, and life-styles. The offenders are overwhelmingly male, but girls too are capable of vicious crimes. . . . What is chilling about many of the young criminals is that they show no remorse or conscience, at least initially. Youth brag about their exploits and shrug off victims' pain.[36]

The author suggested that this recent "upsurge in the most violent types of crimes by teens" began in 1983. However, six years before this "juvenile crime wave" apparently began, *Time* magazine seemed to be just as alarmed about the juvenile crime problem:

Across the U.S., a pattern of crime has emerged that is both per-
plexing and appalling. Many youngsters appear to be robbing and
raping, maiming and murdering as casually as they go to a movie or
join a pickup baseball game. A new, remorseless, mutant juvenile
seems to have been born, and there is no more terrifying figure in
America today.[37]

The author of the 1989 article must have neglected to read this earlier
piece. How could the wave of violence have started in 1983 if it was
already happening in 1977? In fact, these quotations come from a time
when juvenile crime, including serious violence crime, declined by about
one-third. Similar statements can, however, also be found during times
when juvenile crime is increasing. For example, in 1964, the long-time
head of the FBI, J. Edgar Hoover, was similarly convinced that things had
changed.

In the Twenties and Thirties, juvenile delinquency, in general, meant
such things as truancy, minor vandalism and petty theft. Today, the
term includes armed robbery, assault and even murder. . . . We
should not permit actual crimes to be thought of in terms of the
delinquencies of a past era. I am not speaking of the relatively minor
misdemeanors usually associated with the process of growing up. It
is the killings, the rapes and robberies of innocent people by youthful criminals that concern me.[38]

Ten years earlier, in 1954, a New York City judge made a similar statement that was quoted in *Newsweek*, except that he described the low
juvenile crime as being in the 1900s and 1910s, rather than in the 1920s
and 1930s:

Back before the First World War, it was a rare day when you saw a
man under 25 up for a felony. Today it's the rule. And today when
one of these kids robs a bank he doesn't rush for a businesslike get-
away. He stays around and shoots up a couple of clerks. Not long
ago I asked such a boy why, and he said: "I get a kick out of it when
I see blood running."[39]

The article was entitled: "Our Vicious Young Hoodlums: Is There Any
Hope?"
That same year, *Time* magazine ran an article about the "teenage reign
of terror" that has transformed New York City's public school system into
a "vast incubator of crime in which wayward and delinquent youngsters

receive years of protection while developing into toughened and experienced criminals."[40] The article said that in some schools, half the pupils carried switchblades or zipguns, others carried homemade flame throwers or plastic water pistols filled with blinding chemical solutions, and still other students threatened or beat up teachers who gave them poor grades. It suggested that this behavior had begun "in the past few years."

Similar alarms were raised in the 1940s, 1930s, and 1920s.[41] At those times, people believed as they do today that the country was being overwhelmed by a rising tide of juvenile delinquency and crime and that such crime had not been a serious problem only forty or fifty years ago.

Views of Adults as an Aspect that Stays the Same

Juvenile crime itself seems to go up and down, but the feelings about how terrible juveniles are seem to stay the same. Whether juvenile crime is high or low, many people believe that it is worse than before. Thus, we always appear to be in the middle or on the verge of a juvenile crime wave, to which the justice system must respond.

Belief That Juvenile Justice Policy Increases Crime

A fifth aspect of juvenile delinquency and juvenile justice that has stayed the same for at least two hundred years is the belief that the system for processing juvenile offenders increases juvenile crime. This belief seems to be widely held at all times and in all places, whether a lot of delinquency or only a little occurs, and whether juveniles are harshly punished or leniently treated.

Presently, there is growing concern that harsh laws and punishments are leading officials to divert too many youth in need of treatment and rehabilitation away from the juvenile justice system. But that concern tends to alternate in history. Indeed, when the first edition of this book was published in 1991, the previous sentence read "Presently, widespread concern exists that lenient treatment increases juvenile crime."

Concern That Leniency Increases Juvenile Crime

People have always been concerned that lenient treatment will increase crime among juveniles. This was a major point made in the 1977 *Time* magazine article quoted above:

When [a juvenile offender] is caught, the courts usually spew him out again. If he is under a certain age, 16 or 18 depending on the states, he is almost always taken to juvenile court, where he is treated as if he were still the child he is supposed to be. Even if he has murdered someone, he may be put away for only a few months. He is either sent home well before his term expires or he escapes, which, as the kids say, is "no big deal." Small wonder that hardened juveniles laugh, scratch, yawn, mug and even fall asleep while their crimes are revealed in court.[42]

Several years earlier, Ted Morgan argued a similar point in an article entitled "They Think, 'I Can Kill Because I'm 14.'"[43] Ten years before that, J. Edgar Hoover similarly warned against the misguided policies that encourage criminal activity, resulting in the arrogant attitude "You can't touch me. I'm a juvenile!"[44]

Concern About Leniency in Earlier Times

Many people believe that leniency causes juvenile crime and they blame the juvenile justice system for the results of this leniency. They suggest that if juveniles were tried in adult courts and sent to adult institutions, the problem would be solved. But the juvenile justice system was established because the adult courts were believed to be too lenient with juveniles. This suggests that sending juveniles to the adult system will not necessarily result in harsher treatment.

This argument will be discussed in more detail in chapter 4, but there is a basic point to be made here. Before the establishment of the first juvenile institution in New York City, in 1825, only adult prisons were available for punishing juveniles. These adult prisons were viewed as very harsh places that would increase the likelihood of juveniles' committing more crime. Prosecutors, judges, and juries in the criminal courts all naturally tried to avoid sending juvenile offenders to these institutions, with the result that many were freed, with no consequences at all.[45]

The chief judge in New York City was concerned that freeing these juveniles without any consequences for their actions would encourage them to commit further crimes. He helped establish the first juvenile institution to receive these youngsters who otherwise would get off scot-free. One year after the establishment of the institution, the district attorney for New York City stated that the new institution had solved the problem.[46]

Around that same time, officials in London issued a "Report of the Committee for Investigating the Causes of the Alarming Increase of Juvenile Delinquency in the Metropolis" that expressed similar concerns.[47]

The problem, as it existed in both London and New York City, was that because there were only harsh punishments available in the adult system, the natural tendency was to provide more lenient treatments to juveniles, resulting in many of them being let off without any punishment whatsoever. The juvenile justice system was thus invented to correct this problem, and its goal was to provide some consequences for those who otherwise would receive no punishment.

Concern About Harshness Increasing Crime

Just as there have been concerns for a long time that leniency increases juvenile crime, correspondingly, there have been concerns that harsh punishments increase juvenile crime. For example, many law-abiding adults have committed at least some crimes when they were juveniles, for which they might have been sent to an institution. Most of them, however, were not caught or, if caught, received lenient treatment. Most of them then stopped committing crimes, as their earlier behavior was a natural part of their growing up.

Now, suppose instead of receiving lenient treatment they had been sent to an institution. Such harsh punishment might have increased the likelihood that they would continue to commit crimes in the future, rather than simply outgrowing that behavior. This is the purpose of leniency: to allow juveniles to "get out while the getting is good."

Concern About the Harshness of Earlier Times

The effects of harsh punishment on juveniles have not been a concern just in recent times. For example, the 1820s New York City judge quoted earlier who was concerned that letting juveniles off scot-free would encourage them to commit crimes was also concerned that sending juveniles to the prisons and jails would be "a fruitful source of pauperism, a nursery of new vices and crimes, a college for the perfection of adepts in guilt."[48] That is, this judge had to choose between providing harsh punishment or doing nothing at all, and he believed that both choices increased crime among juveniles.

A similar concern in 1899 about the effects of harshness later provided the motivation for establishing the first juvenile court in Chicago (see chapter 5). An Illinois Supreme Court decision made in 1870 severely restricted the lenient handling of juvenile offenders. This meant that juvenile justice officials now faced the same dilemma as did the earlier officials in New York City: they either had to provide harsh punishments to juvenile offenders or they could do nothing at all. Like the

New York City judge, they believed that both choices increased crime among juveniles. The juvenile court was invented then primarily as a middle ground. It would provide lenient treatments for those juveniles who otherwise would be harshly punished in Chicago's jails and poorhouses as well as for those juveniles who otherwise would be let off scot-free.

Concern About Juvenile Justice Policy as an Aspect that Stays the Same

If you think about the problem that officials faced in New York City and London in the early 1800s, and in Chicago in the late 1800s, then it becomes apparent that concerns whether leniency or harshness causes juvenile crime are really two sides of the same coin. Their relationship is what Samuel Walker calls the law of criminal justice thermodynamics: *An increase in the severity of the penalty will result in less frequent application of the penalty.*[49]

This "law" explains the basic problem.[50] Only harsh punishments were available to respond to juvenile crime. Some juveniles received those punishments, but others were let off because the punishments seemed inappropriate and counterproductive. In terms of Walker's law, the penalties were so severe that they were infrequently applied.

Another way to phrase it is to say that certainty and severity are enemies. That is, if you increase the severity of a penalty, you usually decrease the certainty with which it is applied. If you want to increase the certainty with which a penalty is applied, usually you must reduce its severity. This is exactly what criminal justice officials in London, New York City, and Chicago did: they reduced the severity of the penalties for juveniles in order to increase the certainty of applying them. In this way, they established a "lenient" juvenile justice system.

The continued concern about the effectiveness of juvenile justice policies arises from this relationship between certainty and severity. If juvenile justice policies provide harsh punishments, then some juveniles will receive those punishments but others will receive no punishment because the punishments seem inappropriate and counterproductive. But if juvenile justice policies provide lenient treatments, then many juveniles will receive the treatments but some will laugh them off and feel free to commit serious crimes with impunity.

Concern about the effectiveness of harsh punishments arises from the realization that both choices are thought to increase crime. Concern about the effectiveness of lenient policies arises because people believe that "getting tough" with juveniles earlier deters them from committing serious crimes later on.

The Cycle of Juvenile Justice

These five unchanging aspects of juvenile crime and justice give rise to a sixth aspect that has also stayed the same for at least two hundred years: the cycle of juvenile justice. This pattern arises from the fact that, at any given time, many people are convinced that the problem of juvenile crime is a recent event that did not exist in the good old days. These people conclude that the source of the problem is in the policies for handling juvenile offenders, whether these involve harsh punishments or lenient treatments. The result is a cycle of reform in which harsh punishments are replaced by lenient treatments, and then lenient treatments are replaced by harsh punishments.

Regardless of the type of policy in place, people remain convinced that juvenile crime is at an all-time high (whether it actually is or not) and that these high rates are a recent occurrence. This myth that things were better in the "good old days" is one of the primary factors that keep us from breaking the cycle. Instead of looking for times when juvenile delinquency was low and determining the societal factors that led to those low rates, we erroneously look back to policies that were in place thirty or so years ago. Then, regardless of what policy change is implemented, people remain convinced that juvenile crime is still at an all-time high and that things were better in the past.

This cycle cannot be broken by any particular juvenile justice policy, since every conceivable policy confronts the same dilemma: after it is implemented, people will continue to feel that juvenile crime is exceptionally high, that it was not a serious problem in the "good old days," and that it would not be a serious problem today if we only had the proper justice policies in effect. This dilemma dominates not only our current juvenile justice system but also any conceivable future organizational arrangement for processing juvenile offenders. Caught in this cycle, we are doomed to repeat history instead of learning from it and moving toward real progress.

NOTES

1. Travis Hirschi and Michael Gottfredson, "Age and the Explanation of Crime," *American Journal of Sociology* 89 (1983): 552–584. See also Frank R. Donovan, *Wild Kids* (Harrisburg, Pa.: Stackpole, 1967); and Wiley B. Sanders, ed., *Juvenile Offenders for a Thousand Years* (Chapel Hill: University of North Carolina Press, 1970).

2. U.S. Census Bureau, Table 7. Resident Population by Sex and Age: 1980–2008, www.census.gov/compendia/statab/2010/table, accessed February 15, 2010.

3. Howard Snyder, *Juvenile Arrests, 2003*, Juvenile Justice bulletin (Washington, D.C.: Office of Juvenile Justice and Delinquency, U.S. Department of Justice, 2005).

4. Hibberts , 433.

5. Negley K. Teeters and David Matza, "The Extent of Delinquency in the United States," in Ruth Shonle Cavan, ed., *Readings in Juvenile Delinquency* (Philadelphia: Lippincott, 1964), 2–15.

6. James Gilbert, *A Cycle of Outrage* (New York: Oxford University Press, 1986), 24–26.

7. James A. Inciardi, Alan A. Block, and Lyle A. Hallowell, *Historical Approaches to Crime* (Beverly Hills, Calif.: Sage, 1977), 59–89.

8. These articles are described in Archer Butler Hulbert, "The Habit of Going to the Devil," *Atlantic Monthly* 138 (December 1926): 804–806. See also Teeters and Matza, "The Extent of Delinquency."

9. Sanders, *Juvenile Offenders*, 135.

10. Hibberts, 432.

11. Teeters and Matza, "The Extent of Delinquency"; Sophia M. Robison, *Juvenile Delinquency* (New York: Holt, Rinhart and Winston, 1960), chap. 2; Walter C. Reckless and Mapheus Smith, *Juvenile Delinquency* (New York: McGraw-Hill, 1932), chap. 2.

12. Clyde B. Vedder, *The Juvenile Offender* (Garden City, N.Y.: Doubleday, 1954), 26.

13. The year 1952 was the first one in which the tables were labeled as representing arrests in cities with 2,500 or more population. This raises the possibility that part of the rise in proportion of juvenile arrests to adults might result from changes in data collection. See Teeters and Matza, "The Extent of Delinquency."

14. C. Puzzanchera, T. Finnegan, and W. Kang, "Easy Access to Juvenile Populations," prepared by the National Center for Justice for the Office of Juvenile Justice and Delinquency Prevention, U.S. Department of Justice, http://www.ojjdp.ncjrs.gov/ojstatbb/ezapop, accessed 2008.

15. Howard N. Snyder and Melissa Sickmund, *Juvenile Offenders and Victims: A National Report* (Washington, D.C.: Office of Juvenile Justice and Delinquency Prevention, U.S. Department of Justice, 2006).

16. For further discussion of potential biases and interpretations of official crime statistics, see Robert M. O'Brien, *Crime and Victimization Data* (Thousand Oaks, Calif.: Sage, 1985). For a discussion specific to implications for juvenile arrest trends, see Snyder and Sickmund, *Juvenile Offenders and Victims*, 64.

17. Exodus 21:15; Leviticus 20:9.

18. John R. Sutton, *Stubborn Children* (Berkeley: University of California Press, 1988), 11. See also Lee E. Teitelbaum and Leslie J. Harris, "Some Historical Perspectives on Governmental Regulation of Children and Parents," in Lee E. Teitelbaum and Aiden R. Gough, eds., *Beyond Control: Status Offenders in the Juvenile Court* (Cambridge, Mass.: Ballinger, 1977), 1–44.

19. Thomas C. Castellano, "The Justice Model in the Juvenile Justice System: Washington State's Experience," *Law and Policy* 8, no. 4 (October 1986): 479–506.

20. Ira M. Schwartz, *(In)justice for Juveniles* (Lexington, Mass.: D.C. Heath, 1989), 2–3.

21. Gordon A. Raley and John E. Dean, "The Juvenile Justice and Delinquency Prevention Act: Federal Leadership in State Reform," *Law and Policy* 8, no. 4 (October 1986): 397–418.

22. Snyder and Sickmund, *Juvenile Offenders and Victims*.

23. Frederic L. Faust and Paul J. Brantingham, *Juvenile Justice Philosophy* (St. Paul, Minn.: West, 1979), 460.

24. Sir William Blackstone, *Commentaries on the Laws of England*, Vol. IV (London, 1795), 23.

25. See H. Ted Rubin, *Juvenile Justice* (New York: Random House, 1985), chap. 2.

26. Donovan, *Wild Kids*, 11.

27. Harvey Green, "Scientific Thought and the Nature of Children in America, 1820–1920," in *A Century of Childhood, 1820–1920* (Rochester, N.Y.: Strong Museum, 1984), 121.

28. Quoted in Gary F. Jensen and Dean G. Rojek, *Delinquency* (Lexington, Mass.: DC Heath, 1980), 2.

29. Samuel Noah Dramer, "A Father and His Perverse Son," *Crime and Delinquency* 3, no. 2 (April 1957): 169–173.

30. Dr. Don Boys, "Criminal Children: The Lunacy of Leniency," Cornerstone Communications 1997, www.cstnews.com/Code/CrimChld.html, accessed March 30, 2009.

31. These headlines were obtained from "Common Sense about Kids and Guns," www.kidsandguns.org, accessed March 12, 2009.

32. John W. Whitehead, "Kids Today Don't Stand a Chance," www.huffingtonpost.com, March 13, 2008.

33. *Gangs: A Community Response*, Crime and Violence Prevention Center, California Attorney General's Office, June 2003.

34. Quoted in Rick Ruddell and Scott H. Decker, "Kids and Assault Weapons: Social Problem or Social Construction," *Criminal Justice Review* 30, no.1 (2005): 45–63.

35. Peter Annin and Tom Morganthan, "The Lull Before the Storm," *Newsweek*, December 4, 1995, 40.

36. Anastasia Toufexis, "Our Violent Kids," *Time*, June 12, 1989, 52–58. See also the editorial "Meltdown in our Cities," *U.S. News and World Report*, May 29, 1989, for similar arguments.

37. "The Youth Crime Plague," *Time*, July 11, 1977, 18–28.

38. J. Edgar Hoover, "The Crime Wave We Now Face," *New York Times* magazine, April 21, 1946, 26–27; for a similar article written one year earlier, see Judith Viorst, "Delinquency! National Crisis," *Science News Letter* 84 (September 28, 1963): 202–203.

39. "Our Vicious Young Hoodlums: Is There Any Hope?" *Newsweek*, September 6, 1954, 43–44.

40. "The New Three Rs," *Time*, March 15, 1954, 68–70. This is based on a special series appearing in the New York *Daily News* the preceding week.

41. E.g., Hoover, "The Crime Wave"; "Children Without Morals," *Time*, October 5, 1942, 24; Leonard V. Harrison and Pryor M. Grant, "Youth and Crime," *Vital Speeches* 2 (April 20, 1936): 468–472; and "Youth Leads the Criminal Parade," *Literary Digest*, April 23, 1932, 20. For alarms raised in even earlier times, see Hulbert, "The Habit of Going."

42. "Youth Crime Plague," *Time*.

43. *New York Times* magazine, January 19, 1975. A similar article appeared in the same magazine thirteen years earlier, but with an emphasis on the social causes of delinquency rather than on lenient treatment. See Ira Henry Freeman, "The Making of a Boy Killer," *New York Times* magazine, February 18, 1962, 14ff.

44. Hoover, "The Crime Wave," 668.

45. Robert M. Mennel, *Thorns and Thistles* (Hanover, N.H.: University Press of New England, 1973), xxv–xxvi.

46. Bradford Kinney Peirce, *A Half Century with Juvenile Delinquents* (Montclair, N.J.: Patterson-Smith, 1969), 79.

47. Sanders, *Juvenile Offenders*, 111.

48. Quoted in Peirce, *A Half Century*, 41–42.

49. Samuel Walker, *Sense and Nonsense About Crime*, 2nd ed. (Pacific Grove, Calif.: Brooks/Cole, 1989), 46–48.

50. We face similar problems today. For example, homicide is punished more severely than any other crime. Zimring, O'Malley, and found that homicide defendants who did not receive a very severe punishment typically received little or no punishment at all. They concluded: "The problem is not that our system is too lenient or too severe; sadly, it is both"; Franklin Zimring, Sheila O'Malley, and Joel Eigen, "Punishing Homicide in Philadelphia," *University of Chicago Law Review* 43 (Winter 1976): 252. At the other end of the scale, minor delinquencies are punished the most leniently, and often result in diversion from the juvenile justice system. The problem here has been that, because the punishments are so lenient, they have tended to be very broadly applied. The phrase used to describe this is "widening the net"—i.e., diversion programs are compared to a fishing boat's dragging an ever-widening net that sweeps up more and more fish; see James Austin and Barry Krisberg, "Wider, Stronger and Different Nets," *Journal of Research in Crime and Delinquency* 18 (1981): 165–196.

3

The Origin of Juvenile Delinquency

The term "juvenile delinquency" was invented about two hundred years ago. One of its first uses was in the *Report of the Committee for Investigating the Causes of the Alarming Increase of Juvenile Delinquency in the Metropolis*, which was issued in London in 1816.[1] In the United States, the term appears in New York City in 1819, with the founding of the Society for the Reformation of Juvenile Delinquents.[2] Prior to this time, children who committed offenses were simply described as "blackguard children," "stubborn children," poor vagrant children," or simply labeled as young criminals.

The origins of the modern juvenile justice system can be traced back to the establishment of the first juvenile institution in New York City, in 1825. The first juvenile court would be established seventy-five years later, in 1899, in Chicago. Before then, juveniles who committed offenses were tried in the same courts as adults and they received the same punishments as adults. The only difference was that juveniles usually received lesser punishments than adults who had committed the same offenses.

While details on the origin of the juvenile justice system are presented in chapters 4 and 5, this chapter argues that juvenile delinquency itself originated about the same time as did the term "juvenile delinquency." This is a surprising argument, especially for those who believe that juvenile delinquency has remained the same throughout history. It suggests that there really were "good old days" two hundred years ago, before there was any juvenile delinquency—at least in the sense that we mean it today.

Actually, two meanings for the term "juvenile delinquency" emerged around the year 1800. The first refers to delinquency as a modern *phenomenon*. That is, there is a sense in which the behaviors we describe as juvenile delinquency first appeared around 1800 and simply did not exist before then. The second meaning refers to delinquency as a modern *idea*. That is, the term reflects a particular new way of understanding and interpreting youthful offending, which also originated about 1800.

Juvenile Delinquency as a Modern Phenomenon

Juvenile delinquency appears as a modern phenomenon when traditional (i.e., rural and agricultural) societies make the transition to modern (i.e., urban and industrial) societies. The United States and Western European countries made this transition between the years 1760 and 1840, so that was also when the problem of juvenile delinquency first appeared. In the early and middle part of the twentieth century, Eastern European societies made the same transition, and later in that century the developing nations of Asia, Africa, and Latein America started the process. As each country underwent modernization, it confronted the new problem of juvenile delinquency—a phenomenon it did not experience when it was a traditional (rural and agricultural) society.[3]

Five different factors have been identified as associated with the development of this phenomenon, although all are not necessarily involved every time it appears:

- *Traditional mechanisms* for responding to juvenile offending break down as part of the breakdown of the traditional society, which can increase the volume of juvenile offending.
- *Industrialization* increases the number of moveable goods and leads to a rise in property crimes, many of which are committed by juveniles.
- *Urbanization* brings juvenile offenders into close contact with each other and with potential victims, both of which add to the tendency of juveniles to commit offenses.
- *Population growth and composition* shift as a consequence of urbanization and industrialization. Sudden growth in the population of a country or an area (such as a city) can lead to an increased proportion of young people in that population. Since crime is disproportionately committed by young males, this leads to an increase in the total volume of crime. In America, in addition to population growth through new births,

immigration played a large role in the growth and diversification of cities, which meant that not only were there more youths to commit crimes but also there were conflicting cultures and beliefs competing to label and define what was indeed a crime.

- *Societies establish new mechanisms for responding to juvenile offenders* as a response to modernization. These mechanisms, or systems, increase the detection and processing of juvenile offenders, subsequently resulting in higher official statistics on juvenile crime. Moreover, these systems can actually generate juvenile offenders by formally processing and institutionalizing juveniles who, in earlier times, would have remained in the community.

The Breakdown of Traditional Mechanisms

In America, prior to 1760, neither crime in general nor juvenile crime in particular was a serious problem. For example, Theodore N. Ferdinand reports that, in Massachusetts:

Neither adults nor adolescents committed many crimes before the Revolutions (in 1776), and more often than not those few adolescents who were charged with criminal offenses escaped severe punishment by a general unwillingness of juries to convict them. Most of the crimes by adolescents were handled informally in the community by denunciations in church or at town meetings and usually followed by public confessions and pleas for forgiveness. There was no concept of adolescence or juvenile delinquency, and though the crimes of young people were typically less violent than those committed by adults, they were otherwise very similar.[4]

There were no special institutions or facilities for dealing with youthful offenders, so parents were simply required by law and custom to control their own children.[5] This was the major mechanism for controlling delinquency in traditional societies, and it worked well in the small towns and rural areas before 1700. After about 1700, however, there was increasing dissatisfaction with the performance of parents in this traditional task. This resulted in an increasing number of laws being passed that threatened parents who failed in this duty.[6]

For juveniles who could not be controlled by their own families, there was the second traditional mechanism: to bind them out to other families that, it was assumed, would be better at accomplishing this task. These youths usually were required to work as servants to earn their keep.[7]

This second mechanism for controlling delinquency in traditional societies also began breaking down during the 1700s, for several reasons. First, the families that took in these children were increasingly dissatisfied with them, since older and more difficult children were being brought into the system and these children frequently deserted before having served their time.[8] Second, slaves and other indentured servants became more available to fill these worker roles.[9]

Corporal and capital punishments were a third means of control, and these mechanisms had been used with many juvenile offenders. By 1800 or so, these punishments were becoming very unpopular, however, and by law, juveniles were exempted from some forms of corporal punishments in some states. Transportation (e.g., from England to America and Australia) was briefly used as a fourth mechanism after the decline in use of corporal punishment, but soon no places would accept the criminals intended for transport.

Thus, all the traditional means for responding to youthful offenders had broken down by the end of the 1700s. As a result, youthful offenders were boarded out at public expenses or housed in the newly founded adult prisons, often for long periods.[10] These were unpopular options, however, and generally seen as expensive and even counterproductive. Consequently, juries often refused to convict juveniles, preferring to release them with no punishment whatsoever.[11]

Industrialization

Before industrialization, there was a lower total volume of crime, and most were violent crimes such as murder, rape, and assault.[12] After industrialization, there was a higher total volume of crime and most were property crimes such as burglary, robbery, and larceny-theft. This change was a direct result of industrialization itself, which mass-produces moveable goods that can be stolen.

Before industrialization, most of what people owned was not very moveable, so there was very little stealing. For example, until around the year 1300, land was the primary form of wealth, and land could not really be stolen, at least in a modern sense of the term.[13] By about 1500, however, wealth could be accumulated in the form of moveable goods that were either traded for other goods or sold for money. Only at this point could stealing become a real problem.

In England, this led to the famous "carrier's case" in 1473, in which the law of theft took its modern form.[14] The defendant in the case was hired by a merchant to carry some bales to Southhampton, but instead he took the bales for himself. According to the law at the time, this was not considered theft because the merchant had freely given the bales to the carrier. It required an imaginative ruling by the judge in this case to conclude that a theft had taken place. The point is that, as late as 1473 in England, the law of theft was very simple because theft was not much of a problem.

Today, about 90 percent of all crimes are property crimes, such as burglary, larceny, and auto theft. The likelihood that something will be stolen is directly related to how moveable it is. In 1975, for example, $26.44 in motor vehicles and parts were stolen for every $100 that were legally purchased, as compared with only $0.12 worth of furniture.[15] Thus, in the days before industrialization, when most possessions were nonmoveable things like furniture, there was very little stealing.

Juveniles have always committed a larger proportion of property crimes than have adults. As property crimes became the most prominent form of crime, juveniles became a more prominent type of criminal. Thus, this new crime wave came to be seen, to some extent, as a juvenile crime wave.[16]

Urbanization

Before the 1800s, European and American societies were largely rural and agricultural. There were some cities, but European societies before the 1800s were overwhelmingly rural.[17] The cities that did exist were small, with few having more than 10,000 people. The vast majority of people lived in small villages that could not even be called towns, much less cities.

The rural nature of European society persisted into the 1800s. As late as 1801, when the industrial revolution was still getting under way, although the United Kingdom was then the most urbanized nation in the world, it still had only one city of more than 100,000 inhabitants. This city (London), the largest in Europe and probably in the world at the time, accounted for only 4.7 percent of the U.K. population.[18]

America was similarly rural and agricultural. In 1760, a large majority of towns in America had fewer than 1,000 people, and only a few places had more than 2,500.[19] The largest city in the country in that year was Philadelphia, with 23,750 people. New York City had a population of 18,000 and Boston 15,000, but no other city in America had more than 10,000 people.[20]

Industrialization brought with it a vast expansion in urbanization because it freed people from working on the land and it provided them with jobs in factories, which could be located in urban areas. By 1840, Western Europe and America suddenly looked more like our world today—urban and industrial rather than rural and agricultural.

Especially in England and Germany, societies suddenly were trans-formed from almost entirely agricultural to increasingly industrial. By 1841, only about one-third of occupied males in England were employed in agriculture, forestry, and fishing.[21] Before 1800, England had only one city of more than 100,00 people, but by 1851 it had twelve such cities.[22] London's population rose to 2.25 million by 1845.[23] Other cities also experienced explosive growth. For example, in the fifty-seven years between 1774 and 1831, Manchester's population grew from 29,000 to 228,000.[24]

A similar phenomenon occurred in America. In 1820, for example, the population of New York City was about 120,000 and was growing rap-idly in response to immigration.[25] It was becoming a modern city: densely inhabited and increasingly chaotic, with many different racial and ethnic groups. Boston in 1850 had grown to 137,000.[26]

In making the transition to city life, many families simply disintegrated, and homeless children and adolescents began to congregate in groups on the streets of the rapidly growing cities.[27] Many took up stealing as a means of survival since the urban environment brought them into close contact both with likely victims who had moveable goods that could be stolen and with other youths like themselves whom they could cooper-ate with in stealing ventures. In addition, the urban environment offered these youths few other realistic courses of action for their survival.

These children and youths were a new and serious problem, one that did not exist in the "good old days" before urbanization and indu-strialization. Thus, a new term was needed to describe them: juvenile delinquents.

Population Growth and Composition

Two additional and related factors that may have played a role in the new problem of juvenile delinquency are (1) the growth of the overall popu-lation in the United States in particular, its urban centers; and (2) the immigration of many of these youths from diverse cultures.

The size of the crime problem usually is closely linked to the relative proportion of young males in the population, since this group commits more crime than others.[28] A population boom in England during the beginning of the 1800s resulted in a large proportion of young males in London, and that may have contributed to the perception that there was a "juvenile crime wave."

America, and particularly its urban centers, also underwent a popula-tion boom. From 1790 through 1900, the population of the United States in general grew by almost a third each decade.[29] As noted above, this population increase was particularly stark in urban centers such as New York, Philadelphia, and Chicago (cities we will later see at the center of the juvenile justice movement). For example, in the ten years from 1790 to 1800, New York City experienced an 83 percent increase in population, while in the ten years from 1840 to 1850, it grew by another 123 percent. Similar explosive growth occurred in the decade from 1850 to 1860, when Philadelphia and Chicago experienced 365 and 274 percent increases in population, respectively.[30]

While it is difficult to disentangle the effects of increased birth rates from the effects of immigration at this point in time, history does reveal that in middle and latter parts of the eighteenth century, immigration to American no longer primarily comprised English Protestants but also included many Germans, Scottish, Irish, and eventually, Polish and Italians immigrants as well.[31] In general, these newest immigrant groups entered the country at the bottom of the economic ladder and struggled to achieve even the most basic commodities, such as food and housing. As such, the children of these groups were often caught stealing and seen as potential paupers.[32] Thus, this new term of juvenile delinquent was increasing applied to the children of immigrants who had not yet been assimilated into American culture.

Justice System Response

In addition to the influences of urbanization, industrialization, and immigration, system response to young offenders may also have contributed to the definition of juvenile delinquency. For example, there was a large rise in the *rate* of juvenile delinquency occurring in Boston after about 1840 (i.e., holding the youth population constant), as well as in the *seriousness* of the offenses that delinquents committed.[33] After examining a number of possible explanations, Ferdinand concluded that these changes were *caused by* new responses to juvenile crime that allowed even minor status offenders to be locked up in institutions (such as the House of Refuge, discussed in more detail in the following chapter). As noted in chapter 2, official statistics often fall prey to the bias of reflecting changes in system behavior rather than actual changes in offending/offender behavior.

This response contributed to the phenomenon of juvenile delinquency in two ways. First, as the system was more likely to respond to and lock up young offenders, more youth became classified as juvenile delinquents. Second, through their experiences in jails and lockups, the juveniles' future propensity for crime could have been exacerbated rather than reduced.

In sum, juvenile delinquency as a modern phenomenon emerged in Western Europe and America around the year 1800 because that is when those societies underwent the processes of urbanization and industrialization. Urban property crime by lower-class persons became the major type of crime in the whole society. Young people committed more than their share of this crime, and this new type of crime was subsequently described as "juvenile delinquency." Thus, juvenile delinquents originally were lower-class juveniles who stole property from middle- and upper-class adults in urban settings.

Juvenile Delinquency as a Modern Idea

In addition to this new phenomenon of juvenile delinquency, a new way of understanding and interpreting offending behavior by juveniles also arose. As you will see, much of this new way of understanding offending behavior is tied to evolving ideas of the notion of childhood and adolescence. This new idea was then not only applied to the new form of crime that just had appeared on the scene but also used for all other offending behaviors by juveniles that had been around since the dawn of time.

The new idea was that juveniles were vulnerable to the influences of other people, whether good or bad. They were "malleable" like clay— they could be shaped and molded and formed into whatever was wanted. Once they grew up, however, they "set" just like clay that was baked in the oven. The shape became permanent and, whether good or bad, it could no longer be changed.

The "old" idea was that people were largely unchangeable—they were what they were and nothing could be done about it. The new idea was that, while adults were indeed unchangeable, children were not yet "fixed" in a set pattern. They could be influenced toward the good, if one only reached them early enough. The implication was that the good people, the law-abiding citizens, should intervene early and aggressively in the lives of youth who were in danger of being shaped and molded and formed into criminals. These children could be rescued rather easily while they were still young, but as they grew older they would become too set in their ways, and eventually they could not be saved at all.

The invention of the term "juvenile delinquent" reflected this new concept that juveniles were malleable. If you look up the word *delinquent* in the dictionary, you will find that it literally refers to someone who has failed to do what is required of him or her. For example, a person may be delinquent in paying taxes. This term directed attention away from the crimes the child committed and toward the notion that the child was failing to carry out the obligations of a responsible member of society. Thus, whereas the term "young criminal" suggested that we should respond with punishment, the term "juvenile delinquent" suggested that we should respond with efforts to shape and mold and form the youth into a responsible society member.

The Idea of the Juvenile

To have an idea of juvenile delinquency, you must have the idea of "juvenile"—that is, you must think about juveniles as a group of people who are similar to each other and different from other people in at least some ways. You might think that the idea of the juvenile is something that stays the same in history, that everyone would always have recognized juveniles as a group in this sense, and that therefore this idea has not changed in the past and will not change in the future. But in fact, the idea of the juvenile is fairly recent in origin and has varied greatly over time.

Philippe Areis presented the first argument about changes in ideas about childhood over the centuries.[34] Specifically, he said that two separate ideas of childhood prevailed over the centuries, the first emerging around the year 1400 and the second around the year 1600.

The First Idea of Childhood

According to Aries, no idea of childhood was present at all until sometime around the year 1400. Children existed, of course, but there was a sense in which people did not recognize their existence. Children who were still in the care of women (i.e., below the age of 5 or 6) were treated as if they did not exist at all, and children who were older were treated as if they were people like everyone else. Thus, "children" as a category in people's minds did not exist.

This view originated because of high fertility and high infant mortality: people had many children, and a great many of them died before the age of 5 or 6. As late as the 1600s, approximately two-thirds of all children died before the age of 4.[35] The combination of high fertility and high infant mortality meant that the mere birth of a baby did not really count. Many babies were born, but most would soon die and never grow up to become adults.

To protect themselves from the devastation that would come from the child's death, people largely did not become attached to children until they had passed the point at which death was a likely event. Once the child was 6 or 7 and had a fair chance of living to become an adult, then adults began to treat the child as if he or she were real. Before that, people treated the child as if the child had not yet quite achieved the status of a person. Rather, children were seen as being "in a sort of limbo, hanging between life and death, more as a kind of animal than a human being, without mental activities or recognizable bodily shape."[36]

This way of seeing children was not due to ignorance or evil, but to the terrible conditions under which people lived.[37] Around 1400, however, the first idea of childhood developed: it viewed the child as a source of pleasure and joy. Imagine a parent tickling and taking to an infant. The parent talks baby-talk, cuddles and plays with the baby, and generally experiences a lot of pleasure and joy in the infant that comes from the love and attachment the parent feels. According to Aries, the willingness to feel and express this love and attachment arose only when infant mortality had declined—that is, when parents allowed themselves to become attached to infants and thus took pleasure in them. But there was still a strong chance that the infant would die, and so the interaction with the child was still limited.

This first idea of childhood originated with parents, and while it had many positive aspects, it also had negative ones. Because there still was no clear expectation that the child would grow into an adult, there was no special attempt to shape or form the child. Often the child was simply "used" for pleasure, with half a view that the child would die anyway so it didn't matter.[38]

The Second Idea of Childhood

Around the year 1600, the second idea of childhood developed. This idea involved seeing the child as a potential adult. The change occurred because of a further decline in the infant mortality rate, and it remains our view of children today. We expect that each infant who is born will grow up to become an adult, and we treat that infant accordingly.

This idea originated with teachers and moralists rather than with parents.[39] The teachers and moralists were offended by the abuse and neglect of children that arose out of the first idea. But these moralists and teachers added something else: Puritanism was on the rise, and they believed that humans had fallen from grace because of their sin in the Garden of Eden. Therefore, they believed that human nature was fundamentally inclined toward evil. Children, being human, were thought to be inclined toward evil from the very moment of birth.[40]

These moralists were appalled by the behavior of adults in their societies, but the adults seemed to be a lost cause because they were so set in their ways. Children exhibited the same natural inclinations toward evil as adults, but they could still be influenced if proper techniques were used. Children could be shaped and molded and formed into righteous, law-abiding, God-fearing adults.

Thus, the second idea of childhood contained four elements: (1) that the infant was naturally inclined toward evil because of the fallen human nature; (2) that infants will grow up to become adults and become set in their evil ways, when it will be too late to do anything about it; (3) that infants and children were still malleable and could be shaped and molded and formed into righteous, God-fearing, law-abiding adults; and that (4) in the long run this effort would result in a righteous, God-fearing, law-abiding society.

Colleges as the First Great Battleground

At the time this second idea of childhood emerged, around the year 1600, Western Europe was still mostly organized around feudalism, a system in which people were tied to the land in a hereditary network of rights and obligations. Some of those people were peasants and others were nobles, but all were locked in an unchanging system that had been in place for hundreds of years.

Within the heart of that feudal system, however, was a new system slowly growing: capitalism. Under capitalism, people are not tied in fixed and unchanging roles. Instead, they are free to sell their labor to the highest bidder or purchase the labor of anyone willing to sell it. The people who purchased the labor of others (e.g., merchants, bankers, industrialists) increasingly sent their sons to universities, so that they would be educated to take over the family businesses. But up until about the year 1500, universities were pretty loosely organized places. There was no admissions procedure or school calendar; students would just show up and begin to sit in on classes, which were held in rooms rented by the Masters.

There were no dormitories for university students, so they would rent private lodgings, frequently located over a bar and next to a whorehouse. There, they lived totally unsupervised lives. The result was a lot of crime and violence. For example, one contemporary account states: "The students of Paris attacked and slew passersby, carried off the women, ravished the virgins, committed robberies and broke into houses."[41]

The teachers and moralists of the day attempted to get control of this student population by establishing colleges. Colleges originally were boardinghouses for university students and they had rules and supervision. Parents of the students who, like many parents today, had to pay for their child to attend the classes, would pay extra for the student to live in the colleges. That at least gave them some hope that the student might actually learn something.

At the beginning there was an all-out war between the students and the teachers and moralists who ran these colleges. But, in the 1700s the war was largely won, as the social control exerted by the teachers and moralists began to be passed from parent to child. That is, the teachers no longer had to contend with totally unsocialized youth but, rather, their socialized parents had already instilled some control in their children.

Thus, the idea that the young should be shaped, molded, formed, and created into the kind of adults society would want was first applied to the children of the emerging capitalists. It was only later used as the basis of the juvenile justice system, when it would be applied to the children of the urban poor. This transition would be mediated by the emergence of another idea: adolescence.

The Idea of Adolescence

Whereas the second idea of childhood emerged around 1600, the idea of adolescence did not emerge until the 1800s.[42] This new concept extended the second idea of childhood into the teenage years and applied it to the children of the working and lower classes rather than the children of capitalists.

In earlier times, these youths simply were viewed as adults—they left their parents' house, worked like everyone else, married, and had children. But this changed with the urbanization and industrialization that began around 1800. These lower- and working-class young people increasingly lost their economic independence, since they were the last ones hired and the first ones fired in the new industries. They, therefore, remained at home and dependent on their parents for much longer periods.

At the same time, because they were located in urban areas, they were free to roam with other youths who were dislocated and unattached. The result was the same for these poor youths as two hundred years earlier with the children of capitalists: a great deal of crime and violence. So, at that point, teachers and moralists applied the second idea of childhood to lower- and working-class adolescents. These youth were potential adults, and they had not become set in their ways. They could still be shaped and molded and formed into responsible members of society. This could be done only by intervening while they were still adolescents. Once they became adults, they could no longer be changed and would become set in their ways.

The Idea of Juvenile Delinquency

The new idea of juvenile delinquency was formed out of these components: it consisted of the second idea of childhood, extended into the teenage years and redefined as adolescence, applied to the children of the lower and working classes in urban areas, and specifically applied to their behavior in stealing property from wealthier people. These children and adolescents, the new idea held, could be shaped and molded and formed into God-fearing, law-abiding adults. In particular, they could be stopped from committing property crimes.

The battle to control lower- and working-class adolescents, however, could not take place in the colleges, since they did not attend them. Some new system had to be created that could capture these youths so that they could be shaped, molded, and formed. That new system would be the juvenile justice system.

We now turn to the events by which our present juvenile justice system emerged from this philosophical and historical context. The next two chapters focus on two specific times and places: New York City around the year 1825, when the first juvenile institution was founded; and Chicago around 1899, when the first juvenile court was established. These chapters provide specific examples of the general argument made that juvenile delinquency emerged as a modern phenomenon and is a modern idea for interpreting the phenomenon. In both New York and Chicago, adults who created the new juvenile justice institutions and system were responding to a type of crime that simply did not exist when they themselves had been young (the good old days). They did so within the framework of ideas that have formed the basis of our juvenile justice system since that time. But as we will explore in later chapters, those ideas are under escalating attack today.

NOTES

1. The report is partially reprinted in Wiley B. Sanders, ed., *Juvenile Offenders for a Thousand Years* (Chapel Hill: University of North Carolina Press, 1970), 102.

2. Bradford Kinney Peirce, *A Half Century with Juvenile Delinquents* (Montclair, N.J,: Patterson Smith, 1969), 32–38 (originally published in 1869).

3. Louise I. Shelley, *Crime and Modernization* (Carbondale, Ill.: Southern Illinois University Press, 1981), 141–142.

4. Theodore N. Ferdinand, "Juvenile Delinquency or Juvenile Justice: Which Came First?" *Criminology* 27, no. 1 (February 1989): 79–106, esp. 84.

5. Robert H. Bremner, ed., *Children and Youth in America*, Vol. 1 (Cambridge, Mass.: Harvard University Press, 1970), 307.

6. Robert M. Mennel, *Thorns and Thistels: Juvenile Delinquents in the United States, 1825–1940* (Hanover, N.H.: University Press of New England, 1973), xxii.

7. Ibid., xix; Bremner, *Children and Youth*, 64, 104, 263.

8. Mennel, *Thorns and Thistels*, xxii.

9. Bremner, *Children and Youth*, 262.

10. Mennell, *Thorns and Thistels*, xxiv.

11. Ibid., xxv; Bremner, *Children and Youth*, 307; Ferdinand, "Juvenile Delinquency," 84.

12. Howard Zehr, *Crime and Development of Modern Society*, Totowa, N.J.: Rowman and Littlefield, 1976). For an account of violence among primitive peoples and its decline in the modern world, see Martin Daly and Margo Wilson, *Homicide* (New York: Aldine de Greuter, 1988), chap. 10.

13. For a brief history relevant to crime, see Raymond J. Michalowski, *Order, Law and Crime* (New York: Random House, 1985), 84–85.

14. Jerome Hall, *Theft, Law and Society* (Indianapolis: Bobbs-Merrill, 1952).

15. Lawrence E. Cohen and Marcus Felson, "Social Change and Crime Rate Trends, A Routine Activity Approach," *American Sociological Review* 44 (August 1979): 588–608.

16. The beginning stages of industrialization also resulted in a temporary increase in violence crime, which further contributed to the perception that there was a crime wave; see Ted Robert Gurr, "Historical Forces in Violent Crime," in Michael Tonry and Norval Morris, eds., *Crime and Justice*, Vol. 3 (Chicago: University of Chicago Press, 1981), 344; Shelley, *Crime and Modernization*. Violent crime later resumed its long-term downward trend.

17. Gideon Sjoberg, "The Origin and Evolution of Cities," in *Cities: Their Origin, Growth, and Human Impact* (San Francisco: Freeman, 1973), 19.

18. Kingsley Davis, "The Evolution of Western Industrial Cities," in *Cities, Their Origin, Growth, and Human Impact*, 100.

19. David J. Rothman, *The Discovery of the Asylum* (Boston: Little, Brown, 1971), 12.

20. Carl Bridenbaugh, *Cities in Revolt* (New York: Knopf, 1955), 5.

21. Davis, "The Evolution of Western Industrial Cities."

22. Ibid.

23. Josef W. Konvitz, *The Urban Millennium* (Carbondale: Southern Illinois University Press, 1985), 77.

24. Ibid., 96.

25. Peirce, *A Half Century*, 41.

26. Ferdinand, "Juvenile Delinquency," 83.

27. Mennel, *Thorns and Thistels*, xix.

28. Gurr, "Historical Forces," 345–346. For example, the changing proportions of males aged 15 to 29 between 1801 and 1971 in London's population trace a path that is quite similar to the changing volume of felonies in that city over those years. See Ted Robert Gurr, Peter N. Gradosky, and Richard C. Hula, *The Politics of Crime and Conflict* (Beverly Hills: Sage, 1977), 43.

29. Gurr, "Historical Forces."

30. Richard L. Forstall, "Population of the State and Counties of the United States: 1790 to 1990," (Washington, D.C.: U.S. Bureau of Census, 1996).

31. Ibid.

32. Encyclopaedia Britannica online, www.britannica.com., accessed April 25, 2008.

33. Ferdinand, "Juvenile Delinquency."

34. Philippe Aires, *Centuries of Childhood* (New York: Knopf, 1962).

35. Ibid., 38.

36. Arlene Skolnick, *The Intimate Environment* (New York: Little, Brown, 1973), 333.

37. Lawrence Stone, "The Massacre of the Innocents, *New York Review* 14 (November 1974): 25–31.

38. The "negative" aspects of the first conception of childhood are emphasized in the discussion by LaMar Empey, *American Delinquency* (Homewood, Ill.: Dorsey, 1982), chaps. 2–3.

39. Aries, *Centuries*, 330–412. See also Lloyd de Mause, ed., *The History of Childhood* (New York: Psychohistory Press, 1974).

40. Joseph E. Illick, "Child Rearing in Seventeenth Century England and America," in de Mause, ed., *The History of Childhood*, 316–317.

41. Frank R. Donovan, *Wild Kids* (Harrisburg, Pa.: Stackpole, 1967), 67.

42. Joseph F. Kett, *Rites of Passage* (New York: Basic Books, 1977); John Demos and Virginia Demos, "Adolescence in Historical Perspective," *Journal of Marriage and the Family* 31 (1969): 632–638.

4

The Origin of Juvenile Justice

Juvenile Institutions

This chapter examines New York City around the year 1825, when the first institution devoted specifically to the confinement and care of juveniles in America was opened. In doing so, this chapter provides specific examples of the general process described in the last chapter—that is, it shows how a new term emerged to describe a new phenomenon. The term itself described a new idea, a new way of interpreting and understanding offending behavior by juveniles. That new idea became the basis for new organizations: the first juvenile institutions.

There is a saying, "Sometimes you can't see the forest for the trees." When you are in a forest, you are so close to it that you can only see individual trees, not the larger patterns and shapes of the forest itself. A person flying over the forest in a plane, in contrast, can see the forest much better but cannot see the trees as well.

The people we study in this chapter were embedded in their historical "forest" so that they could see smaller events (e.g., trees) very easily, but they could not see the larger patterns and shapes very well. We observe these people from the vantage point provided by almost two hundred years—like people flying over a forest in an airplane. While we may miss some details, it is easier for us to recognize the larger patterns and shapes of history.

Historical Context: New York City Around 1820

In 1820, the leaders of the United States were mainly Protestant gentlemen who had been born before the American Revolution into prominent and wealthy families and lived in small, tightly knit towns. For example, imagine one such leader who was 65 years old in 1820. That man would have been born in 1755, when a larger majority of towns in the United States had fewer than 1,000 people, and only a few places had more than 2,500.[1] New York City had fewer than 15,000 people in that year.[2]

That man would have been 21 years old in 1776, when the Declaration of Independence was signed, and 34 years old in 1789, when the United States Constitution was ratified. By 1820, when the man was 65 years old, the population of New York City would have been about 120,000 and was growing rapidly in response to immigration.[3] It was quickly becoming a modern city: densely inhabited and increasingly chaotic, with many different racial and ethnic groups. However, it was governed by these well-born Protestant gentlemen who had grown up in quiet and orderly small towns where people were pretty much the same and everyone knew his or her place and kept to it.

This was the beginning of the transformation of America from a rural and agricultural society into an urban and industrial society. From our vantage point today, we can see the larger patterns and shapes of the changes that were going on, but they could not. All they knew was that they had fought and died to establish a new and noble nation, and now things were apparently breaking down.

Something had gone wrong. Young ruffians ran in gangs through the streets, and watchmen found hungry urchins asleep under doorsteps. Beggars and cutpurses jostled the wealthy on busy thoroughfares. It had been fewer than fifty years since the supposedly perfect nation had been devised, but the noble plans of the forefathers already seemed in jeopardy. Even while the blood of life still coursed through the veins of Thomas Jefferson and John Adams, the perfect experiment seemed on its way to destruction.[4]

In the small, tightly knit towns in which these gentlemen had been born and raised, it was natural for prominent citizens to come together into voluntary associations to resolve community problems.[5] So when New York City began to experience problems, these gentlemen naturally gathered together to discuss what might be done.

The Society for the Prevention of Pauperism

Faced with a disturbing breakdown of quiet and order, the gentlemen held a meeting on December 16, 1817, at the request of John Griscom, a professor of chemistry and natural philosophy, and Thomas Eddy, a financier who had been instrumental in building the Erie Canal. Both were Quakers interested in prison reform. The group constituted itself into a Society for the Prevention of Pauperism, and appointed a committee to write "a statement of the prevailing causes of pauperism, with suggestions relative to the most suitable and efficient remedies." They met again two months later to review what was considered to be a "full and elaborate report."[6]

Paupers as "Undeserving" Poor

The problem was defined as *pauperism*, not as poverty or crime or delinquency. Paupers were "undeserving" poor people—those undeserving of charity because of their wicked and dissolute ways. Paupers were deceitful, traitorous, hostile, rude, brutal, rebellious, sullen, wasteful, cowardly, dirty, and blasphemous. Paupers were lazy and refused to work, they got drunk and passed out in the gutters, they stole things and got into fights with each other, and they let their children run around without proper care and supervision.

Prominent citizens at the time generally believed that paupers were poor *because* they were corrupt and vice-ridden. That is, paupers became poor because it was what they deserved. If they were honest and hardworking, then they would earn an adequate livelihood and would not be poor.

There were, of course, some people who were poor through no fault of their own. These were the "deserving" poor—the poor who were "deserving" of any charity that the wealthy elite of a small town might provide. An example would be the God-fearing widow who scrubbed laundry all night and then gathered up her eight small children to take them to church in the morning.

Such people were poor but they were not a problem—as the Bible says, "the poor you have always with you." The problem was pauperism. Paupers were poor people who had a whole list of nasty characteristics and were poor precisely because of those characteristics. They were the reason that New York City was descending into chaos. In the good old days, the law-abiding citizens would run those people out of town. But suddenly, in New York City, thousands of these paupers were cluttering up the streets—too many to run out of town. Something would have to be done.

The Reports on Pauperism

The first report to the Society was presented in February 1818, and it focused on the conditions in New York City's penitentiaries. Twenty years earlier, Thomas Eddy, one of the two Quakers who called the meeting about paupers, had organized the construction of the first penitentiaries in New York City and had served as its first warden.[7] Prisoners worked in silence, making goods to be sold to pay for their keep. They could also save any additional money they made.

However, free merchants thought this was unfair competition, so a law was passed in 1801 that required all goods to be labeled as prison-made.[8] Sales dropped off dramatically, and things quickly went downhill. In 1802, a major riot occurred at the prison that had to be put down by the military. Conditions continued to deteriorate, and Eddy decided the penitentiary had been a bad idea.

A second report, written in 1819, called attention to the fact that there were no separate facilities for juveniles in these penitentiaries. This was followed by a third report, written by Cadwallader Colden, who was mayor of New York City and the presiding judge of the municipal court[9] (remember, New York had only 120,000 people at this time). Colden was particularly concerned that many youths came before his court who had not received proper care from their parents and they had been charged with relatively minor offenses. Juries would refuse to convict these youths because of their age, but Colden believed that this encouraged the youths to commit more crimes. When they were convicted and sent to the penitentiary, however, Colden believed they were harmed by association with adult criminals. Colden concluded that, for these youths, "the penitentiary cannot but be a fruitful source of pauperism, a nursery of new vices and crimes, a college for the perfection of adepts in guilt." [10]

The fourth report, issued in 1822, took the natural next step of recommending the establishment of a separate penitentiary for juvenile offenders. But they also took another natural step. Remember, this was a society for the *prevention* of pauperism, so they suggested that the new institution focus on the *reform* of the offenders, not on the punishment of offenses: "These prisons should be rather schools for instruction than places for punishment like our present State prisons. . . . The wretchedness and misery of the offender should not be the object of the punishment inflicted; the end should be his reformation and future usefulness."[11]

The focus on prevention was advanced further by Thomas Eddy, who suggested that they bring in youths who had not committed any offenses but were in danger of doing so:

European institutions had been constructed for young criminals, but no one had secured the power from the State of withdrawing, from the custody of weak or criminal parents, children who were vagabonds in the streets and in peril of a criminal life, although no overt act had been committed. The mayor [Colden] well remarks: "Deprived of this power, the institution would lose much of its influence."[12]

This focus on prevention, particularly the focus on juveniles who had not yet committed any crime, was the unique contribution of the New York House of Refuge, and it is why we consider this institution as marking the origin of the modern juvenile justice system.

The New York House of Refuge

The society renamed itself the Society for the Reformation of Juvenile Delinquents,[13] and it developed plans for establishing a "house of refuge" for children in danger of growing up to be paupers and criminals. This first juvenile institution, called the New York House of Refuge, was opened on New Year's Day, 1825, at the present site of Madison Square Garden. At the time, this was about a mile north of the most recently built houses in the city and "was surrounded by cultivated farms, groves, open and rough fields blooming in their season with wild flowers."[14]

Juvenile Penitentiary or Juvenile Poorhouse?

The New York House of Refuge received few, if any, youths who would have been sent to the penitentiary. For example, nine of the first sixteen children sent to the institution had not committed any punishable offense at all.[15] By the end of its first year, the House of Refuge had received a total of seventy-three children.[16] The most serious offender had been convicted of grand larceny. Nine additional children had been sent for petty larceny, and the remaining sixty-three were there for vagrancy, stealing, and running away from the poorhouse.

Of the youths committed to the House of Refuge for punishable offenses, most would not have been sent to the adult penitentiary because of the general reluctance of juries to convict young offenders and place them in adult prisons. That is, they would have gotten off scot-free as earlier indicated. Later in 1825, the New York City district attorney described this situation, in a speech at the House of Refuge:

Before the establishment of the House, a lad of fourteen or fifteen years of age might have been arrested and then tried four or five times for petty thefts, and it was hardly ever that a jury would convict. They would rather that the culprit, acknowledged to be guilty, should be discharged altogether, than be confined in the prisons of our State and county. This rendered the lad more bold in guilt, and I have known instances of lads, now in the House, being indicted half a dozen times, and as often discharged to renew the crimes, and with the conviction that they might steal with impunity.[17]

Because there were few genuinely "criminal" youth, Douglas Rendlemen argued that the House of Refuge really was a juvenile poorhouse rather than a juvenile penitentiary: an institution for poor youth who were in danger of growing up to be paupers.[18] Regardless of whether one agrees with that argument, almost all the children who were sent to this first House of Refuge were poor, but most of those children were not criminals.

In addition, two practices in the House of Refuge were consistent with practices in the poorhouses. First, these juveniles were not sentenced for a certain length of time, proportionate to their offense, as was the case for criminal courts. Rather, boys were committed until their 21st birthday and girls until their 18th birthday (the latter was later amended to be the same as for the boys).[19] Second, commitment to the institution did not require a criminal conviction. A city alderman could simply issue an order admitting the youth, or a parent could apply to the board of the House of Refuge for the youth's admittance.[20]

Also consistent with the practice in the poorhouses was the House of Refuge's heavy emphasis on work.[21] Commentators on the situation in the House of Refuge emphasized the connection between idleness and temptation:

These children come to the institution almost universally heedless and indolent. They have never been put to serious labor, and seem almost to have lost the capacity of entering upon any work requiring intelligence and skill. This condition of mind has rendered their attendance upon school almost profitless, even if they have been sent. . . .

Indolence is the mother of ignorance and impiety. It is the aimlessness and helplessness of these vagrant children than make them so certainly the victims of temptation. Every inmate leaving a reformatory should be able to say: *I learned to work there.* [emphasis in original][22]

The opening paragraph of the first "rules and regulations" of the House of Refuge stated:

The introduction of labor into the House of Refuge, will be regarded principally with reference to the moral benefits to be derived from it. If the employment should be unproductive of much pecuniary profit, still the gain to the city and State will eventually prove considerable, from the reformation and consequently the reduced number of offenders.[23]

The children in the House of Refuge worked for eight hours per day at chair-making, tailoring, brass-nail manufacturing, and silver-plating, in addition to spending four hours a day for their schooling.[24]

The Causes and Cures of Pauperism and Crime

The reformers of this era believed that there were three possible causes of the problems of pauperism and crime among these juveniles: "weak and criminal parents," "the manifold temptations of the streets," and "the peculiar weakness of (the children's) moral nature."[25] The House of Refuge addressed all three problems by removing the children from their parents and from the streets, and by placing them in a highly disciplined program to reinforce their weak moral natures. Thus, the reformers believed that the House of Refuge would successfully cure delinquency.

These reformers, however, tended to focus on the inadequacies of the parent and the child, as opposed to the temptations of the streets. Since many of the urban poor were recent immigrants, whereas the gentlemen reformers were native-born Americans, it has been suggested that these gentlemen reformers tended to see the immigrants as inferior. This tendency was exacerbated when the great Irish immigration took place as a result of the potato famine of the 1840s. Most of the gentlemen reformers were of English extraction, and they looked down on the Irish; in addition, they were Protestant, whereas the Irish immigrants were Roman Catholics. The children of these Irish Catholic immigrants soon came to dominate the population inside the House of Refuge.[26] The gentlemen reformers naturally understood this as a reflection of the inferior racial stock of the Irish rather than attributing the problem to the difficult circumstances under which these people were forced to live.

The managers of the institution were satisfied that the House of Refuge would cure this malady. In their fourth yearly report, they described their many successes:

In almost every case, we do not say in all cases, the discipline of the institution works a reformation. The moral faculties are awakened, the thoughts of the young offender are turned, often with regret, upon his past life, and he is led to resolve on a better course. In many instances, the child not only thinks of his future condition in this world, but his mind is filled with a concern for his eternal as well as his temporal welfare; a conviction is produced that our happiness in this life, as well as in that which is to come, depends on a due application of our moral and physical faculties. The transition of a hopelessness, to the enjoyments in the Refuge of comfort, to the relief which is afforded to the mind by constant and useful employment, to the knowledge of good and evil, to the hope of obtaining an honest living, and to the consolations of religion, must be to him as a new birth.[27]

The "Placing Out" System

There was such a great supply of these potential paupers that the House of Refuge was soon filled, and the question arose as to what to do with all of them. Even though the youths were all committed until they turned 21, "it was never proposed to retain the inmates longer than to become satisfied of their reformation."[28] Yet, sending them back to "the streets" clearly was a bad idea.

By 1828—only three years after the founding of the House of Refuge—the practice was begun of sending youth to work on farms in the newly settled states, such as Ohio, Indiana, and Illinois. This was consistent with the practices of the poorhouses, which had been apprenticing out poor youths since around the year 1600.[29] This apprenticing had not been associated with the penitentiaries, but it supports the argument that the original House of Refuge was really a poorhouse for juveniles, rather than a penitentiary.

Thus, the House of Refuge quickly became a shipping station for poor children who were thought to be in danger of growing up to be paupers. They would be removed from their families and would spend about a year in the House of Refuge, learning good work habits. They then would be placed on trains headed west, where they would be indentured out for service until they reached 21. These apprenticeships soon accounted for 90 percent of the releases from the House of Refuge, with the remainder consisting of deaths, escapes, transfers to adult prisons, and a few outright releases.[30]

This transfer function was later taken over by the Children's Aid Society. For example, in 1854, the society took forty-six boys and girls on a train to a church in a small town in Michigan. The society's journal recorded what happened: "At the close of the sermon the people were informed of the object of the Children's Aid Society. It met with cordial approval of all present and several promised to take the children. . . . Monday morning the boys held themselves in readiness to receive application from the farmers . . . and before Saturday they were all gone."[31]

In other places the children were sent, they would all get off the train in a particular town, where they would be picked over by local farmers. Those who were not chosen to work would get back on the train and move on to the next town. In short, over 50,000 children were removed from New York City in this way.[32]

Most of the time, there was no investigation of the family prior to the placement, nor was there any check on how the child was treated afterward. Many children were never heard from again. Many others became problems in their new homes, either because they were problems to being with or because they were so badly treated. Later on, many Western states passed laws forbidding this practice or required that the Children's Aid Society post a bond for each child to ensure that he or she did not become a public burden.

The natural parents of these children were not usually told where the child had ended up, nor were they allowed further contact with the child, since they were usually seen as the source of the problem. Managers sent glowing reports to the parents about how healthy and happy the children were, but recent historical research has turned up letters from the children relating the terrible conditions under which they lived.[33] These letters were not forwarded to the parents.

Juvenile Delinquent vs. Potential Pauper

Perhaps the best way to understand this new institution is to realize that the original idea of the "juvenile delinquent" was identical with the earlier idea of youths being in danger of growing up to be "paupers." Although the terms sound quite different, at the time they had almost identical meanings.

As mentioned in the previous chapter, the literal meaning of the adjective *delinquent* is that of neglecting or failing to perform tasks required by law or duty, such as failing to pay taxes on time. That meaning is quite similar to the noun *pauper*, which refers to a poor person who neglects or fails to perform the tasks required by law and duty in society: hard, honest work. But while the terms are quite similar in meaning, *juvenile* derives from the second idea of childhood described in chapter 3 and essentially refers to a "potential adult." Considered literally, a juvenile delinquent is a certain kind of potential adult—one who will neglect or fail to perform the hard, honest work required by law and duty.

Because the idea of the juvenile delinquent was so similar to the idea of the potential pauper, the procedures for handling juvenile delinquents resembled the procedures that had long been used to handle potential paupers. Since at least the Poor Law of 1601, in England, young paupers from urban areas had been taken into poorhouses and then apprenticed out to rural areas.[34] This practice was transplanted to the American colonies, and was in frequent and customary use thereafter.[35] With the establishment of the House of Refuge, that practice continued, directed at the same poor population and with the same intent: to ensure that these poor youths grew up to become honest, hard workers.

Part of the reason that juvenile delinquency as an idea and the House of Refuge as an institution were so successful is that they fit comfortably into the ideas and practices of the day. Although it sounded like a new and different idea at the time, the concept of juvenile delinquency was really just a minor variation on the old and well-established idea of potential pauperism. Similarly, while it seemed like a new and promising practice, the House of Refuge was really a minor variation on the old and well-established practice of placing potential paupers from urban areas into a poorhouse for a period of time and then apprenticing them out to rural areas where they could learn the benefits of honest, hard work.

Legal Issues Related to the Juvenile Institutions

The idea of the House of Refuge spread quickly, and a second house was established in Boston, in 1826 (one year after the first one, in New York City). A third house was established in Philadelphia the following year. Thus began some legal challenges to the system.

The Case of Mary Ann Crouse

Mary Ann Crouse was a girl who was sent to the Philadelphia House of Refuge. Like many other youths, she had not committed a criminal offense, but she was a poor child who appeared to be in danger of growing up to become a pauper. On the complaint of her mother, she was brought into court and committed to the House of Refuge. Her father objected to this, and he filed a writ of *habeas corpus* (a legal demand for the state to explain why it is holding someone).

Mary Ann's father thereby raised a crucial legal issue. A very basic principle of criminal law is that there should be no punishment unless a crime has been committed. But Mary Ann had not committed any crime.

Her father argued that the state had no right to punish her, so she should be released.

The case went to the Pennsylvania Supreme Court, which handed down its opinion in 1838. In it, the court rejected the father's arguments and held that sending Mary Ann to the House of Refuge was perfectly legal:

> The object of the charity is reformation, by training its inmates to industry; by imbuing their minds with principles of morality and religion; by furnishing them with means to earn a living; and, above all, by separating them from the corrupting influence of improper associates. To this end, may not the natural parents, when unequal to the task of education, or unworthy of it, be superseded by the parens patriae, or common guardian of the community? . . . The infant has been snatched from a course which must have ended in confirmed depravity; and not only is the restraint of her person lawful, but it would be an act of extreme cruelty to release her from it.[36]

Four points in this quotation form the basis of the decision. Each is important for later developments in the juvenile justice system. First, the state court argued that Mary Ann was being *helped*, not punished. The House of Refuge was a *charitable school*, not a prison. The objective of the House was to *save* her from a terrible fate, not to punish her for criminal offenses. The question of whether children in juvenile institutions are being punished or helped is one that comes up again and again in the history of the juvenile justice system.

Second, the state court compared the *good intentions* of those who ran the House of Refuge with the *actual performance* of Mary Ann's parents. In fact, by 1838, the juvenile institutions had already abandoned most elements of rehabilitation and had become heavily oriented toward custody. The rigid routine was marked by numerous escape attempts and inmate uprisings, which were followed by whippings and leg irons and cold showers in the middle of winter.[37] If the court had compared the *actual* performance of the House of Refuge with the good intentions of Mary Ann's parents, it might have reached the opposite decision. The comparison between good intentions and actual performance is one that will be made several more times in the legal history of the juvenile justice system.

Third, the state court argued that it was legal to "help" Mary Ann because of the state's role as *parens patriae*.[38] This Latin phrase means "parent of the country," and it was originally used in the 1500s in England in connection with children whose parents had died, leaving an estate. In such cases, a special court (called a chancery court) would manage the estate until it could be turned over to the child at the age of 21. This was done on the theory that, when the child's natural parents were dead, the state, as parent of the country (*parens patriae*), would take over the role of the child's parent.

The case of Mary Ann Crouse was the first time that this concept was applied to a poor child whose parents were still alive (rather than to a presumably wealthy child whose parents had died and left an estate). There was a certain similarity: in the one case, the parents were dead, while in the other, the parents were "unequal to the task of education, or unworthy of it." Sixty years later, the concept of *parens patriae* would become the legal foundation of the first juvenile court. The question of whether *parens patriae* was a legitimate or appropriate rationale for sending children to institutions, however, would continue to be debated.

Fourth, because the Pennsylvania Supreme Court held that Mary Ann was not being punished, it also held that she did not need any protections of formal due process granted to defendants in a criminal trial. One of those protections was the legal doctrine that there should be no punishment without a crime. Mary Ann had been brought into a criminal court and sent to an institution when she had not committed any crime. But the court held that she was not being punished, so it did not matter that she had not committed a crime. The question of whether juveniles are entitled to the formal protections of due process is one that continued to be raised in legal cases involving the juvenile justice system.

This was the first legal challenge to the increasingly widespread practice of bringing children who had not committed any criminal offense into criminal court and committing them to a House of Refuge until they were 21 years old. This was part of Thomas Eddy's original idea in his proposal to establish the New York House of Refuge. While the court upheld the practice in this case, another case arose thirty years later that produced the opposite result.

The Case of Daniel O'Connell

By 1868, over twenty houses of refuge had sprung up all over the country, and through the years they housed between 40,000 and 50,000 youths.[39] After 1850, however, the apprenticing system began to break down, and it became harder and harder to place children in jobs when they were released.[40] Accordingly, the number of outright discharges increased, and children were simply sent back to their homes. Increasing levels of violence occurred in the Houses of Refuge, and, in general, they were no longer existed in such an idealized glow.

One of the newer Houses of Refuge had been established in Chicago, and through its doors came a boy named Daniel O'Connell. Like Mary Ann Crouse, he had not committed any criminal offense, but he had appeared to be in danger of growing up to become a pauper and was committed to the school until his 21st birthday. Daniel's parents objected and, like Mary Ann's father, filed a writ of *habeus corpus*.

This case went to the Illinois Supreme Court, which ordered Daniel released in 1870.[41] Thus, the court reached the opposite decision in a case that was almost identical to that of Mary Ann Crouse. The legal reasoning of that latter decision can be compared with the legal reasoning in the *Crouse* case, on each of the four points described above.

First, in the O'*Connell* case, the Illinois Supreme Court concluded that Daniel was being *punished*, not helped, by being sent to the reform school:

> Why should minors be imprisoned for misfortune? Destitution of proper parental care, ignorance, idleness and vice, are misfortunes, not crimes. . . . This boy is deprived of a father's care; bereft of home influences; has not freedom of action; is committed for an uncertain time; is branded as a prisoner; made subject to the will of others, and thus feels he is a slave.[42]

Recall that the Pennsylvania Supreme Court took the opposite stance: that Mary Ann was being *helped*, not punished, by being sent to the House of Refuge.

Second, in the O'*Connell* case, the state court described the harsh realities of the Chicago Reform School, but it seemed to grant the benefit of the doubt to Daniel's parents, who were presumed to care for the boy and want to provide good "home influences." That is, in the O'*Connell* decision, the court compared the *actual performance* of the Chicago Reform School with the *good intentions* of Daniel's parents. The Pennsylvania Supreme Court had taken the opposite stance, describing the House of Refuge in idealistic terms and Mary Ann's parents in harsh ones. This change reflected the fact that reform schools were now almost fifty years old and much of the idealism concerning them had faded.

Third, the Illinois Supreme Court rejected the *parens patriae* doctrine as the basis for dealing with juveniles. The Illinois Supreme Court simply viewed Daniel as being "imprisoned," so its decision focused on legal doctrines related to criminal courts and criminal punishments.[43] The doctrine of *parens patriae*, and related concepts like chancery courts and the "best interests" of children, were irrelevant and did not enter into the decision.

Fourth, once the idealized and romanticized view of the House of Refuge as a solution for juvenile delinquency was discarded, the need for the formal due process protections became obvious:

> Can the State, as *parens patriae*, exceed the power of the natural parent, except in punishing crime? These laws provide for the "safe keeping" of the child; they direct his "commitment" and only a "ticket of leave" or the uncontrolled discretion of a board of guardians, will permit the imprisoned boy to breathe the pure air of heaven outside his prison walls. . . . The confinement may be from one to fifteen years, according to the age of the child. Executive clemency cannot open the prison doors for no offense has been committed. The writ of *habeas corpus*, a writ for the security of liberty, can afford no relief, for the sovereign power of the State as *parens patriae* has determined the imprisonment beyond recall. Such restraint upon natural liberty is tyranny and oppression. If, without crime, without the conviction of an offense, the children of the State are thus to be confined for the "good of Society," then Society had better be reduced to its original elements and free government acknowledged a failure. . . . Even criminals cannot be convicted and imprisoned without due process of law.[44]

Similarities Between the Two Cases

The similarities and differences in these two cases can be summed up in table 4.1.

What is remarkable, given the fact that they reached opposite decisions, is that these two cases presented the judges with virtually identical sets of facts. Neither juvenile had committed a criminal offense, but both were committed to a juvenile institution until they were 21. Both fathers

Table 4.1.   A Comparison Between the *Crouse* and *O'Connell* Cases

	Crouse Case	*O'Connell* Case
Court focused on	Good intentions	Actual performance
Juveniles were said to be	Helped and treated	Punished
Legal basis of court's decision	*Parens patriae*	Criminal law
Decision	Due process is not required	Due process is required

sought release of their child by filing a writ of *habeus corpus*. Each case went to the state supreme court, where opposite decisions were reached.

The *Crouse* court warmly viewed the House of Refuge, while coldly glaring at the inadequacies of Mary Ann's parents. They concluded that she was being helped by the House of Refuge, that she did not need to be protected from this help by the formal requirements of due process, and that the legal basis for all of this was the *parens patriae* doctrine that the state could step in as parent when the natural parents failed in their role. While so strong a stance is rarely taken today, many people view juvenile justice in essentially similar terms.

The O'*Connell* court, in contrast, coldly glared at the inadequacies of the Chicago Reform School, but cast warm glances in the direction of the (supposedly) loving parents. They concluded that Daniel was being treated like a criminal even though he had not committed a crime. The legal protections of formal due process, therefore, were as important to him as to an adult, and the doctrine of *parens patriae* was irrelevant. Many people continue to view juvenile justice in essentially similar terms today.

The Larger Impact of These Cases

The O'*Connell* case set the stage for the founding of the first juvenile court in Chicago, in 1899. The judge had ruled that it was illegal to send poor children to reform schools unless they had committed a felony offense. As a result of that case, "by 1890 the Illinois system of handling delinquent children, haphazard at best, had virtually evaporated."[45]

Many people at the time believed that sending poor children to institutions, even though they had committed no crimes, had been a good practice and was best for the children themselves. The O'*Connell* ruling, therefore, outlawed a practice that they thought was good, just, and important. These people went looking for a new legal basis to continue this practice, even though the court had defined it as illegal. They created that new legal basis by founding the first juvenile court.

Essentially, the juvenile court was invented to get around the O'*Connell* ruling. It allowed Illinois once again to send to juvenile institutions poor children who had not committed a criminal offense. Thus, the juvenile court did not establish a new practice for juvenile justice. Rather, it allowed Illinois to return to the old practice with a new mechanism and a new legal rationale. As we will see later, however, the establishment of the juvenile court did not provide a final end to this debate, as we will see these same issues revisited in future cases.

The Lessons of History

Several lessons emerge from this discussion of the early attempts to deal with the rise of juvenile delinquency that we will see again and again throughout the cycle of juvenile justice. In particular these lessons help us to understand why a particular reform became popular at a given historical time. As we saw in this chapter, juvenile delinquency as an idea and the House of Refuge as a practice spread quickly throughout the country. They did not solve the problem of urban property crime by lower-class youth, but they did win the competition with other interpretations of this phenomenon and other ways of responding to it. As such, they became the basis of the present juvenile justice system while other ideas and other reforms faded away, leaving no trace in today's world.

We can ask why this particular idea and this particular reform were "successful" in comparison with other possible ideas and reforms. Other ideas besides that of juvenile delinquency can be used for understanding and interpreting urban property crime by lower-class youth. There also are other mechanisms besides a "house of refuge" for responding to this phenomenon. So, why did this particular idea and this particular policy succeed at the time and become the basis for our modern juvenile justice system? Phrased bluntly, why did this idea and reform "sell" better than others?

The Cycle of Juvenile Justice

The problem faced by the gentlemen reformers in New York City in the early 1820s fits into the cycle of juvenile justice, as described in chapter 1. High juvenile crime rates were accompanied by a firm belief that juvenile crime had not been a problem back in the good old days. Harsh punishments were available, but the reluctance of officials to impose these punishments meant that many youth were let off scot-free. Officials at the time, such as Mayor Colden, thought both of these alternatives increased juvenile crime.

The House of Refuge was designed to provide a middle ground between punishing harshly and doing nothing at all. It offered leniency for those who would have been harshly punished, and it provided some response for those juveniles who would have otherwise received no punishment.[46]

Thus, the cycle begins with a sense of the problem and an attempt at reform. If the cycle exists as we have described it, then we can expect to find that the juvenile crime rates will remain high despite the introduction of leniency and that many people will remain convinced that the rates can be reduced through appropriate (e.g., more harsh) justice policies.

The Idea of Juvenile Delinquency: Potential Pauper

The idea of juvenile delinquency, as proposed by the gentlemen reformers in New York City, sounded new and different, as well as exciting and promising. But in reality it was just a slightly revised version of the old and popular idea that poor youths are potential paupers. Taken literally, the two terms—delinquents and paupers—have almost identical meanings.

Though the idea of juvenile delinquency seemed new, it did not require people to think differently from how they had thought in the past. By its fitting comfortably into the historical and philosophical context of the day, people felt satisfied believing that they were taking a new look at things without experiencing the trouble and inconvenience of actually having to grapple with new concepts and ideas.

The Idea of Juvenile Justice: House of Refuge

The House of Refuge as a method for responding to the delinquency problem seemed new and different, as well as exciting and promising. Because it seemed innovative, people were optimistic that it would solve the problems of delinquency. In fact, however, the House of Refuge was just a slightly modified version of the well-established method for handling paupers: put them in an institution for a period of time and then apprentice them out to rural areas until they become adults. Like the new idea of juvenile delinquency, the House of Refuge was popular in part because it sounded new and different even though it wasn't.

The House of Refuge did establish a new legal basis for the old practice. The old legal basis was in the poor laws, but these had begun to disappear by the end of the 1800s.[47] The new legal basis was found in the *Crouse* decision, thus the practice was able to survive and grow as its former legal basis was dying.

Economic Interests of the Rich and Powerful

The gentlemen reformers believed that delinquency had three causes: "the peculiar weaknesses of (the children's) moral natures," "weak and criminal parents," and "the manifold temptations of the streets." Our perspective today assigns the major problem to the "streets" rather than inherent weaknesses in parents or children—that is, we attribute the causes of those crimes to the conditions under which poor parents and children lived.

Today, we know that those poor parents and children at the time found themselves in a new historical situation, with the beginning of urbanization and industrialization. We also know that every time this historical situation has occurred, the modern problem of juvenile delinquency has soon followed.[48] Thus, it is reasonable for us to conclude that these parents and children probably were no "weaker" or "more criminal" than parents and children at other times when, and other places where, the problem of delinquency does not appear.

But, as a reform measure, the House of Refuge did not attempt to change the streets in any way. Instead, it removed children from the streets who were thought to have "weak moral natures" and "weak and criminal parents." The major thrust of the House of Refuge was to address these supposed weaknesses in the child and the parent, yet today it seems clear that these weaknesses were not the real problem.

Would it have been possible at the time to change "the streets"—that is, the conditions under which poor people lived? To ask the question might provoke protests that nothing could have been done anyway, and so there is no point in thinking about it. We argue that this simply is not true. There were at least some things that could have been done at the time to improve the conditions under which poor people lived. In fact, there were people espousing those policies at the time.[49] However, these ideas were not implemented because prominent and powerful people were unwilling to consider them. It was much easier for the wealthy and powerful to believe that something was wrong with poor children and their parents than to think that something was wrong with this new urban society.

From our vantage point almost two hundred years later, we can argue that the idea of juvenile delinquency as potential pauperism, and the House of Refuge as a policy response, succeeded at the time in part because they were convenient for the rich and powerful people of the day to believe. Other ideas and other policy responses, especially those that would have attempted to change the conditions under which poor people lived, would have been inconvenient, in that they would have threatened the economic interests of the rich and powerful. Those ideas were developing at the time, but they were not implemented.

Moral and Intellectual Superiority of the Reformers

Reformers in New York City confronted a world that they did not understand. There was an enormous social distance between the small group of prominent and powerful gentlemen who ran the city and the large number of poor immigrants with whom they were so concerned. Faced with the uncertainty of the new and unknown, these reformers chose to believe that children with "peculiar weaknesses of moral nature" were being raised by "weak and criminal parents."

We have argued that this interpretation was convenient, in that it did not challenge the reformers' economic interests. But this interpretation also reinforced a sense of moral and intellectual superiority. By believing that immigrant groups were morally inferior, the gentlemen reformers correspondingly believed that they were morally superior.[50] People always like to believe good things about themselves. How much better it must have felt to think that these "others" were morally inferior than to see their problems as arising from social conditions that they and their rich friends had created, maintained, and profited from? Their sense of moral superiority, then, justified taking control of the situation and fed the vast optimism about the effectiveness of their actions.

The Unfair Comparison

Vast optimism is a natural reaction whenever people undertake a reform, particularly when approaching difficult problems such as delinquency. Like today, people at that time wanted a sure cure for the problem.[51] They wanted to believe that everything would work out just fine, and they tended to believe anyone who promised that it would.

As evident in the *Crouse* decision, this optimism was supported by focusing on the reformer's good intentions, and by assuming that the actual practices associated with those reforms would fulfill those intentions. The founders of the New York House of Refuge assumed that things would work out in practice according to their good intentions; if there were problems, it was just a question of working out the details. In their idealism, the reformers did not anticipate the many difficult and ultimately insoluble problems that would develop in these houses of reform.

This vast optimism about the future was further supported by comparisons to the highly critical, pessimistic views of prior policies. This is a common practice for reformers, who usually emphasize the failures and inadequacies of past policies, portraying them as much worse than they really are. Pessimistic assessments of the past are based on actual practices, whereas potential is based on good intentions.

The unfair comparison, then, is that between an optimistic, idealistic assessment of the future, based on good intentions, and a pessimistic, cynical assessment of the past, based on the actual performance. Structuring the comparison this way fuels the drive for change.

This is the comparison found in the *Crouse* and *O'Connell* cases. In the *Crouse* case, the good intentions of those running the House of Refuge were compared to the actual performance of Mary Ann's parents. In the *O'Connell* case, the actual performance of the Chicago Reform School was compared to the good intentions of Daniel's parents. In each situation, an unfair comparison was used to justify the court's decision, whereas a fair comparison would have made the decisions appear less certain and more problematic.

It is usually easy to make an unfair comparison at any time of reform. Reformers propose new policies that are not yet implemented or have only just been implemented. Good intentions are in abundance, but actual practices are scarce. Thus, it is easy to gaze lovingly at the good intentions of reformers while casting a sideways glance at what actually happens.

In contrast, past policies have been in effect for years, so the actual practices are apparent. Whatever lofty idealism accompanied those policies when established has been worn down by the intractable problems that the policies created, leaving cynical and burnt-out people as their advocates. Even if the good intentions remain, their proponents lack the fervor, excitement, and certainty that were there initially. Ignorance, after all, is bliss.

Expansion of State Power

Ultimately, bright hopes for the future, based on the moral superiority and good intentions of the reformers, justified an expansion of state power. The Pennsylvania Supreme Court found that Mary Ann Crouse did not need due process protections because she did not need to be protected from those well-intentioned reformers. The reformers were granted this power because of an optimistic assessment that they would use it for Mary Ann's own good.

Expansion of state power, therefore, was linked with optimism about the effectiveness of the House of Refuge. The optimism itself was not justified by the actual performance of that institution, which had already degenerated substantially, but by the good intentions of its founders. When the *O'Connell* court later found that juveniles did need due process, it was because the court had looked at actual performance rather than at good intentions.

Reformers usually want to expand state power rather than limit it. They usually believe in their ability to do good things, and they do not want their efforts to be restricted by laws and due process rights. How comfortable the *Crouse* decision must have felt with these reformers, so sure of their ability to do good. How uncomfortable the *O'Connell* decision must have felt, with its implication that Daniel needed protection from these very reformers.

If these lessons of history are correct, then we will find the same patterns accompanying the next attempt at reform: the founding of the first juvenile court in Chicago, in 1899. Ultimately, the question is whether, and in what way, such lessons might apply today.

NOTES

1. David J. Rothman, *The Discovery of the Asylum* (Boston: Little, Brown, 1971), 12.
2. Ibid., 13.
3. Bradford Kinney Peirce, *A Half Century with Juvenile Delinquents* (Montclair, N.J.: Patterson Smith, 1969), 41 (originally published in 1869).
4. Robert S. Picket, *House of Refuge* (Syracuse: Syracuse University Press, 1969), xviii–xix, quoted in Harold Finestone, *Victims of Change* (Westport, Conn.: Greenwood, 1976), 19.
5. For a discussion of the role of prominent gentlemen in colonial America, see Paul K. Longmore, *The Invention of George Washington* (Berkeley: University of California Press, 1988).
6. Peirce, *A Half Century*, 32–38.
7. Blake McKelvey, *American Prisons* (Montclair, N.J.: Patterson Smith, 1977), 8.
8. Joseph J. Senna and Larry J. Siegel, *Introduction to Criminal Justice* (St. Paul: West, 1978), 366.
9. Peirce, *A Half Century*, 40.
10. Ibid.
11. Ibid., 41–42.
12. Ibid., 34; see also 54.
13. Ibid., 63, 65.
14. Ibid., 74.
15. Robert H. Bremner, ed., *Children and Youth in America*, Vol. 1 (Cambridge, Mass.: Harvard University Press, 1970), 13.
16. Sanford Fox, "Juvenile Justice Reform: An Historical Perspective," *Stanford Law Review* 22 (1970): 1187 pl. 1192.
17. Peirce, *A Half Century*, 79.
18. Douglas Rendleman, "Parens Patriae: From Chancery to the Juvenile Court," *South Carolina Law Review* 23 (1971): 205, reprinted in Frederic L. Faust and Paul J. Brantingham, *Juvenile Justice Philosophy* (St. Paul, Minn.: West, 1979), 58–96.

19. Peirce, *A Half Century*, 105.

20. Ibid., 82–83.

21. A similar connection between prisons and productive labor has been documented in Dario Melossi and Massimo Pavarini, *The Prison and the Factory: Origins of the Penitentiary System* (London: Macmillan, 1979).

22. Peirce, *A Half Century*, 84–85.

23. Quoted in ibid., 86.

24. Ibid., 87.

25. Ibid., 82.

26. Finestone, *Victims of Change*, 31.

27. Peirce, *A Half Century*, 110

28. Ibid., 105.

29. Rendlemand, "Parens Paatriae," 62.

30. Robert M. Mennel, *Thorns and Thistles* (Hanover, N.H.: University Press of New England, 1973), 22–23.

31. Quoted in Walter I. Trattner, *From Poor Law to Welfare State* (New York: Free Press, 1974), 103.

32. Ibid., 104.

33. Bremner, *Children and Youth*, 22–26. As late as 1894, an overseer of the poor in Pennsylvania was prosecuted for indenturing a 7-year-old boy to a cruel farmer. The overseer had been warned about the farmer and visited the boy after he was indentured, but did not find anything wrong. The boy died of starvation and overwork after only a few months. See *Commonwealth v. Coyle*, 160 Pa. 36, 28 A. 576, 28 A. 634 (1894), cited in Rendleman, "Parens Patriae," 63, n. 29.

34. Trattner, *From Poor Law to Welfare State*, 10–12.

35. Stefan A. Riesenfield, "The Formative Era of American Public Assistance Law," *California Law Review* 43, no. 2 (1955): 175–233.

36. Mennel, *Thorns and Thistles*, 14.

37. Ibid., 19–20. Mennel quotes a disgruntled former employee who wrote an "exposé" about the place (p. 27). See also John Mahony's account of his experiences as a boy in the House of Refuge in Charles Sutton, *The New York Tombs* (New York: U.S. Publishing, 1874), 171–176 (reprinted Montclair, N.J.: Patterson-Smith). Mahony describes how "my first promptings towards crime originated in the House of Refuge." He concludes: "I have been a prisoner in Sing Sing State Prison when it was at its worst, but in many respects, I would rather be confined in Sing Sing than in the House of Refuge, as the "Refuge" was conducted when I was there."

38. Rendleman, "Parens Patriae."

39. Peirce, *A Half Century*, 78.

40. Mennel, *Thorns and Thistles*, 62.

41. *People v. Turner*, 55 Ill. 280 (1870).

42. Quoted in Mennel, *Thorns and Thistles*, 125.

43. Only twelve years later, the same court reversed itself and approved, in a roundabout way, the concept of *parens patriae*. This was the Ferrier case

(103 Ill. 367, 1882). Rendleman, "Parens Patriae," (82) states: "The Illinois Supreme Court, by striking down the legislature's idea that poor children could be taken from their parents [in the *O'Connell* case], gave the onus to the legislature to develop an alternative. The legislature came back with more of the same and the court receded [in the *Ferrier* case].

44. Quoted in Anthony Platt, *The Child Savers* (Chicago: University of Chicago Press, 1977), 103–104.

45. Mennel, *Thorns and Thistles*, 127–128.

46. In terms of the law of criminal justice thermodynamics, introduced in chapter 2, the House of Refuge reduced the severity of the penalty so as to increase the frequency of its application. See Samuel Walker, *Sense and Nonsense About Crime*, 2nd ed. (Pacific Grove, Calif.: Brooks/Cole, 1989), 46–48; see also chapter 2 for a discussion of this concept.

47. Rendleman, "Parens Patriae."

48. Louise Shelley, *Crime and Modernization* (Carbondale: Southern Illinois University Press, 1981).

49. See Philip Jenkins, "Varieties of Enlightenment Criminology," *British Journal of Criminology* 24, no. 2 (April 1984): 112–130, for a discussion of more "radical" theories developing around that time.

50. In general, see Emile Durkheim on crime as "normal" in society, summarized in George B. Vold, Thomas J. Bernard, and Jeffrey B. Snipes, *Theoretical Criminology*, 5th ed. (New York: Oxford University Press, 2002).

51. James O. Finkenauer, *Scared Straight! And the Panacea Phenomenon* (Englewood Cliffs, N.J.: Prentice-Hall, 1982).

5

The Origin of Juvenile Justice

The Juvenile Court

Thomas Eddy had come up with the idea that children in danger of growing up to be paupers and criminals could be taken away from their parents (even though they had not committed any offense) and placed in institutions where they would be trained to be hard-working, God-fearing, law-abiding citizens. His idea spread throughout the country during the 1800s, but then it was largely dismantled in Illinois due to the *O'Connell* decision in 1870. Many prominent and powerful people in the state had favored this system, and thus they were in the market for a new legal mechanism for reestablishing it. They succeeded in creating it by founding the first juvenile court.

This new juvenile court was not a junior criminal court as we think of it today. It was a social welfare agency, the central processing unit of the entire child welfare system. Children who had needs of any kind could be brought into the juvenile court, where their troubles would be diagnosed and the services they needed provided by court workers or obtained from other agencies.

One aspect of this system was similar to the criminal courts; that is, the juvenile court had coercive powers. Other welfare agencies were voluntary, so that children or parents who did not wish to receive the services could simply refuse them. The new juvenile court, in contrast, was endowed with even greater coercive powers than criminal court. Parents and children had almost no ability to resist the court's efforts to "help." With such great power in the service of so noble an undertaking, the founders of the juvenile court were certain that the problem of juvenile delinquency would soon be solved.

As in New York City seventy-five years earlier, when the first House of Refuge was established, the views that led to the establishment of this court can be understood only by analyzing their context. We begin by looking at conditions in Chicago around the year 1900.

Historical Context: Chicago at the Turn of the Century

No other city ever grew as rapidly as Chicago did in the 1800s.[1] A person who was born in Chicago in 1840 started life in a village of 5,000 people. By the time that person was 60 years old, in 1900, Chicago was a gigantic metropolis of 1.5 million. This growth was fueled by wave upon wave of immigrants. In 1890, 70 percent of the people who lived in Chicago had been born in foreign countries. Most of the remainder were first-generation Americans whose parents had been born abroad.

In this enormous city, only a small group of people had been in America for several generations, but this group controlled almost the entire political life and business establishments in the city. Like the gentlemen reformers who had founded the first juvenile institution in New York, members of this group were quite wealthy and almost all of them had been born in small towns or villages. Like those earlier reformers, these people were profoundly disturbed at the breakdown of social order and the seeming chaos that Chicago had become, and they focused their attention on the children, since the adults seemed to be lost causes. Again, like the reformers before them, they generally believed that there were three "causes" of this disorder: weak and criminal parents, the manifold temptations of the streets, and the peculiar weakness of the juveniles' moral natures.

The Latest Scientific Thinking

The latest scientific thinking supported these general beliefs. In 1859, Darwin published his book on the theory of evolution, and he applied that theory to human beings in 1871.[2] The theory that human beings had evolved from lesser species led rather quickly to the view (called social Darwinism) that some racial or ethnic groups of people were more highly evolved than others. In particular, the view became popular among white Anglo-Saxon Protestants that their group was the most highly evolved, and that other groups were biologically inferior.

In 1876, the Italian physician Lombroso used evolution to explain crime.[3] He argued that criminals were biological throwbacks to an earlier evolutionary state, that they were "less civilized" and more inclined to engage in violence and theft. This was called the theory of the "atavistic" criminal, and it became very popular among groups that considered themselves more highly evolved.

Thus, the latest thinking in biological evolution suggested that some people were less evolved than others, and the latest thinking in criminology suggested that less evolved people tended to commit more crimes. As it happened, virtually all of the powerful people in Chicago were white Anglo-Saxon Protestants, while a great majority of the recent immigrants were not. This meant that, aside from other possible explanations, it could be argued that crime and disorder resulted because members of these immigrant groups were biologically inferior.

This gave powerful people a sense of certainty in their own views, since they believed themselves superior and the other groups inferior. Unfortunately, this sense of certainty and superiority was combined with at least some ignorance of the supposedly inferior people. And that ignorance was generated by the enormous social distance that existed between the very small group of wealthy, powerful, native-born Americans and the vast bulk of poor immigrant people.[4]

The Position of Women

Whereas the first juvenile institutions had been founded by men, the first juvenile court was largely the result of the work of women. Anthony Platt examined the work of these women and presents a rather cynical view that illustrates the social distance, sense of superiority, and feeling of certainty that dominated their accomplishments.[5]

According to Platt, these women were not progressives, leading the charge for social reform. Such progressive women were active at the time, but they were being arrested and imprisoned for advocating such dangerous ideas as the use of birth control and granting women the right to vote. In contrast, the women who founded the first juvenile court were relatively conservative politically. They primarily were the wives and daughters of the prominent and powerful men who ran Chicago's political and business establishments. Like those men, they were wealthy, white, Anglo-Saxon, and Protestant. And like them, they had a sense of their own superiority and of their God-given, natural status at the peak of the social hierarchy.

These women were in a dilemma. They were energetic, educated, talented, and perceptive, and they believed that the wealthy had an obligation to return something to society through public service. But they were also conservative, and they believed in the traditional woman's role as related to home, family, and children. Finally, they were wealthy, with plenty of servants to cook and clean for them and to raise their children. Since their traditional woman's role as keeper of the house and hearth was assumed by servants, in a very real sense these women had nothing else to do.

Thus, they solved this dilemma by addressing the problems of poor children. Taking care of children was at the heart of the traditional woman's role, so these wealthy women used their energies, talents, and abilities to achieve what they perceived was appropriate work for women. Initially, this drive led them into the slums of Chicago to work with the children directly. Ultimately, they extended their efforts to going before the city council and state legislature, arguing for major policy changes in the handling of juvenile offenders. Unless the subject was directly related to the problems of children, such involvement by women in the political process would have been incompatible with their traditional role, so taking on this effort had considerable benefits for them.

The First Juvenile Court

These women confronted a criminal justice system that had, in their view, largely broken down. For most of the century, a "preventive" system had been in place, taking poor children in danger of becoming paupers and criminals out of their homes and putting them into reform schools where they could be helped. But this system had been derailed by the O'Connell case, which declared the practice illegal. After that ruling, only children who had been convicted of felonies could be sent to reform schools.[6] According to Richard Tuthill, who later became the first juvenile court judge, this decision "overthrew the whole prospect we then had of getting a chance to aid the boys."

The Problem and the Solution

Attention was increasingly focused on children who could not be sent to the reform schools because they had not committed felonies. Judges continued to believe that it was important to remove these children from the influence of their weak and criminal parents, as well as the manifold temptations of the streets, so the children often ended up in poorhouses, police lockups, or county jails.

How many children fell into this category? Julia Lathrop, who was later chief of the Federal Children's Bureau, reported that in the six months prior to the establishment of the first juvenile court, 332 boys between the ages of 9 and 16 were sent to the city prison in Chicago.[7] Of that number, 320 were sent based on a blanket charge of "disorderly conduct," which could represent a variety of offending behaviors from trivial to fairly serious. About one-third of these were pardoned by the mayor, usually as a favor to the local alderman.

> But the significant fact which must not be overlooked is that, even if "let off" by the justice or pardoned by the mayor, no constructive work was done in the child's behalf. He was returned to the same surroundings that had promoted his delinquency, in all probability to be caught again and brought before another justice who, knowing nothing of the previous arrests, would discharge or find him again as seemed wise at the time. . . . Boys were kept in "Lockups" and in jails in the company of adult prisoners, under circumstances which were a guaranty of ruined character, and were "let off with a scolding" by the justices because a jail sentence, however well deserved according to the law, was so manifestly bad for the boy.[8]

From this description, it is apparent that officials in Chicago faced the same dilemma as did officials in New York City seventy-five years earlier: either punish harshly or do nothing. Both options seemed to increase crime among juveniles.

As a member of the Board of State Commissioners of Public Charities, Lathrop inspected all these facilities and raised a public outcry about the treatment of these children. Her report was presented in 1898, and contained arguments about preventing pauperism similar to those made earlier in New York:

> There are at the present moment in the State of Illinois, especially in the city of Chicago, thousands of children in need of active intervention for their preservation from physical, mental and moral destruction. Such intervention is demanded, not only by sympathetic consideration for their well-being, but also in the name of the commonwealth for the preservation of the State. If the child is the material out of which men and women are made, the neglected child is the material out of which paupers and criminals are made.[9]

Later that year, as a result of pressures generated by Lathrop and others, the annual meeting of the Illinois Conference of Charities voted to recommend the establishment of a separate court for juveniles. The idea was suggested by Frederick Wines, one of the most prominent penologists in the country, and it quickly gathered wide support. The measure was passed unanimously by the Illinois Legislature on January 1, 1899, and it went into effect six months later.

The Legal Model of the Original Juvenile Court

The legal problem that had been raised by the *O'Connell* decision was the inability to deal with the "neglected child" who was "the material out of which paupers and criminals are made." The court ruled that such children could not be sent to reform schools. In contrast, serious juvenile offenders were not a problem because they already could be sent there. So, if the new court was to be a solution to this legal problem, it had to get around the *O'Connell* ruling. A way to do this was found in the decision of the earlier *Crouse* case.

As was explained in the previous chapter, in that case, the judge argued that it was legal to commit Mary Ann Crouse to the House of Refuge because of *parens patriae*—the idea that the state is the ultimate parent of all of its citizens. The objection raised in the *O'Connell* case was that the state had no right to do this in criminal court. *Parens patriae* was, however, a power held by the Chancery court, which was a court in England that administered the property of orphans who had inherited estates. Legally, the Chancery court was supposed to preserve the best interests of the child until the child was old enough to take control of the estate. These courts had existed in England since the 1500s.

The solution, then, was to define the new juvenile court as a chancery court, not as a criminal court. This suited the purpose admirably. Chancery court was designed to help children who lacked proper parental care because their parents had died. But delinquent children lacked proper parental care because their parents were "weak and criminal." Chancery court had nothing to do with punishment, but it operated in the best interests of the child. If the new juvenile court had nothing to do with punishment, but only operated in the best interests of the child, then the legal objection raised in the *O'Connell* case would not apply.

Legal Steps to Establish the Juvenile Court

To establish a juvenile court as a chancery court required two separate steps: jurisdiction over juveniles had to be (1) removed from criminal court, and (2) established in the new juvenile court. These two steps were contained in the legislation passed by the Illinois Legislature in 1899.

The first step was accomplished by raising the age of criminal liability to 16. Recall that under English common law, children under the age of

7 could not be convicted of a crime, no matter what they did, because it was held that they did not have sufficient reasoning ability to form *mens rae* (criminal intent).

The Illinois legislature raised this age to 16 in 1899, and eight years later, it raised it to 17 for boys and 18 for girls.[10] As a result, those children who were younger than these ages could not be charged with a crime in criminal court because legally they did not have sufficient reasoning ability to form criminal intent. This change in the age of criminal liability removed jurisdiction over juveniles from the criminal court.

Crime consists of *actus rea* (the behavior itself) and *mens rea* (the criminal intent).[11] If juveniles could not legally form *mens rea*, then they legally could not commit a crime. They could still kill people and force them to have sex, beat people up and break into houses, and knock old ladies down and take their purses. However, these would not be crimes; rather, they were acts that would be a crime if committed by an adult. Similarly, people who are totally insane cannot commit crimes, but they can commit acts that would be crimes if committed by sane persons.

After jurisdiction was removed from adult criminal court, the legislature established a new court that would have jurisdiction over youth who committed these acts. The jurisdiction of the juvenile court was defined in the Illinois law as including youth who violated "any law of this State or any City or Village ordinance."[12] That is, the new juvenile court had jurisdiction over any youth who committed an act that would be a crime if committed by an adult. This seemingly strange phrase remains in the language of the juvenile court today.

This legislation accomplished the transfer of youths who had violated criminal laws from the criminal court to the new juvenile court, but remember that criminal offenders were not the main problem—it was the juveniles who had *not* committed any criminal offenses but who were in danger of growing up to be paupers and criminals. The new court, thus, must include jurisdiction over these youths or it would not calm the basic concerns of the reformers. Thus, the Illinois legislature included in the jurisdiction of the new juvenile court:

Any child who for any reason is destitute or homeless or abandoned; or dependent on the public for support; or has not proper parental care or guardianships; or who habitually begs or receives alms; or who is found living in any house of ill fame or with any vicious or disreputable person; or whose home, by reason of neglect, cruelty or depravity on the part of its parents, guardian or other person in whose care it may be, is an unfit place for such a child; and any child under the age of 8 years who is found peddling or selling any article or singing or playing any musical instrument upon the street or giving any public entertainment.[13]

It is difficult to imagine any poor child who would not fit within one or another of these provisions; in fact, this law was written so that the juvenile court could, if it wanted to, take jurisdiction over every poor child in the city of Chicago. Of course, the authors of the law did not anticipate that all poor children would be brought under the court's jurisdiction. Rather, they wanted the court to take jurisdiction only when the child's best interests would be served. It was left to the court workers to make these decisions. That is, this law provided court workers with virtually unlimited power over poor children, on the assumption that they would use that power for the good of the children.

The new juvenile court, acting in its role as *parens patriae*, could take poor children out of their homes and place them in reform schools so that they would not grow up to become paupers and criminals. In summary, this practice was originally carried out under the Poor Laws, but their authority had eroded. Then it was implemented through the House or Refuge, but the *O'Connell* decision had undermined that legal basis. Now it was to be carried out through the new juvenile court. At last, there appeared to be a secure legal basis for this practice.[14]

Characteristics of the Original Juvenile Court

The flavor of the new juvenile court can be sensed by comparing some terms used in that court with those used in the criminal court. The terms as applied in the criminal court convey a sense of fault, blame, accusation, guilt, and punishment, while those in the juvenile court depict a sense of problems, needs, concerns, helping, and caring (see table 5.1).

Table 5.1.   Comparison of Terms in Juvenile and Criminal Courts

Criminal Court	Juvenile Court
Indictment	Petition
Arraignment	Intake hearing
State v. John Doe	*In re John Doe*
Plead guilty or not guilty	Admit or deny offense
Trial	Adjudication
Pre-sentence investigation	Social history
Sentence proportionate to offense	Disposition in best interests of child

In criminal court, the process begins when the defendant is indicted. An *indictment* is a formal, written accusation that the person has committed a crime. In the new juvenile court, the process began with a petition. A *petition* is a written request for something—a student might petition to get a grade changed, for example. The petition in juvenile court was, then, a formal request for the court to look into the case of this particular child, to see if there is reason to take jurisdiction. The child was not accused of anything particular, then, only identified as possibly in need of help and attention.

The first phase of the trial process in criminal court is the *arraignment*, where charges are formally read. The term *arraign* means to "call to account" or "accuse." In contrast, the first phase of the juvenile court is the *intake hearing. Intake* indicates only that a case is to be opened. The petition alleges certain facts that, if found to be true, give the court the right to take jurisdiction over the child, but the child is not "called to account" or "accused" at this hearing.

The petition can allege that the juvenile committed an act that would be a crime if committed by an adult, or it can allege that the juvenile for some other reason is in danger of growing up to be a pauper or criminal (e.g., the very lengthy list of conditions previously cited under the Illinois law). It should be noted that later on this portion would be restricted to what we now call status offenses—mainly truancy, incorrigibility, and running away.

In criminal court, the case itself is named *State v. John Doe*. That terminology implies a contest or fight between the state and the defendant, who must protect himself against the accusations made by the state. In juvenile court, the case name was then (and still is) typically expressed as *In re John Doe*. This *In re* phrase means "in the matter of" or "concerning." There is no expression in the terminology that the state opposes John Doe or that John Doe must defend himself.

Defendants who plead not guilty in criminal court then face a *trial*, usually in front of a *jury* of twelve peers. The term *trial* originally meant "to settle a dispute by a test or contest in which the two sides fight it out." Thus, at a criminal trial, the prosecution and defense fight it out. In the new juvenile court, a juvenile who denied the allegations received an *adjudication hearing.* The term *adjudication* has the same root as the word *judge.* That is, at this hearing, a judgment is going to be made about whether these facts are true (as alleged in the petition) or false (as alleged by the juvenile). There is no implication in the term that the state is going to fight it out with the juvenile.

The outcome of a criminal trial is *conviction*, the original meaning of which was "to overcome." A person who is convicted has been overcome in the trial in which the prosecution and defense have fought it out. In the juvenile court, however, the juvenile is to be *adjudicated*; that is, the judge formally states that the facts alleged in the petition are found to be true. The juvenile court, therefore, takes jurisdiction, which means that the court asserts the legal authority to decide what is in the juvenile's best interests.

Once an adult is convicted, often a presentence investigation is undertaken in order to make a recommendation about the appropriate *sentence*. This investigation primarily includes information on the adult's prior offending and specific circumstances surrounding the current offense (such as injury to the victim and malicious intent) that relate to the severity of the punishment deemed appropriate, or *proportionate*, to the offense. In juvenile court, a *probation officer* prepares a social history of the juvenile in order to recommend a *disposition*. The term *disposition* refers to "putting things in order," or making a proper or orderly arrangement. Having declared the right to take jurisdiction over this youth, the judge then decides what will put the case in a proper order. Unlike the term *sentence*, a disposition contains no implication that the juvenile is to be punished.

In criminal court, the sentence is supposed to be proportionate to the seriousness of the offense. In contrast, the disposition is supposed to be in the best interests of the child. The phrase "best interests" was taken from the British Chancery court, where it was used to describe the obligation to preserve the estate of the orphan. In juvenile court, it means that every juvenile requires the love, care, and attention of a kindly (if firm) parent. When the child's natural parents cannot or do not provide this, the original Illinois law charged the juvenile court with the responsibility to so do.

The Juvenile Court and the Social Work Movement

Today, we usually think of the juvenile court as a version of the criminal court. But originally, the juvenile court was not a criminal court at all, as demonstrated by the terminology reviewed above. It was really a coercive casework agency. *Casework* is a term taken from the social work movement.

The social work movement was founded in Chicago about the same time as the juvenile court,[15] and some of the same people were involved in both.[16] The movement originally emphasized social reform; that is, it focused on changing the social conditions that gave rise to poverty and dependency. Social workers dealt primarily with the agents of the larger society, such as city and state officials and the leaders of the business community. The focus on social reform implied that the "blame" for poverty and dependency lay in the social conditions created and maintained by these powerful people, rather than in the poor and dependent individuals themselves.

Social work soon shifted its focus from social reform to casework. That is, social workers stopped working with business and political leaders to change the urban environment, and they began working with poor and dependent individuals to help them adapt to that environment. The new focus on casework implied that the "blame" for poverty and dependency lay in the poor individual's failure to adapt, rather than on the urban environment itself. Casework then became the primary focus of the social work movement.

The original emphasis on social reform was consistent with a view of the poor as "deserving"—that is, the poor deserved help and assistance because poverty and dependency were the result of larger social conditions, not the people's own failings and shortcomings. The later emphasis on casework, however, was consistent with the view of the poor as paupers—people thought to be poor because of their own failings and shortcomings, which needed to be corrected. Because of their emphasis on casework, most social workers in both England and America opposed financial aid to the poor, since they believed it would only "pauperize" the people further by making them dependent.[17]

The first law providing direct financial aid to poor children (now called Aid to Families with Dependent Children, or AFDC) was passed in Illinois in 1911, as an amendment to the Juvenile Court Act. Its purpose was to provide the court with an additional disposition for adjudicated juveniles:

> The Illinois Board of Charities, in arguing for the relief program, continuously stressed the causal connection between poverty (dependency) and delinquency. The juvenile court had available a variety of dispositions ranging from institutionalization to probation. The Funds to Parents Act amendment, in effect, gave the court another disposition. If the parents were "proper guardians" but "poor and unable to properly care" for the dependent child, then the court could grant aid.[18]

This law illustrates the prevailing view at that time that some poor people were "deserving" while others were "undeserving paupers." The deserving poor could receive direct financial aid to alleviate their poverty and help them raise their children in an appropriate way. The undeserving poor (i.e., paupers) would not receive this money, since they presumably would squander it. Instead, their children would be taken from them by the state, acting as *parens patriae*, and they would be left to fend for themselves.

This law illustrates the close connection between the social work movement—a forerunner of our modern welfare system—and the original juvenile court. As conceived, the juvenile court was essentially a case-work agency. That is, it helped individual children, especially poor children, to adapt to their environment.

The Juvenile Court as Central Referral Unit

The juvenile court was to be the central referral agency for the entire child welfare system. The founders of the court did not distinguish between children who committed crimes (whom we call delinquent children today) and children whose parents were unwilling or unable to provide adequate care and supervision for them (whom we call depen-dent or neglected children today).

In their view, it was the natural state of all children to be dependent. When children did not receive proper parental care and supervision, a variety of harmful effects could result, including crime and delin-quency. But a child who committed a crime was not essentially differ-ent from a child who was merely neglected or dependent. The fact that a child had committed a crime was a minor point that had no real importance, other than supplying proof positive that the child lacked the proper parental care and supervision that all children, by their very nature, need.

Thus, all needy children, regardless of whether they had committed a crime or not, could be brought into juvenile court, where their "best interests" would be assessed and a recommendation would be made about the services needed to achieve them. The child would then receive needed services either from court workers or through a referral to people and agencies in the community.

Juvenile Court as a Coercive Casework Agency

The juvenile court was to be not only a casework agency but also a coer-cive casework agency. Other casework agencies were strictly voluntary: any individual who did not wish to be helped could simply refuse the services. But children whom the juvenile court wished to help could not refuse, any more than children could refuse services from their natural parents. The court, after all, acted as *parens patriae*, as the ultimate parent of the child. This positioned the juvenile court midway between case-work agency and criminal court (see table 5.2).

Table 5.2.   Juvenile Court as a Coercive Casework Agency

Casework Agency	Juvenile Court	Criminal Court
Voluntary treatment	Coerced treatment	Coerced punishment

The idea of coerced treatment was the centerpiece of the original juvenile court. This idea was applied mainly to "salvageable offenders" such as exemplified by Mary Ann Crouse and Daniel O'Connell, who had committed either status offenses or minor criminal offenses. Juveniles who committed serious criminal offenses continued to be sent to criminal courts.[19]

In that sense, the original juvenile court was an addition to, rather than a replacement for, the adult criminal court. Juveniles could be sent to juvenile court first, where the attempt would be made to salvage them. If that attempt failed, then they could always be sent on to criminal court, where they would have gone originally.

Legal Issues Concerning the Juvenile Court

Just as the placement of youths in the House of Refuge was first brought into question in the *Crouse* case, the new practice of processing and committing youths through a separate juvenile court would soon be brought into question as well. Because this new court was a civil court and not a criminal court, young defendants brought within its jurisdiction did not enjoy the due process protections of the Bill of Rights. However, similar to the House of Refuge, this court could confine youth up until their 21st birthday. This practice of confinement (e.g., punishment or treatment) without the benefit of due process protections would receive its first legal test in the case of Frank Fisher.

The Case of Frank Fisher

Shortly after the Illinois law was passed, Pennsylvania established its own juvenile court. The case of Frank Fisher was one of the first tests of the legal authority of this new court. Frank Fisher was a 14-year-old boy who had been indicted for larceny in Philadelphia. His case was sent to this newly established court, from which he was sent to the same House of Refuge that had received Mary Ann Crouse sixty years earlier.[20]

Like Mary Ann's (and Daniel O'Connell's) father, Frank's father objected and filed a writ of *habeus corpus* in an attempt to get Frank released. Frank had been charged with (not convicted of) larceny, a criminal offense, so the "no punishment without a crime" principle implied that, when a crime was committed, the punishment should be proportionate to the seriousness of the offense. Frank had committed a minor offense, but he could be held in the House of Refuge until his 21st birthday, a total of seven years. This was a much longer confinement than he would have received in criminal court, and it seemed disproportionate to the seriousness of his offense.

The case went to the Pennsylvania Supreme Court, which had also heard the *Mary Ann Crouse* case sixty years earlier. As it did before, it rejected the arguments of Frank Fisher's father, with its decision containing essentially the same points as found in the earlier *Crouse* decision. Specifically, the court asserted that Frank was being *helped, not punished*, by being confined in the Philadelphia House of Refuge. Also, in making this assertion, the court focused on the *good intentions* of the state, especially in comparison to the *poor actual performance* of Frank's parents. The court then argued that helping Frank was legal because of the *parens patriae* powers of the state, now embodied in the juvenile court. Lastly, because Frank was being helped and not punished, the court held that he had no need for due process protections:

> To save a child from becoming a criminal, or from continuing in a career of crime, to end in maturer years in public punishment and disgrace, the Legislature surely may provide for the salvation of such a child, if its parents or guardian be unable or unwilling to do so, by bringing it into one of the courts of the state without any process at all, for the purpose of subjecting it to the state's guardianship and protection. The natural parent needs no process to temporarily deprive his child of its liberty by confining it in his own home, to save it and to shield it from the consequences of persistence in a career of waywardness; nor is the state, when compelled, as *parens patriae*, to take the place of the father for the same purpose, required to adopt any process as a means of placing its hands upon the child to lead it into one of its courts.[21]

Here, we have a third legal case in which the *Fisher* decision represents another swing of the pendulum between two separate lines of reasoning (see table 5.3). The differences in these decisions do not arise out of differences in the facts of the cases—the circumstances of the cases could be rotated and you would get the same decisions out of these courts. Our argument here is that these decisions turn on whether or not the court

Table 5.3.   A Comparison of the *Crouse, O'Connell,* and *Fisher* Cases

	Crouse and *Fisher* Cases	*O'Connell* Case
Court focused on	Good intentions	Actual performance
Juveniles were said to be	Helped and treated	Punished
Legal basis of court's decision	*Parens patriae*	Criminal law
Decision	Due process is not required	Due process is required

was idealistic or realistic in its view of what was happening in the juvenile justice system.

The *Crouse* decision was handed down only thirteen years after the founding of the first juvenile institution. Hope still burned brightly for the wonderful good that would be accomplished in these marvelous institutions. But thirty years later, in the *O'Connell* decision, those bright hopes for a solution to the problem of delinquency had faded into an increasingly ugly reality, and the court took a sober, realistic, even critical view of these institutions.

The founding of the juvenile court infused new hope for idealistic dreams. There was vast optimism that this new mechanism would soon solve the problem of delinquency. The *Fisher* decision, handed down only six years after the founding of the first juvenile court, returned to the logic and language of the *Crouse* decision.

In the following chapter, we will show how sixty years after the *Fisher* case, the *Gault* case would find its way to the U.S. Supreme Court. Its facts would be similar to the facts in the three earlier cases, and all four circumstances could be rotated among the courts without influencing the decisions. At that point, the passage of time would again have dimmed the bright hopes for a solution, and the Supreme Court would return to the language and logic of the *O'Connell* decision.

The Lessons of History

The founders of the juvenile court proposed a new idea of juvenile delinquency: instead of being a potential pauper, a juvenile delinquent was thought to be a dependent or neglected child. This new idea of the delinquent won the competition against other such ideas and became the dominant view of youthful offending for the next seventy years. Only after 1970 did the popularity of this idea begin to fade and other interpretations begin to compete with it.

Associated with this new idea of delinquency was the new idea of juvenile justice, or the juvenile court. Like the juvenile institutions established seventy-five years earlier, the idea of the juvenile court generated great optimism that it would solve the problem of urban property crime committed by lower-class youths. This, of course, did not happen. But the juvenile court succeeded in the sense that it triumphed over other possible policies for responding to this problem. By 1925, all but two states had juvenile courts, with the last state establishing its court in 1945.[22]

As was done in the last chapter, we can ask why these ideas were so appealing to so many people at the time. Simply put, we can ask why the new juvenile court and the new definition of juvenile delinquency "sold" so well.

The Cycle of Juvenile Justice

Like the problem faced by the gentlemen reformers in New York City in 1825, the problem reformers in Chicago faced in 1899 fits nicely into the cycle of juvenile justice as we have defined it earlier. High juvenile crime rates at the time were accompanied by a firm belief that these rates could be lowered by the proper policy response. Harsh punishments were available for juvenile offenders, but lenient treatments were not. Officials were often reluctant to impose harsh punishments, so many youths were simply released. Officials at the time, such as Julia Lathrop, thought that both choices increased juvenile crime.

As with the juvenile institutions, the juvenile court was designed to provide leniency for those who would have been harshly punished by being sent to Chicago's jails and poorhouses, and to do something for juveniles for whom nothing otherwise would have been done by the adult criminal justice system. That is, it was designed to provide a middle ground between punishing harshly and doing nothing at all.[23]

The reformers in Chicago, therefore, were in the same position as the New York City reformers had been in seventy-five years earlier. What had happened in those intervening years that caused the juvenile justice system to return to where it had started?

In the middle years of the 1800s, there appears to have been a gradual evolution in thought, fueled by the belief that juvenile crime rates were unusually high and could be lowered with the proper policy response. The House of Refuge originally had been a lenient response that handled minor criminal offenders and status offenders. When it failed to solve the problem of delinquency, the natural response was to make it tougher. As it became tougher, justice officials increasingly sent the more serious offenders to the House of Refuge, who otherwise would have been sent to adult jails and penitentiaries. These officials also increasingly let the minor criminals and status offenders off scot-free, because they did not want to impose these harsh penalties and they did not want to house them with more serious criminal youths.

Eventually, justice officials once again found that they had to choose between imposing harsh punishments and doing nothing at all. Juvenile crime rates remained high, and now they were attributed to the "forced choice" between two bad alternatives. These sentiments were reflected in the O'Connell decision, thus a new alternative—the juvenile court— appeared on the scene as a way to reintroduce leniency in order to solve the problem.

The Idea of Juvenile Delinquency: Dependent or Neglected Child

The idea of juvenile delinquency proposed by the gentlemen reformers in New York City was a slightly modified version of the popular idea that poor youths were "potential paupers." This idea remained popular throughout the 1800s, but it failed to reduce delinquency and so it was vulnerable to attack by new ideas.

As mentioned above, the new idea introduced by the founders of the juvenile court was that juvenile delinquents were dependent and neglected children. These founders argued that the natural state of all children was to be dependent and that they require the care and supervision of a kindly but firm parent. Children who lack such care and supervision exhibit problem behaviors, one of which is to engage in criminal activities and status offenses. But the participation in criminal offenses by itself does not mean that these children are different from other children who were dependent and neglected; it just means that they are manifesting different symptoms of the same underlying problem. Thus, dependency and neglect are the center of attention, rather than the criminal behavior itself.

One reason that this new idea became so popular at the time was probably that, like the earlier definition of the delinquent as a potential pauper, the new view sounded new and different but it actually wasn't. Many forms of child protection legislation had been passed in the country since the mid-nineteenth century,[24] and the social work movement had become prominent in the latter part of that century. Thus, the concept of neglected and dependent children was widely known. The "new" idea of juvenile delinquency was really just an old and well-established idea that was newly applied to juvenile offenders.

This new idea, therefore, did not require that people think anything different from what they had been thinking before. Fitting comfortably into the historical context of the day, this idea ensured that people felt satisfied in believing that they were taking an entirely new way of looking at things, but demanded of them none of the trouble and inconvenience of actually grappling with a new concept or idea.

The Idea of Juvenile Justice: Juvenile Court

As a method of responding to delinquency, the juvenile court also seemed new and different. Because it *appeared* so innovative, people were optimistic that it would be effective in solving the problems of the day. In practice, however, the juvenile court returned to handling juvenile offenders as they had been handled before the O'*Connell* decision. As with the new idea of juvenile delinquency, the juvenile court was probably popular in part because it sounded new and different but actually wasn't new or different.

The juvenile court established a new legal basis for the old practice of sending poor urban children to rural institutions for their own good. Originally, the legal basis had been found in the poor laws, but that basis had been eroded and was replaced by criminal laws in the *Crouse* decision. The O'*Connell* decision had found the criminal-law basis inadequate, thus the juvenile court established an even newer legal basis, adopting the *parens patriae* doctrine from British Chancery Court. Thus, the older method of dealing with juvenile offenders was continued, even as its legal basis was changed.

Economic Interests of the Rich and Powerful

In chapter 4, we said that the gentlemen reformers who founded the House of Refuge had not tried to do anything about the "manifold temptations of the streets" but, rather, just to remove the children from those streets. From our perspective today, it seems reasonable to conclude that the major problem was in the streets—that is, the conditions under which poor children and their parents lived, rather than anything inherent in the children and parents themselves. Similar children and parents had lived under other conditions, in which no comparable problem of delinquency had appeared. Although it would have been possible to do something about these poor living conditions, nothing was done and the idea was never even seriously considered. The reason no attempts were made is probably that such actions would have threatened the economic interests of rich and powerful people.

A similar situation seems to have happened with the juvenile court movement. The social work movement originally focused on reforming people's social conditions, but later the focus was changed to casework—that is, on changing individuals so that they were able to function under the existing social conditions. One can speculate that one of the reasons this shift took place was that the efforts to reform society simply were not successful. No one likes to beat his head against a wall. Eventually, social workers stopped trying to change the rich and powerful, and they started trying to change the poor and powerless. The seeds of both casework and social reform had been planted at the beginning of the juvenile court movement, but only the seeds of casework were able to take root and grow. The seeds of social reform withered and died.

As with the conditions in New York City, it seems reasonable to conclude that the social conditions in Chicago were probably the principal cause of the wave of delinquency that engulfed the city. Poor parenting, with the resulting dependency and neglect, may have caused delinquency among some poor children, but it was not the main cause. The concept of the juvenile court triumphed in its competition with other possible policies, precisely because it failed to address delinquency's principal cause: the social conditions under which poor people lived.

Moral and Intellectual Superiority of the Reformers

As with the gentlemen reformers in New York City, in Chicago there was great social distance between the small group of prominent and powerful people who ran the city and the large number of poor immigrants with whom they were concerned. Chicago's reformers also chose an interpretation of delinquency that reinforced their sense of moral and intellectual superiority. They believed that poor children lacked proper parental care and supervision, and therefore were dependent and neglected. They also believed that, acting through the power of the state, the reformers would be able to provide the proper care and supervision that the natural parents could not.

With the perspective of 100 years of history, it seems reasonable for us to conclude that parental neglect was not the central problem. The poor parents at that time and in that place probably were no more neglectful than poor parents have been at any other time and place, when no comparable problem of delinquency existed. So, what was it about that interpretation that led the reformers to embrace it? In particular, why was this "moral superiority" interpretation adopted over the view proposed by the social work movement—that delinquency was a problem that originated in the social conditions existing in Chicago at the time?

We suggest that viewing delinquents as dependent and neglected children preserved the reformers' sense of moral and intellectual superiority. This view would have been especially important for the women who founded the court, given their commitment to the traditional role of women as mothers. By focusing on the inadequacies of these children's parents, these women were able to validate their own moves out of the home and into the larger society to use their talents and abilities. In contrast, the social-reform view would have implied that the source of the delinquency problem lay in the economic activities of their own wealthy and powerful husbands and fathers. This view, we argue, would have been too threatening for them to consider for any length of time.

The Unfair Comparison

The "unfair comparison" likens an optimistic, idealistic assessment of the future, based on the good intentions of the reformers, with a pessimistic, cynical assessment of the past, based on actual performance. This comparison was discussed in chapter 4 with respect to the *Crouse* and the *O'Connell* decisions. In part, the unfair comparison fueled the spread of the House of Refuge reform, and the same type of comparison was used to promote the juvenile court as a reform.[25]

When the unfair comparisons are viewed from today's perspective, it would seem that the founders of the first juvenile court made excessively optimistic appraisals of how effective this new organization would be in resolving the problem of delinquency. In particular, they genuinely believed that the problem could be resolved in fairly short order with this new mechanism. That appraisal was based on an assumption that their good intentions would be directly translated into good practices. This, of course, was not to be.

At the same time, these reformers pessimistically viewed the actual practices of the policies that existed before the establishment of the juvenile court. They focused on the dismal conditions in which juveniles were being held at the time, systematically ignoring anything good about those practices and magnifying anything that was bad about them. At no point was there any mention of the good intentions of those who had set up this system.

Once their own reforms had been implemented, however, these same reformers no longer focused on actual practices. Rather, in the face of increasingly awful conditions, they remained focused on their good intentions, just as the founders of the juvenile institutions had done. To do otherwise would have challenged their sense of moral and intellectual superiority. The road to hell may be paved with good intentions; likewise, no one wants to believe that his or her own good intentions can produce hellish results.

Expansion of State Power

The procedures for processing juveniles did not change much with the establishment of the juvenile court. The terminology changed, since the court was conceived as a coercive casework agency rather than as a criminal court; however, each new term was parallel to an existing term in the criminal court. In practice, the names changed but the game remained the same.

There was one important change brought about by the establishment of the juvenile court: the expanded power of the state to intervene in the lives of poor children. The new juvenile court could take jurisdiction over virtually every poor child in the city of Chicago, as long as the caseworker thought it was in the best interests of the child. It was no longer necessary for the child to have committed a criminal offense of any sort, much less a felony, for the court to send the child to an institution. The few due process protections that had been provided to juveniles previously were wiped out by the establishment of the new juvenile court.

Once again, an optimistic projection of the effectiveness of the new reform, based on the good intentions and the moral and intellectual superiority of the reformers, was used to expand the state's power to intervene and limit poor children's power to resist. Those legal protections were thought to be unnecessary because the state's power would be used for the good of these children.

Generalizing the Lessons of History

The lessons of history to be derived here are quite similar to those derived in chapter 4 regarding the founding of the first juvenile institution in New York City. These two events are sufficiently distant from us that we can have some perspective on them; that is, we can see the shapes and patterns of the forest rather than just the branches and leaves of individual trees. Gaining such perspective is harder in the remaining chapters of this book, since those chapters concern events much closer to our own time. Before we discuss more recent events, however, we want to generalize the lessons of history so as to ponder whether these lessons can apply to events in our own time.

Lesson 1: The Cycle of Juvenile Justice. The widespread perception that juvenile crime rates are unusually high is accompanied by a widespread belief that these rates can be lowered by appropriate juvenile justice policies. This results in a continuous cycle of reform that consists of establishing lenient treatments in a major reform, gradually toughening up those treatments over a long time so that officials end up choosing between harsh punishments and doing nothing at all, and then reestablishing lenient treatments in another major reform.

Lesson 2: Ideas of Juvenile Delinquency. Ideas of delinquency that "sell" (i.e., that succeed in the competition with other possible ideas) propose that delinquents are a subgroup within some larger problem group (e.g., paupers, dependent and neglected children) with which the public is already familiar. The prevailing idea of delinquency and delinquents thus drives the idea of what juvenile justice should be.

Lesson 3: Ideas of Juvenile Justice. Responses to delinquency that "sell" (i.e., that succeed in the competition with other possible responses) are slightly modified versions of responses to the larger problem group of which delinquents are thought to be a subgroup (potential paupers, dependent and neglected children, etc).

Lesson 4: Economic Interests of the Rich and Powerful. Responses to delinquency that "sell" focus on the behavior of poor and powerless people but ignore the behavior of rich and powerful people. In particular, responses that focus on poor people's behavior do not harm the economic interests of the rich and powerful—that is, they aim to remove delinquents from the streets rather than change conditions on the streets.

Lesson 5: Moral and Intellectual Superiority of Reformers. Responses to delinquency that "sell" imply that delinquents and their parents are morally and intellectually inferior, and that the reformers themselves are morally and intellectually superior.

Lesson 6: The Unfair Comparison. Reformers "sell" their own reforms by an unfair comparison, in which a harsh assessment of actual practices of past policies is compared with an optimistic assessment of reforms, based on good intentions. Because they assume that good intentions directly translate into good practices, reformers promise to solve the problem of juvenile delinquency.

Lesson 7: The Power of the State. Reforms that "sell" increase the power of the state, based on optimistic assessments of how effective the reform will be in solving the problem. The power of the state usually continues to expand regardless of the specific content or nature of the reform.

NOTES

1. See Harold Finestone, *Victims of Change* (Westport, Conn.: Greenwood Press, 1976), 38–42.

2. Charles Darwin, *On the Origin of the Species* (London: John Murray, 1859); Charles Darwin, *Descent of Man* (London: John Murray, 1871.

3. See George B. Vold and Thomas J. Bernard, *Theoretical Criminology* (New York: Oxford University Press, 1986).

4. For a contemporary example, see C. R. Henderson, "The Relation of Philanthropy to Social Order and Progress," in Frederic L. Faust and Paul J. Brantingham, eds., *Juvenile Justice Philosophy* (St. Paul, Minn.: West, 1979), 48–58 (originally published in 1899 in Chicago).

5. Anthony Platt, *The Child Savers* (Chicago: University of Chicago Press, 1977).

6. Robert M. Mennel, *Thorns and Thistles* (Hanover, N.H.: University Press of New England, 1973), 127.

7. Julia Lathrop, "Introduction," in Sophonisba P. Breckinridge and Edith Abbott, *The Delinquent Child and the Home* (New York: Arno, 1970), 2–4 (original edition 1912).

8. Ibid.

9. Quoted in Mennel, *Thorns and Thistles,* 129.

10. "Testimony of Judge Merritt W. Kinckney," in Sophonisba P. Breckinridge and Edith Abbott, *The Delinquent Child and the Home* (New York: Arno, 1970), 203 (original edition 1912).

11. See, for example, Joel Samaha, *Criminal Law* (St. Paul, Minn.: West, 1983), chap. 3.

12. Quoted in Mennel, *Thorns and Thistles,* 130.

13. Ibid., 131.

14. See Platt, *The Child Savers,* 135; Sanford Fox, "Juvenile Justice Reform," *Stanford Law Review* 22 (June 1970): 1187–1239; and John Hagan and Jeffrey Leon, "Rediscovering Delinquency," *American Sociological Review* 42 (1982): 587–598, for arguments that the founding of the juvenile court codified existing practices rather than changed them.

15. Walter I. Trattner, *From Poor Law to Welfare State* (New York: Free Press, 1974), 136ff.

16. Mennell, *Thorns and Thistles,* 151–152.

17. Joel F. Handler, *Reforming the Poor* (New York: Basic Books, 1972), 6–10.

18. Ibid., 11.

19. Fox, "Juvenile Justice Reform"; Mennel, *Thorns and Thistles,* 133.

20. 213 Pa. 48, 62 A. 198. The decision is reproduced in Faust and Brantingham, *Juvenile Justice Philosophy,* 156–162.

21. Ibid.

22. Mennel, *Thorns and Thistles,* 132.

23. In terms of criminal justice thermodynamics, the juvenile court reduced the severity of the penalty to increase the frequency of its application. See Samuel Walker, *Sense and Nonsense About Crime* (Pacific Grove, Calif.: Brooks/Cole, 1989), 46–48. See also chapter 2 for a discussion of this concept.

24. Douglas Rendleman, "Paarens Patriae: From Chancery to the Juvenile Court," *South Carolina Law Review* 23 (1971): 205.

25. E.g., see statements by Julian Mack and Merritt Pincknewy, both of whom were juvenile court judges in Chicago, in Sophonisba P. Breckinridge and Edith Abbott, *The Delinquent Child and the Home* (New York: Arno, 1970). Mack's article is partially reprinted in Faust and Brantingham, *Juvenile Justice Philosophy* (St. Paul, Minn.: West, 1979), 97–114. Breckinridge and Abbott founded the social work movement, and the book is introduced by Julia Lathrop.

6

The Supreme Court and Due Process

By the 1950s, optimism about the juvenile court had broken down and a more realistic view of the situation began to emerge. This view was based on an assessment of the actual performance of the juvenile court rather than on the good intentions of its founders. In practice, the juvenile court often did not "treat" juveniles or act in their "best interests" but, rather, punished them for their offenses.

This new realism laid the basis for a reintroduction of due process protections; that is, if juveniles are being punished, then they need at least some of the protections provided to adults in criminal court. Thus, there was a shift away from the language and logic of the *Mary Ann Crouse* and *Frank Fisher* cases and back to the language and logic of the *Daniel O'Connell* case.

By 1962, the two largest states—New York and California—had passed laws reflecting this new realism. These laws separated the handling of juveniles who had committed criminal offenses from those who had committed only status offenses, and they provided some due process protections, including the right to be represented by a lawyer.[1] But the complete return to the language and logic of the *O'Connell* case would be accomplished by the U.S. Supreme Court.

The U.S. Supreme Court and the Juvenile Court

In the 1960s, the U.S. Supreme Court issued a number of decisions that expanded the due process rights of criminal defendants generally. Under the leadership of Chief Justice Earl Warren, the Court was concerned with civil liberties and human rights, and these concerns were reflected in its many decisions of this decade. In general, the Court believed that criminal defendants were citizens who were presumed innocent until they had been proven guilty beyond a reasonable doubt. As citizens, criminal defendants were entitled to the rights and privileges guaranteed by the U.S. Constitution. Two of the Court's more important decisions on this matter were *Mapp v. Ohio* (1961), which concerned the Fourth Amendment prohibition of "unreasonable searches and seizures," and *Miranda v. Arizona* (1965), which concerned the Fifth Amendment privilege against self-incrimination.

The Court also, for the first time, addressed the operation of the juvenile justice system. Five key decisions were issued between 1966 and 1975 that changed the face of juvenile justice: *Kent v. United States* (1966), *In Re Gault* (1967), *In Re Winship* (1970), *McKeiver v. Pennsylvania* (1971), and *Breed v. Jones* (1975).

The *Kent* case was the first juvenile case ever heard by the Supreme Court. The *Crouse* and *Fisher* cases had gone to the Pennsylvania Supreme Court, while the *O'Connell* case had gone to the Illinois Supreme Court. So, the very fact that the U.S. Supreme Court had accepted this case signaled its intention to consider applying constitutional protections to the juvenile process. By the time the *Breed v. Jones* decision appeared nine years later, juveniles had some (but not all) of the due process rights adults have in criminal court. The language and logic of the *Crouse* and *Fisher* cases were gone, and in their place were the language and logic of the *O'Connell* case.

Briefing Cases

In discussing these five cases, we use a modified version of the legal brief. First, the *facts* of the case are presented, which include both a description of the crime that was committed and the process by which the case made its way to the U.S. Supreme Court. Second, the *issues* are described that the Supreme Court used to consider the case. Third, the *decision* of the Court is given. Fourth, the *reasons* that the Court gave in reaching that decision are explained. Fifth, any significant *dissent* to the opinion is discussed—that is, we consider the reasons given by the judges who voted against the decision and who wrote an opinion expressing a minority view. Sixth, some *comments* that put the case in its historic and political context are offered.

The Case of Morris Kent

Facts

In 1959, 14-year-old Morris A. Kent Jr. was arrested and charged with several housebreakings and an attempted purse snatching. He was placed on probation and returned to the custody of his mother, who had been separated from his father since Morris was 2 years old.

On September 2, 1961, while still on probation, Kent broke into a woman's apartment, raped her, and stole her wallet. He was arrested for this crime three days later and interrogated until 10 P.M. that night, during which time he apparently confessed to several such break-ins and rapes. He was also interrogated for all of the next day, at which time his mother retained a lawyer.[2]

The lawyer quickly filed a motion for a hearing on whether to waive jurisdiction to criminal court, along with an affidavit from a psychiatrist asserting that Kent was "a victim of severe psychopathology" and recommending hospitalization. Given the seriousness of the offense, the lawyer assumed that the judge might want to waive jurisdiction, and he wanted the opportunity to argue against it. The lawyer also filed a motion to obtain the records that the probation office had kept on Kent over the last two years. He wanted to use those records to support the argument that Kent should not be waived to adult court.

The judge received these motions but did not rule on them. He also received a new report from the probation department, dated September 8, that described Kent's "rapid deterioration of personality structure and the possibility of mental illness." The judge then entered a motion stating that "after full investigation, I do hereby waive" jurisdiction over the case, and ordered that Kent be held for trial in adult criminal court.

This precise phrase was important because the judge was required by the District of Columbia's Juvenile Court Act to conduct a "full investigation." However, the judge gave no indication of what that investigation was or why he had reached the decision to waive jurisdiction.

On September 25, about three weeks after the crime, Kent was indicted in (adult) criminal court on eight counts of housebreaking, robbery, and rape, and one additional count of housebreaking and robbery. The lawyer moved to dismiss the indictment on the grounds that the waiver from juvenile court had been invalid. In addition, the lawyer appealed the waiver itself to the Municipal Court of Appeal, and he also filed a writ of *habeas corpus*, demanding that the state justify Kent's detention.

The municipal court did not hand down its decision for a year and a half, until January 23, 1963. In its final decision, the court rejected the appeal of the waiver and the writ of *habeas corpus*, and it held that the only valid way to review a waiver decision was to move to dismiss the indictment in criminal court.

The court then took up the question of whether to dismiss Kent's indictment. The problem for the municipal court was that the juvenile court judge had given no indication of what investigation he had conducted or his reasons for the waiver. The municipal court decided it would not "go behind" the judge's statement that he had conducted a "full investigation." It therefore ruled that the waiver had been valid and refused to dismiss the indictment.

For most of this time, Kent was in a hospital for the criminally insane, where he was diagnosed as schizophrenic. Following the municipal court decision, he was tried and found guilty by a jury on six counts of housebreaking and robbery. The judge sentenced him to five to fifteen years on each count, for a total of thirty to ninety years in prison. The jury, however, found him not guilty on the rape charges, on the grounds that he was insane. While this did not appear to be a sane verdict, Kent was sent back to the same mental hospital. If that hospital ever decided that his sanity was restored, he would be transferred to prison to complete the unexpired portion of his thirty- to ninety-year sentence.

Issues

Kent's lawyer argued that the District of Columbia statutes, especially the Juvenile Court Act, had been violated by the police and the judge in their handling of the case. In particular, he alleged that the judge had failed to make a "full investigation" before waiving Kent to criminal court. The lawyer also argued that the U.S. Constitution had been violated because Kent was denied various due process rights to which he would have been entitled if he were an adult.

Decision

The court decided the waiver violated the District of Columbia's Juvenile Court Act. Because it was based on District of Columbia statutes, the decision applied only to the District of Columbia.

The court ruled that Kent had been entitled to a waiver hearing, that he was entitled to have legal counsel at that hearing, that the hearing itself should have measured up to the essentials of due process of law, that the counsel should have had access to all records related to the juvenile, and that the judge should have made a statement of reasons for his decision. Finally, the U.S. Supreme Court issued a series of guidelines to consider in making a waiver decision, and ordered a new hearing to be held to determine whether Kent's waiver had met those guidelines.

Reasons

Two decisions had been handed down by the court of appeals between Kent's crime and trial (1961 to 1963) and the Supreme Court decision in the case (1966). The *Watkins* decision in 1964 ruled that a juvenile's lawyer should have access to social service files in waiver cases, and the *Black* decision in 1965 held that a juvenile was entitled to a lawyer in a waiver hearing. The Supreme Court affirmed these two lower court decisions and used relatively simple logic to extend them: if a juvenile is entitled to a lawyer at a waiver hearing and if the lawyer has the right to see the files in the case, then the juvenile must be entitled to the hearing itself, which Kent had not received.

In addition, the Municipal Court of Appeals had ruled that a waiver could be reviewed by moving to dismiss the indictment in criminal court. In this case, the Supreme Court used relatively simple logic to extend this decision: since the waiver decision is reviewable, the judge must state in writing the reasons for the waiver so that the review can be meaningful.

Comments

While this decision applied only to the District of Columbia, it had great national importance because of the general perspective the Court took on the issues. Throughout the decision, there were numerous references to the need for due process protections in juvenile court.

For example, the Court held that the waiver hearing must "measure up to the essentials of due process and fair treatment." This perspective was a radical departure from the traditional juvenile court view that due process was unimportant because the "best interests" of the child were to be pursued. Stating that the hearing must be "fair" suggests that the youth is being subjected to possible punishment.

But beyond that general perspective, the Court actually described a specific line of reasoning for a future constitutional challenge to the juvenile court. In its view, this case raised a constitutional issue involving the equal protection clause of the Fourteenth Amendment. That clause says: "no state may deny any person, under its government, equal protection of the law." In the past, the Supreme Court had interpreted this clause to mean that people could receive "less protection" from the law only if they also received some "compensating benefit" that they could not obtain without sacrificing that protection. Juvenile courts provide juveniles with "less protection" than the criminal courts provide adults, but juveniles were supposed to receive a "compensating benefit," in that the juvenile court looked after their "best interests," so that they were being helped and not punished.

The Supreme Court questioned whether this "compensating benefit" really existed. Specifically, the Court stated that this case raised:

> [a] basic issue as to the justifiability of affording a juvenile less protection than is accorded to adults suspected of criminal offenses, particularly where, as here, there is an absence of any indication this denial of rights available to adults was offset, mitigated, or explained by action of the government, as *parens patriae*, evidencing the special solicitude for juveniles, commanded by the Juvenile Court Act.

In answering this question, the Court indicated that it would look at how juveniles were really treated in juvenile court, not merely at what the law "commanded." The focus was on the *actual performance* of the court, not just its *good intentions*. The Court went so far as to speculate that juveniles did not merely fail to receive special care and treatment, but that they actually received the "worst of both worlds":

> While there can be no doubt of the original laudable purpose of juvenile courts, studies and critiques in recent years raise serious questions as to whether actual performance measures well enough against theoretical purpose to make tolerable the immunity of the process from the reach of constitutional guaranties applicable to adults. There is much evidence that some juvenile courts, including that of the District of Columbia, lack the personnel, facilities and techniques to perform adequately as representatives of the State in a *parens patriae* capacity, at least with respect to children charged with law violation. There is evidence, in fact, that there may be grounds for concern that the child receives the worst of both worlds: that he gets neither the protections accorded to adults nor the solicitous care and regenerative treatment postulated for children.

The Court said "we do not pass upon these" constitutional questions because local statutes had been violated. Courts always rule on the narrowest possible grounds, so the Court did not make a constitutional ruling in this case. But interested lawyers would interpret the above statements as an invitation to send the Supreme Court a case that did not violate local statutes but that raised the same constitutional issues.

Morris Kent himself got nothing out of this decision. Kent received a new hearing from the local criminal court on whether his waiver had conformed to the guidelines set forth in the Supreme Court decision. The criminal court found that it had. Kent was returned to the mental hospital, to be transferred to prison if he was ever found to be sane. Thus, the decision did him no good at all.

The decision had a major national impact, however. The decision applied only to the District of Columbia because it was based on local law, but courts across the nation adopted its guidelines on the assumption that a failure to do so would result in a successful appeal to the Supreme Court.

The decision also served notice that the U.S. Supreme Court would consider cases involving the juvenile justice system—after all, this was the first juvenile case it had ever heard. The Court also made it clear it would view the juvenile justice system from a due process perspective. Thus, *parens patriae* was dead, and rising to take its place was the equal protection argument outlined in the *Kent* decision. A new juvenile court was being born.

The Case of Gerald Gault

Facts

Gerald Gault, a 15-year-old boy who lived in Gila County, Arizona, had been on probation for about three months for being in the company of another boy who had stolen a wallet from a lady's purse. On June 8, 1964, he and his friend Ronald Lewis called their neighbor Mrs. Cook and asked her: "Do you give any?" "Are your cherries ripe today?" and "Do you have big bombers?"

Mrs. Cook called the sheriff, who arrested the boys and placed them in detention. When Gerald's mother came home at dinnertime, she thought Gerald was over at the Lewis's and sent her older son to get him. The Lewis family informed him that Gerald had been arrested.[3]

The next day, Gerald's mother and brother went down to a hearing. No record was kept of this hearing and Mrs. Cook did not appear. The judge later said Gerald admitted making the obscene remarks, whereas the Gaults said that Gerald only admitted dialing the phone. The judge said he would "think about it." Gerald was released from detention two or three days later.

A second hearing was held on June 15, with Gerald's mother and father both attending. No record was kept of the hearing and Mrs. Cook did not appear. Mrs. Gault asked that Mrs. Cook identify which boy made the remarks, but the judge said it was not necessary.

The judge then committed Gerald to the State Industrial School for Boys until his 21st birthday. That meant he could be held for up to six years, although he probably would be held between six and eighteen months. If he had been an adult, the maximum penalty for this offense would have been a fine of $5 to $50 and imprisonment for not more than two months.

The Gaults then retained a lawyer, who filed a writ of *habeas corpus*, demanding that the state justify holding Gerald. This writ ultimately made its way to the U.S. Supreme Court.

Issues

In the lower courts, the lawyer argued that Gerald's treatment had violated both Arizona statutes and the U.S. Constitution. But in presenting the case to the U.S. Supreme Court, the lawyer narrowed the issue down to the denial of six specific constitutional rights in Gerald's adjudication hearing: (1) the right to notice of the charges,(2) the right to counsel, (3) the right to confront and cross-examine witnesses, (4) the privilege against self-incrimination, (5) the right to a transcript of the proceedings, and (6) the right to appellate review of the case.

Decision

The Supreme Court ruled that in adjudication hearings that might result in the youth being sent to an institution, juveniles had four of these six rights: (1) the right to adequate, written, and timely notice; (2) the right to counsel; (3) the right to confront and cross-examine witnesses; and (4) the privilege against self-incrimination. Because the decision was based on the Constitution, it applied to the entire nation, not just to Arizona.

The Court did not rule on the right to a transcript and appellate review, although it encouraged states to provide those rights to juveniles. The Court also did not rule on due process rights at other stages of the juvenile justice system, or in adjudication hearings that could not result in institutionalization (e.g., in some states juveniles cannot be sent to an institution for a status offense).

Reasons

The Court first presented a general line of reasoning for why due process protections should be introduced into the juvenile court. It included all the arguments made in the O'*Connell* decision and also added the equal protection argument outlined in the *Kent* decision.

First, the Supreme Court concluded that Gerald was being *punished, not helped*:

> It is of no constitutional consequence—and of limited practical meaning—that the institution to which he is committed is called an Industrial School. The fact of the matter is that, however euphemistic the title, a "receiving home" or an "industrial school" for juveniles is an institution of confinement in which the child is incarcerated. . . . Instead of mother and father and sisters and brothers and friends and classmates, his world is peopled by guards, custodians, state employees, and "delinquents" confined with him for anything from waywardness to rape and homicide.

Second, the conclusion that he was being punished was based on an assessment of the *actual performance* of the juvenile justice system, not its *good intentions*: "It is important, we think, that the claimed benefits of the juvenile process should be candidly appraised. Neither sentiment nor folklore should cause us to shut our eyes [to failures of the juvenile court]."

Third, the Court questioned, and ultimately rejected, the *parens patriae* doctrine: "its meaning is murky and its historic credentials are of dubious relevance. . . . There is no trace of the doctrine in the history of criminal jurisprudence. . . . The constitutional and theoretical basis for this peculiar system is—to say the least—debatable."

Fourth, given a realistic appraisal of the juvenile justice practices, the Court concluded that there was a need for *due process protections*: "The essential difference between Gerald's case and a normal criminal case is that the safeguards available to adults were discarded in Gerald's case. The summary procedure as well as the long commitment was possible because Gerald was 15 years of age instead of over 18."

Thus, all four arguments that had appeared earlier in the O'*Connell* case reappeared in the *Gault* case. Added to these arguments was the equal protection argument that had been outlined in the *Kent* decision. Advocates of the juvenile court had maintained that juveniles were required to give up some of the law's protection in order to receive as compensating benefits the special care and concern afforded to juveniles. In contrast, the Supreme Court held that they could receive that special care and concern without giving up any of the law's protection:

It is claimed that juveniles obtain benefits from the special procedures applicable to them which more than offset the disadvantages
of denial of the substance of normal due process. As we shall discuss, the observance of due process standards, intelligently and not
ruthlessly administered, will not compel the States to abandon or
displace any of the substantive benefits of the juvenile process. . . .
We do not mean to denigrate the juvenile court process or to suggest that there are not aspects of the juvenile system relating to
offenders which are valuable. But the features of the juvenile system which its proponents have asserted are of unique benefit will
not be impaired by [due process protections].

In this argument, the Supreme Court claims that the benefits of the
juvenile court are available *without* any reduction in the law's protection. Thus, no constitutional basis exists for providing less protection to
juveniles than to adults. The Court went on to argue that due process
itself offers an additional benefit: "The appearance as well as the actuality of fairness, impartiality and orderliness—in short, the essentials of
due process—may be a more impressive and more therapeutic attitude
so far as the juvenile is concerned [than the informality of juvenile
court]."

The Court then concluded that the denial of due process to juveniles
violates the equal protection clause: "In view of this, it would be extraordinary if our Constitution did not require the procedural regularity and
the exercise of care implied in the phrase 'due process.' Under our constitution, the condition of being a boy does not justify a kangaroo
court."

Having completed its general line of reasoning, the Court made specific arguments about each of the six specific rights Gerald's attorney
claimed he had been denied. As noted above, it ruled that juveniles were
entitled to the first four of those rights. In each case, the Court emphasized how important these rights were for preparing an adequate defense.
As originally conceived, of course, it was not necessary for juveniles to
prepare a defense because juveniles did not have to defend themselves
against a court that would act in their "best interests."

The Supreme Court did not rule on whether juveniles have a right to
appellate review and to a transcript. These two issues are linked, since the
transcript is legally important only when it is used for appellate review.
The Court pointed out that, although all states provide appellate review
for adults, they are not required to do so by the Constitution. Thus, the
Court encouraged states to provide this for juveniles but did not require
them to do so.

Dissent

An important dissenting opinion was written by Justice Stewart, who held on to at least some aspects of the language and logic of the *Crouse* and *Fisher* cases. Stewart implicitly accepted the *parents patriae* doctrine, describing juvenile courts as "public social agencies" rather than criminal courts. He focused on the good intentions of the juvenile court rather than its actual performance:

> Whether treating with a delinquent child, a neglected child, a defective child, or a dependent child, a juvenile proceeding's whole purpose and mission is the very opposite of the mission and purpose of a prosecution in a criminal court. The object of the one is correction of a condition. The object of the other is conviction and punishment for a criminal act.

Justice Stewart granted that the reality had not always lived up to this good intention, so that some juveniles may be punished rather than treated. But he argued that the intentions should be retained rather than rejected:

> There can be no denying that in many areas the performance of these agencies has fallen disappointingly short of the hopes and dreams of the courageous pioneers who first conceived them. For a variety of reasons, the reality has sometimes not even approached the ideal. . . . But I am certain that the answer does not lie in the Court's opinion in this case, which serves to convert a juvenile proceeding into a criminal prosecution.

Finally, he acknowledged the need for some modest infusions of due process, but not the wholesale injection that the court was granting:

> For example, I suppose all would agree that a brutally coerced confession could not constitutionally be considered in a juvenile court hearing. But it surely does not follow that the testimonial privilege against self-incrimination is applicable in all juvenile proceedings. Similarly, due process clearly requires timely notice of the purpose and scope of any proceedings affecting the relationship of parent and child. But it certainly does not follow that notice of a juvenile hearing must be framed with all the technical niceties of a criminal indictment.

This dissent contains the basic arguments, even if modified and restrained, of the *Crouse* and *Fisher* decisions. The courts have good intentions even if actual practice has not measured up. They treat juveniles, and do not punish them. Thus, due process protections are not really needed, at least not to the extent that the Supreme Court is granting them.

Comments

The *Gault* case is the fourth in an alternating series of cases that began in 1938 with *Mary Ann Crouse*. The crucial element of each decision is whether the Supreme Court focused on the good intentions or on actual performance of the juvenile justice system.

If the Supreme Court focused on good intentions, then it ruled that juveniles are being helped and therefore do not need due process protections in juvenile court. If the Supreme Court focused on actual performance, then it ruled that juveniles are being punished and therefore need due process protections, just as adults need them in criminal court. These alternating decisions were not the result of differences in the facts of the case. Rather, the facts in these four cases are sufficiently similar that they could be rotated and the decisions would remain the same.

The lines of reasoning are available to the Court, each legally sufficient. The courts alternate between these two lines of reasoning based on whether they are idealistic or cynical about the ability of the juvenile justice system to help children. The *Crouse* case came only thirteen years after the founding of the first juvenile institution, and the Pennsylvania Supreme Court was still very optimistic about how well those institutions would work. The *O'Connell* case came thirty years later, and the failure of the institutions was much more apparent. The vast optimism was renewed by the establishment of the first juvenile court in 1899. The *Fisher* case came only six years later, and reflected the firm belief that this new mechanism would work extremely well. Sixty years later, the *Gault* decision affirmed an awareness of the failures of that same mechanism. See table 6.1 for a comparison of these three cases.

Table 6.1.   A Comparison of the *Crouse, O'Connell, Fisher,* and *Gault* Cases

	Crouse and *Fisher* Cases	*O'Connell* and *Gault* Cases
Court focused on	Good intentions	Actual performance
Juveniles were said to be	Helped and treated	Punished
Legal basis of court's decision	*Parens patriae*	Criminal law
Decision	Due process is not required	Due process is required

As for Gerald Gault, he was later released from the institution and joined the military, from which he eventually retired as a master sergeant. In 1997, he and his family appeared at a conference celebrating the fortieth anniversary of the *Gault* decision, where he stated that he had no idea what was happening to him in court until the judge said he was being sent to an institution until he was 21.[4]

The Case of Samuel Winship

Facts

In 1967, 12-year-old Samuel Winship was charged with stealing $112 from a woman's pocketbook at a furniture store in the Bronx. A saleslady said she saw him dash from the store and then the woman found the money missing. A defense witness, however, said the saleslady was in another part of the store at the time and could not have seen Winship. By New York State law, the judge was required to find a "preponderance of the evidence" in order to adjudicate. "Preponderance" meant that more evidence existed to indicate Winship did it than that he didn't. Winship was adjudicated delinquent and committed to a juvenile institution for an initial period of eighteen months, subject to annual extensions for up to six years.[5]

"Preponderance" is the standard used in civil courts because civil cases involve a conflict between two citizens—for example, the name of the case would be *John Doe v. Jane Smith*. Using this standard, the judge decides which citizen is able to marshal more evidence. The judge then rules in favor of that citizen. "Preponderance" had always been the standard of evidence used in juvenile courts because they were considered civil, not criminal, courts.

In contrast, "beyond a reasonable doubt" is the standard used in criminal courts. "Beyond a reasonable doubt" is a much higher standard of evidence than "preponderance"—it means there is so much evidence of the person's guilt that there is no reasonable doubt left. This higher standard has been used in criminal court because the power of the state is arrayed against an individual citizen—the name of the case would be *State v. John Doe*. The founders of the United States were very concerned about abuses of power by the state, and were always seeking ways to limit that power. Thus, they set a very high standard that the state must meet before the judge can decide in the state's favor that is, the state must prove its case "beyond a reasonable doubt." In contrast, the standard for the defendant was quite low: if defendants can establish that there is a "reasonable doubt" about their guilt, then they are to be acquitted.

Winship's lawyer claimed to have established "reasonable doubt" about Winship's guilt by presenting a witness who said the saleslady was in another part of the store at the time. But the judge held that the preponderance of the evidence was that Winship had taken the $112. The lawyer did, however, get the judge to acknowledge that this was the basis for his decision in the court record:

> COUNSEL: Your Honor is making a finding by the preponderance of the evidence.
> COURT: Well, it convinces me.
> COUNSEL: It's not beyond a reasonable doubt, Your Honor.
> COURT: That is true. . . . Our statute says preponderance and a preponderance it is.

The lawyer then appealed this case all the way to the U.S. Supreme Court.

Issue

The legal issue in this case was "whether proof beyond a reasonable doubt" is among the "essentials of due process and fair treatment required during the adjudicatory stage when a juvenile is charged with an act which would constitute a crime if committed by an adult."[6]

Decision

The "beyond a reasonable doubt" standard is required in adjudication proceedings in which the juvenile is charged with an act that would constitute a crime if committed by an adult. The "preponderance" standard may still be used in adjudication hearings that consider only status offenses.

Reasons

"Beyond a reasonable doubt" had never been held to be the constitutional standard in (adult) criminal court, although it was used in all such courts and was assumed in a number of earlier Supreme Court decisions. To remove any doubt about the standard, the Supreme Court first held that "the Due Process Clause protects the accused against conviction except upon proof beyond a reasonable doubt of every fact necessary to constitute the crime with which he is charged."

The Supreme Court then turned to the use of the standard in juvenile court. It first considered the arguments of the New York Court of Appeals, which earlier had rejected Winship's claim. The New York Court of Appeals had argued that the juvenile court is designed "not to punish, but to save the child," and thus there is no need for due process protections; that the addition of due process protections would risk the destruction of the benefits now afforded to juveniles; and that there is only a "tenuous difference" between the preponderance and the reasonable doubt standards.

In rather sarcastic language, the Supreme Court argued that the first two of these arguments had already been rejected in the *Gault* decision. It then called the "tenuous difference" argument "singularly unpersuasive" in light of the lengthy history of the reasonable doubt standard and the fact that the juvenile court judge had said on the record that there was a preponderance of the evidence, but it was not beyond a reasonable doubt. This indicated a clear difference between the two standards, not merely a "tenuous" difference.

Dissent

Justice Stewart dissented from this opinion, as he had from the *Gault* decision. This time he was joined by the new Chief Justice, Warren Burger, who had been appointed by President Nixon to replace Chief Justice Earl Warren. Their dissent again contained the essence of the *Crouse* and *Fisher* arguments, focusing on the good intentions of the juvenile court while conceding that its actual practice had not always matched the ideal. They argued that due process protections were not required and would only make things worse:

> The original concept of the juvenile court system was to provide a benevolent and less formal means than criminal courts could provide for dealing with the special and often sensitive problems of youthful offenders. . . . I dissent from further straight-jacketing of an already overly restricted system. . . . My hope is that today's decision will not spell the end of a generously conceived program of compassionate treatment intended to mitigate the rigors and trauma of exposing youthful offenders to a traditional criminal court.

Comments

Two years later, the Supreme Court made the *Winship* decision fully retroactive.[7] This meant that youths who had been adjudicated on a preponderance of the evidence would either have to be released from institutions or readjudicated by evidence that was beyond a reasonable doubt. This was an unusual step—normally, decisions apply only after they are announced.

This unusual move indicated how important the *Winship* decision was. The "beyond a reasonable doubt" standard was issued to ensure that when the court finds that someone has committed a criminal act, that finding is accurate. Adjudications based on a preponderance of the evidence were held to be not accurate enough to warrant continuing to keep someone in an institution. This same focus on accurate fact-finding appears in the next case, where it involved the right to a jury trial.

The Case of Joseph McKeiver

Facts

In 1968, 16-year-old Joseph McKeiver of Philadelphia was charged with robbery, larceny, and receiving stolen goods. These three felony charges arose from an incident in which McKeiver and twenty or thirty other youth chased three younger teenagers and took 25 cents from them. McKeiver had never been arrested, was doing well in school, and was gainfully employed, and the testimony of two of the three witnesses against him was described by the juvenile court judge as somewhat inconsistent and weak.[8]

At the beginning of the hearing, McKeiver's lawyer said he had never met McKeiver before and was just interviewing him. The judge allowed five minutes for the interview. The lawyer then requested a jury trial, which was refused, and McKeiver was adjudicated and placed on probation.

The case was appealed to the Pennsylvania Supreme Court, where it was joined to another juvenile case in which a jury trial had been requested. Fifteen-year-old Edward Terry, also from Philadelphia, had hit a police officer with his fists and with a stick when the officer attempted to break up a fight Terry was watching. After denying a jury trial, the judge adjudicated Terry and committed him to an institution.

These two cases were appealed to the U.S. Supreme Court, where they were joined to two North Carolina cases that also involved juveniles' requesting jury trials. Barbara Burris and about forty-five other black children between 11 and 15 years old had been arrested and charged with obstructing traffic as the result of a march protesting racial discrimination in the county schools. They had refused to get off the paved portion of a highway when told to do so by police. In a separate incident arising out of the same protest, James Howard and fifteen others created a disturbance in a principal's office. He was charged with being disorderly and defacing school property. The judge adjudicated all these youth and committed them to institutions. He then suspended the commitments and placed them on probation for terms ranging from twelve to twenty-four months.

Issue

"These cases present the narrow but precise issue whether the Due Process Clause of the Fourteenth Amendment assures the right to trial by jury in the adjudicative phase of a state juvenile court delinquency proceeding."[9]

Decision

The court ruled that the Constitution did not require trial by jury at the adjudication stage of juvenile court processing.

Reasons

Unlike the New York Court of Appeals in the *Winship* case, the Pennsylvania Supreme Court presented a rationale for rejecting McKeiver's claim that incorporated a careful and thoughtful reading of the *Gault* and *Winship* decisions. The U.S. Supreme Court liked it so much that it relied heavily on it for its own decision.

The Pennsylvania Supreme Court argued that the U.S. Supreme Court had attempted to strike a balance that would preserve the benefits of the juvenile court while incorporating sufficient procedural regularity "to impress the juvenile with the gravity of the situation and the impartiality of the tribunal." The state court then argued that (1) although faith in judges is no substitute for due process, juvenile court judges do try to handle cases differently than criminal court judges; (2) despite shortcomings, the rehabilitative facilities available to juvenile courts are superior to those available to criminal courts; (3) despite the fact that it is a punishment, adjudication of delinquency is less onerous than conviction of a crime; (4) despite its failures, current practices may contain "the seed from which a truly appropriate system can be brought forth"; and (5) of all the due process rights, jury trial is likely to be the one that would most disrupt and destroy the "unique nature of the juvenile process."

The U.S. Supreme Court agreed with this line of argument and expanded on it. The main function of a jury trial in the criminal justice system is to limit possible abuses of state power, since conviction then requires the agreement of twelve ordinary citizens. The right to a jury trial, therefore, makes it hard for the state to use convictions as a political weapon. The Supreme Court held that this function was less important in the juvenile justice system than in the (adult) criminal justice system.

On the other hand, all the rights given in *Gault* and *Winship* had been designed to ensure accuracy in fact-finding during the adjudication hearing. Juries, however, have never been said to be more accurate in fact-finding than judges—if anything, research suggests that juries are less accurate. In addition, juries would be highly disruptive of the informal, cooperative atmosphere in which everyone tried to find the child's best interest, and would tend to create an adversarial atmosphere in which each side attempted to win the case. Thus, the Supreme Court held that juries were not required in juvenile adjudication hearings.

Dissent

A dissent was written by Justice Douglas and joined by Justices Black and Marshall. These judges argued that juveniles were being punished, not helped, and therefore they were entitled to due process rights, including trial by jury: "In the present cases imprisonment or confinement up to 10 years was possible for one child and each faced at least a possible five-year incarceration. No adult could be denied a jury trial in those circumstances."

They also argued that jury trial, like the earlier rights given juveniles, can contribute to the juvenile's sense that the proceedings are fair, which can help in the effort to rehabilitate. Finally, they argued that jury trials "provide the child with a safeguard against being prejudged by a judge who may well be prejudiced by reports already submitted to him by the police or caseworkers in the case."

Comments

The *Kent* and *Gault* decisions had been written by Justice Fortas, who was one of the most liberal members of the already liberal Warren Court, headed by Chief Justice Warren. By the time of the *McKeiver* case, both Chief Justice Warren and Justice Fortas were gone, replaced by President Nixon's conservative appointments of the new Chief Justice Burger and Justice Blackman.

Justice Blackman wrote the *McKeiver* decision, and he was joined by Justice Stewart and Chief Justice Burger[10] The argument in this decision is similar to Stewart's dissent to *Gault* and to Stewart's and Burger's dissent to *Winship*. Specifically, it focused on preserving the original good intentions of the juvenile court, despite conceding that actual practice had not always lived up to the ideal. Given this focus, the opinion opposed further straitjacketing of the system with due process rights.

One could argue that the Supreme Court reversed itself in the *McKeiver* case—that is, that the dissenting opinions of Stewart and Burger in the *Gault* and *Winship* decisions became the majority opinion in the *McKeiver* decision. One might further argue that this change occurred because of the departure of liberals Fortas and Warren and their replacement by conservative Justices Burger and Blackman, who then joined Stewart in his opinion. This interpretation would be consistent with the fact that Justices Douglas and Marshall,[11] two of the remaining liberal members of the Warren Court, dissented from the *McKeiver* opinion.

That is one possible interpretation. However, it is also true that in many ways the *McKeiver* decision was consistent with, and extended, the *Kent*, *Gault*, and *Winship* decisions. In the *Kent* decision, Justice Fortas accused the juvenile court of providing the "worst of both worlds," and in *Gault*, Fortas tried to preserve the benefits of the juvenile court while adding the benefits of the criminal court. That suggests that he wanted the "best of both words," and not merely to replace the juvenile court with a criminal court for juveniles.

The *McKeiver* decision, then, focused on preserving the "best" of the juvenile court world, whereas *Gault* and *Winship* had added the "best" of the criminal court world. In that sense, the *McKeiver* decision was consistent with, not a reversal of, the *Gault* and *Winship* decisions. The fifth and final case, written by Chief Justice Burger and joined by the new conservative majority, again focused on preserving the ideals of the original juvenile court.

The Case of Gary Jones

Facts

On February 8, 1970, 17-year-old Gary Jones committed an armed robbery in Los Angeles with a loaded gun. He was arrested and placed in detention that same day. On March 1, Jones was adjudicated a delinquent on that charge, along with two other charges involving robberies with a loaded gun. The case was continued for several weeks so the probation officer could prepare a social history and recommend a disposition, and Jones was returned to detention.[12]

On March 15, the court reconvened for the disposition hearing, but the judge announced instead that he would waive jurisdiction to the criminal court. Jones's lawyer expressed surprise and requested a continuance in order to prepare arguments about the proposed waiver. The court continued the case for another week, then heard arguments on the waiver issue and ordered Jones tried as an adult.

Jones's lawyer filed a writ of *habeas corpus*, alleging that Jones had already been tried in juvenile court for this offense, and could not be tried again in criminal court without violating the double-jeopardy clause in the Fifth Amendment to the Constitution, which holds that no person shall "be subject for the same offense to be twice put in jeopardy of life or limb."

This petition was denied because the court held that a juvenile adjudication was not a criminal trial, so that Jones had not been placed in "jeopardy of life or limb" at it. Jones, therefore, was tried and convicted in criminal court and sentenced to prison.

Issue

The issue was "whether the prosecution of respondent as an adult, after Juvenile Court proceedings which resulted in a finding that respondent had violated a criminal statute and a subsequent finding that he was unfit for treatment as a juvenile," violated the double-jeopardy clause of the U.S. Constitution.

Decision

With respect to double jeopardy, juvenile adjudication is the same as a criminal trial. Someone who has been adjudicated in juvenile court for an offense cannot also be tried in adult court for the same offense.

Reasons

The double-jeopardy clause states that a person should not twice be placed at risk of punishment for the same offense. The question before the Court, therefore, was whether the juvenile adjudication hearing constituted jeopardy, in that the juvenile faced the risk of punishment for the offense.

Relying on arguments made in the *Gault* and *Winship* decisions, the Supreme Court said yes:

We believe it is simply too late in the day to conclude, as did the District Court in this case, that a juvenile is not put in jeopardy at a proceeding whose object is to determine whether he has committed acts that violate a criminal law whose potential consequences include both the stigma inherent in such a determination and the deprivation of liberty for many years.

They then stated the precise point at which jeopardy attaches, so the case can no longer be waived: "We therefore conclude that respondent was put in jeopardy at the adjudicatory hearing. Jeopardy attached when respondent was 'put to trial before the trier of the facts,' that is, when the Juvenile Court, as the trier of the facts, began to hear evidence."

The Supreme Court listed several reasons for selecting this point, but concluded with one that was consistent with its goal of trying to preserve the best of the original juvenile court while introducing some protections from criminal court. In the original juvenile court, the juvenile could be trusting and open with the judge because the disposition of the case would be made on the basis of the juvenile's "best interests." But a juvenile could not be trusting and open if the judge might turn around and waive jurisdiction to criminal court. The Supreme Court argued that the juvenile court judge's actions had placed Gary Jones in a dilemma that undermined the very trust that the original juvenile court tried to nurture.

If he appears uncooperative, he runs the risk of an adverse adjudication, as well as of an unfavorable dispositional recommendation. If, on the other hand, he is cooperative, he runs the risk of prejudicing his chances in adult court if transfer is ordered. We regard a procedure that results in such a dilemma as at odds with the goal that, to the extent fundamental fairness permits, adjudicatory hearings be informal and non-adversary. Knowledge of the risk of transfer after an adjudicatory hearing can only undermine the potential for informality and cooperation which was intended to be the hallmark of the juvenile-court system.

Comments

The *Jones* decision was written by Chief Justice Burger and joined by all members of the Court. From the point of view of the conservative members, this decision preserved aspects of the original juvenile court, while from the point of view of the liberal members, it added one more due process right to those granted in the *Gault* and *Winship* decisions.

This unanimous decision marked the end of the Supreme Court's restructuring of the juvenile court. It had begun in 1966, with the activist liberals of the Warren Court, but by 1975, the Supreme Court had itself been transformed by President Nixon's appointment of four conservative justices. Enough is enough, said the new conservative majority; it is time to preserve what was good about the original juvenile court.

The Lessons of History

On the surface, the Supreme Court's reform does not seem consistent with the "lessons of history" derived from studying the earlier reforms in New York and Chicago, and presented in the conclusion of chapter 5. Below, we consider each lesson in turn, noting both potential consistencies and inconsistencies.

Lesson 1: The Cycle of Juvenile Justice. The widespread perception that juvenile crime rates are unusually high is accompanied by a widespread belief that these rates can be lowered by appropriate juvenile justice policies. This results in a continuous cycle of reform that consists of establishing lenient treatments in a major reform, gradually toughening up those treatments over a long time so that officials end up choosing between harsh punishments and doing nothing at all, and then reestablishing lenient treatments in another major reform.

The Supreme Court's reform, on the surface, does not seem to fit into this cycle because it neither established new lenient treatments in a major structural reform nor gradually toughened existing punishments over a long period of time. One would have expected that the next step in this cycle would have been the gradual toughening of punishments because juvenile justice officials were not yet confronted with a forced choice between harsh punishments and doing nothing at all. If Lesson 1 is correct, the Supreme Court's reform would have appeared strangely out of place, more or less irrelevant to the general concerns of the public about juvenile justice.

Looking back with a perspective of over forty years, we can see how the Supreme Court was influenced by the larger social and political movements of the time. First, the national focus on civil rights and personal liberties of the 1960s and early 1970s infiltrated both the adult and the juvenile courts. The Warren Court was responding to civil unrest that was deeply rooted in other social movements of the time. The baby boomer generation (i.e., the very large number of children born shortly after 1945, when veterans returned to the United States from the Second World War) was now entering adolescence, and all social institutions dealing with youth, including the juvenile courts, were overwhelmed with the rising numbers of adolescents they needed to serve.

Second, and perhaps even more important, the migration of large numbers of African Americans from rural southern locations to the urban northern locations resulted in what was called at the time "white flight." Whites moved to the suburbs, so the inner cities became the home to African American families that were not well equipped to compete in the industrial economy of the time. Much like the children of European immigrants decades before, the children of these African American families became the foremost "clientele" of the juvenile court. Meanwhile, the civil rights movement was gaining momentum, bringing to the national forefront issues of government oppression of minorities in multiple arenas, such as school, employment, housing, and, of course, the justice system.[13]

Given this historical context, it is not surprising that the Supreme Court at this time tended to focus on the actual practice (punishment) of the juvenile system rather than its stated good intentions (rehabilitation). Moreover, while some of the ideals set forth by the Supreme Court do not necessarily appear to fit within the context of the cycle, we will find that their actual implementation does. The gradual toughening up of the system would be only temporarily kept at bay, until the dust began to settle from the political unrest of this historical time.

Lesson 2: Ideas of Juvenile Delinquency. Ideas of delinquency that "sell" (i.e., that succeed in the competition with other possible ideas) propose that delinquents are a subgroup within some larger problem group (e.g., paupers, dependent and neglected children) with which the public is already familiar. The prevailing idea of delinquency and delinquents thus drives the idea of what juvenile justice should be.

The Supreme Court proposed that juvenile delinquents were indeed a subgroup of a larger group with which the justices themselves were quite familiar: criminal defendants who were citizens of the United States, who were presumed innocent until proven guilty, and who therefore deserved the rights and protections guaranteed by the U.S. Constitution. This is much different than the previous notion of juvenile delinquent which was that of a needy and dependent child. This earlier idea of delinquent went hand in hand with the development of the juvenile court as a civil court and its deep connections with the social work movement. Before that, the notion of juvenile delinquents as a subgroup of paupers fit nicely with the poor laws of the days and the House of Refuge movement. This "new" idea appears to take us even further back in time, before the House of Refuge, when juvenile delinquents were simply handled as small criminals in adult courts and adult prisons. It suggests a response to juvenile delinquents that we are all familiar with: the criminal justice system.

Lesson 3: Ideas of Juvenile Justice. Responses to delinquency that "sell" (i.e., that succeed in the competition with other possible responses) are slightly modified versions of responses to the larger problem group of which delinquents are thought to be a subgroup (potential paupers, dependent and neglected children, etc).

Based on the above notion of the juvenile delinquent as a subgroup of criminal defendants, the new response was to view the juvenile court as a slightly modified version of the adult criminal court, rather than a modified version of a social welfare agency or a chancery court. To the liberals on the Supreme Court at the time, this view served to better protect the juveniles from receiving punishments without a fair hearing characterized by due process. However, we will see in the following chapters how this same view set the stage for a further redefinition of the juvenile delinquent as a "small criminal" and how that proved a catalyst for the implementation of increasingly harsh punishments, while largely sidestepping many of the due process protections proposed by the Court.

In particular, while the idea that juvenile delinquents are citizens who are presumed innocent and who have constitutional rights never "sold" very well to the general public, the notion of the juvenile delinquent as a small criminal fits well within the upcoming "war on crime."

Lesson 4: Economic Interests of the Rich and Powerful. Responses to delinquency that "sell" focus on the behavior of poor and powerless people but ignore the behavior of rich and powerful people. In particular, responses that focus on poor people's behavior do not harm the economic interests of the rich and powerful—that is, they aim to remove delinquents from the streets rather than change conditions on the streets.

The Supreme Court's reform did not attempt to change the behavior of the rich and powerful, but it could have harmed their economic interests. A constitutional juvenile court would be more expensive, which would result in tax increases. In addition, a constitutional juvenile court would provide due process protections to juvenile defendants, which could result in "guilty" juveniles being freed to commit more crimes. These are relatively minor points, but it is clear that the Supreme Court's reform did not fall into the mainstream of what we would expect from this particular lesson. However, it is important to note that the Court did indeed strike down the one reform that would have been the most costly to the taxpayers: provision of trial by jury.

Lesson 5: Moral and Intellectual Superiority of Reformers. Responses to delinquency that "sell" imply that delinquents and their parents are morally and intellectually inferior, and that the reformers themselves are morally and intellectually superior.

The idea of juvenile delinquents as defendants with rights conveys the image of a complete and whole person, not someone assumed to be morally and intellectually inferior. In addition, by providing the juveniles with due process rights, the Court assumed that delinquents needed protection from agents of the larger society, including the justices of the Supreme Court itself. This appears to contradict the basic premise of Lesson 5. Yet the same basic argument of the *Gault* decision appears previously in history in the *O'Connell* decision handed down by the Illinois State Supreme Court, which held that O'Connell did indeed need protection from the state. That decision did not "sell" very well, and so the "morally and intellectually superior" reformers found a way around it by creating the juvenile justice court itself. If these Supreme Court decisions are equally unsuccessfully at selling, then it seems likely that reformers will find other ways to achieve their supposedly lofty goals.

On the other hand, as we previously noted in Lesson 2, applying due process rights does redefine juvenile delinquents as a subgroup of "criminal offenders" rather than merely needy children. This definition has the potential to further justify the reformers in their definition of themselves as morally superior. In our society, the mere commission of a criminal offense is enough to deem a person to be of poor moral character, as is exemplified in the denial of professional licensure in over 800 professions to convicted offenders based on the notion that, by definition, they cannot be of "good moral standing."[14] To the extent that this redefinition promotes the image of the reformer as morally superior, it may indeed "sell."

Lesson 6: The Unfair Comparison. Reformers "sell" their own reforms by an unfair comparison, in which a harsh assessment of actual practices of past policies is compared with an optimistic assessment of reforms, based on good intentions. Because they assume that good intentions directly translate into good practices, reformers promise to solve the problem of juvenile delinquency.

Consistent with this lesson, the Supreme Court provided a harsh assessment of the actual practices of past policies, and it compared that assessment with its optimistic view that the reform would improve conditions for juveniles. Inconsistent with this lesson, however, is the fact that the Court did not propose to "solve" the problem of delinquency. Its proposed reform might decrease delinquency, at least somewhat, because it would create greater respect for the law for juvenile offenders, who would deem their treatment by the system as fair and just. An optimistic promise to make the system fair, however, probably would not "sell" nearly as well as a reform that promises to solve the problem of delinquency.

Lesson 7: The Power of the State. Reforms that "sell" increase the power of the state, based on optimistic assessments of how effective the reform will be in solving the problem. The power of the state usually continues to expand regardless of the specific content or nature of the reform.

Inconsistent with this lesson, the Supreme Court restricted the power of the state to intervene in the lives of delinquents by providing delinquents with a means for resisting such intervention. For the first time, the power of delinquents and their families was expanded and the power of those who worked with delinquents was limited. The Supreme Court took this stance because, like the founders of the U.S. government, they did not believe that government officials were necessarily morally or intellectually superior. While not consistent, then, with lessons of history, the decisions are consistent with the history of our nation and with the role of the separate branches of government in a system of checks and balances to restrict the abuse of power.

The Supreme Court's reform was, for the most part, inconsistent with the lessons from history. If these lessons are correct, then we can expect this reform to only partially "sell." That is, those parts of the reform that can be used to the benefit of the reformers and the state will be implemented, while those portions of the decisions that do not hold such potential will fall by the wayside.

NOTES

1. Paul J. Brantingham, "Juvenile Justice Reform in California and New York in the Early 1960s," in Frederic Faust and Paul J. Brantingham, *Juvenile Justice Philosophy*, 2nd ed. (St. Paul, Minn.: West, 1979), 259–268.

2. *Kent v. United States,* 383 U.S. 541 (1966). Reprinted in Larry J. Siegal and Paul E. Tracy, eds., *Juvenile Law: A Collection of Leading U.S. Supreme Court Cases* (Englewood Cliffs, N.J.: Pearson Prentice Hall, 2008).

3. *In Re Gault,* 387 US 1 (1967). Reprinted in Siegal and Tracy, eds., *Juvenile Law.*

4. Robert E. Shephard Jr., "The Juvenile Court at a Hundred Years," *Juvenile Justice* 6, no. 2 (December 1999), Office of Juvenile Justice and Delinquency Prevention, National Institute of Justice, United States Department of Justice.

5. *In Re Winship,* 397 U.S. 358 (1970). Reprinted in Siegal and Tracy, eds., *Juvenile Law.*

6. Recall that juveniles cannot commit crimes per se because the law establishing the juvenile court raised the age of criminal liability. Thus, they can only commit acts "which would constitute a crime if committed by an adult."

7. *Ivan V. v. City of New York*, 407 U.S. 203, 92 S.Ct. 1951, 32 L.Ed.2d 659 (1972).

8. *McKeiver v. Pennsylvania*, 403 U.S. 528 (1971). Reprinted in Siegal and Tracy, eds., *Juvenile Law*.

9. Ibid.

10. Justice White concurred in this opinion for a simpler reason that focused more tightly on the intention of the juvenile court to help, not punish, juveniles. Justice Harlan concurred in the decision, but for a different reason. He argued that jury trials are not constitutionally required in adult criminal courts, so they are not required in juvenile courts, either.

11. Justice Brennan, another liberal member of the court, dissented in the North Carolina cases, but he concurred in the Pennsylvania cases. In his view, jury trial was not required if the public and press were admitted to adjudication hearings, as was the case in Pennsylvania.

12. *Breed v. Jones*, 421 U.S. 519 (1975). Reprinted in Siegal and Tracy, eds., *Juvenile Law*.

13. For more complete discussions of African American migration to northern cities, as well as the influence of racial conflict on the juvenile justice system, see Barry Feld, *Bad Kids: Race and the Transformation of the Juvenile Court* (New York: Oxford University Press, 1999); Dougless S. Massey and Nancy A. Denton, *American Apartheid: Segregation and the Making of the Underclass* (Cambridge, Mass.: Harvard University Press, 1993); Nicholas Lemann, *The Promised Land: The Great Black Migration and How It Changed America* (New York: Vintage Books, 1992).

14. Paul Cromwell, Leanne Fiftal Alarid, and Rolando V. del Carmen, *Community-Based Corrections*, 6th ed. (Belmont, Calif.: Thomson Wadsworth, 2002).

7

Due Process and Adjudication Hearings

An Idea That Didn't Sell

The U.S. Supreme Court established a new constitutional juvenile court that was supposed to provide juveniles with "the best of both worlds." Adjudication hearings were to provide juveniles with the due process protections that were found in the criminal court, while disposition hearings were to provide them with the care and treatment that had been found in the original juvenile court. But this smooth blending of two worlds was not to be.[1]

The "best" of the criminal court world was to be the due process protections in the juvenile court's adjudication hearings. We examine adjudication hearings in this chapter and conclude that, for various practical reasons, this promise was not kept. Similar to previous reforms, the good intentions of the Supreme Court simply did not translate into the actual practices of the juvenile court.

The next chapter, chapter 8, discusses what actually happened in the disposition hearings. These hearings were supposed to continue the "best" of the juvenile court world: a focus on care and treatment and the "best interests" of the child, as opposed to the punishments provided in criminal courts. As it turned out, disposition hearings ended up being driven by the broader "get tough" movement that emphasized a greater focus on punishment than on treatment of juvenile offenders.

Adjudication Hearings: The Discretion vs. Due Process Dilemma

The central issue in the Supreme Court decisions had been whether the adjudication hearings would be characterized by the discretion and informality of the original juvenile court or by the formal due process procedures of adult criminal court.

It must be remembered that introducing the due process rights ordered by the Supreme Court would require a change in thinking on the part of juvenile justice officials, as well as changes in practice. The point of view of the founders of the juvenile court was that due process protections would interfere with the ability of the court to help the children. Because it is very complicated to try to help children, while it is fairly simple to punish them, the founders of the juvenile court believed that juvenile justice officials needed great flexibility in their jobs, giving them the freedom to respond to different cases differently and to individual children individually. Juvenile justice officials at this time, just as the child-savers of the past, believed deeply in their ability to properly assess, treat, and ultimately reform juvenile offenders. Discretion and informality were seen as the keys to the system's "success."

The Supreme Court, however, took the view of the founders of our nation, who, when faced with the same choice between discretion and due process, decided in favor of due process. Having just rebelled against what they believed was a tyrannical government, they did not trust the good intentions of government officials, and they created a government based on a separation of powers and a system of checks and balances. In criminal court, the founders restrained the power of the state by providing defendants with due process rights.

These same considerations motivated the Supreme Court to give due process rights to juveniles. The dominant thread of reasoning through all of the Supreme Court decisions was that the juvenile had to be given sufficient due process rights to ensure accuracy of fact-finding in the adjudication hearing. Like the founders of the United States, the Supreme Court knew that many "guilty" juveniles would be freed by their decision. For example, they went so far as to make the *Winship* decision retroactive, which freed from institutions many juveniles who had committed serious offenses but had been convicted only on a preponderance of the evidence. But the Supreme Court believed that this was better than adjudicating some juveniles who had not actually committed the alleged offenses. This view reflected the position of the founders of the United States, who made it quite difficult to convict criminal defendants.

An old saying expressed their sentiment: "Better a hundred guilty people go free than one innocent person be convicted."[2]

In contrast, compare the above saying to the broad discretion allotted the first juvenile court. Under the provisions of the Illinois Juvenile Court Act of 1899, children could fall under the jurisdiction of the court for, among many other reasons, being homeless, abandoned, lacking proper parental care, begging, or simply selling any article or singing or playing a musical instrument on the street. In fact, we earlier argued that it is difficult to imagine any child from a poor family who could not fit under at least one provision of this original act. The sentiment behind this act might be summarized by a saying such as: "Better a hundred nonneedy children receive services than one needy child be denied."

These two lines of thinking are, thus, inherently inconsistent. To adhere to the decisions set forth by the Supreme Court, drastic change in the juvenile proceeding would be required. To understand more fully the extent of change, let us first take a closer look at a typical, pre-*Gault* adjudication hearing.

Adjudication Hearings Before *Gault*

Justice Fortas described the juvenile court that adjudicated Gerald Gault as "a kangaroo court." While the term seems appropriate for what happened to Gault, most youth processed by juvenile courts did not receive such outrageous treatment. Most juveniles were treated fairly and at least somewhat reasonably, with court officials trying to promote the child's best interests as much as possible. "Kangaroo" juvenile courts were the exception, not the rule, in the pre-*Gault* era.[3]

On the other hand, juvenile courts as envisioned by their founders were very informal. The typical hearing involved the juvenile, a probation officer, and the judge. Attorneys were usually not present at such hearings. In fact, estimates are that attorneys appeared in fewer than 5 percent of all cases at this time.[4]

The role of the probation officer was to investigate the child's home life and social situation, and thereby determine his or her need for services. The role of the child was to be open and honest with the judge and probation officer in order to allow them to make a determination in the best interests of the child. The role of the judge was, then, to make a judgment about (i.e., to adjudicate) two questions: whether the juvenile committed the act in question; and if so, whether the child was in need of services.

We would not necessarily characterize such a proceeding as a "kangaroo court," but it is apparent that there is room for a lot of looseness and discretion in such a hearing. This looseness meant that few "guilty" juveniles were freed while relatively many juveniles who were otherwise "innocent" were adjudicated. Consider, for example, the cases that reached the U.S. Supreme Court as described in chapter 5. These were not unusual cases in terms of the way they were handled. No formal evidence was taken against Gerry Gault, and it was not clear that he had actually committed the offense. The judge agreed there was "reasonable doubt" about whether Winship really had stolen the money. The evidence against McKeiver was described as "weak and inconsistent," and in the North Carolina cases that were joined to *McKeiver*, the juvenile court was essentially used to suppress the civil rights movement. Only the cases against Morris Kent and Gary Jones were solid enough to warrant conviction in criminal court, and both of them were, in fact, waived to criminal court.

The point is that, in the juvenile court, judges often were not overly concerned with whether the juvenile really committed the offense. Rather, they often looked at the case in terms of whether the juvenile needed help. If so, they would adjudicate the youth a delinquent so that the needed services would be provided.

Expected Changes

After the Supreme Court decisions, juveniles would have the power to fight against the state. They would have the right to be represented by an attorney at waiver and adjudication hearings, and the state would now have to prove its case "beyond a reasonable doubt." If the juvenile court implemented the Supreme Court's newly granted due process rights, we would expect to see a great increase in the percentage of juveniles who were represented by defense counsel. We also would expect to see a large increase in formal adjudication hearings in juvenile court, where juveniles contest the charges against them. Finally, we would expect to see an increase in the percentage of juveniles who were acquitted of the charges and released.

Adjudication Hearings After *Gault*

The Supreme Court decisions generally resulted in some shift away from the "loose" attitude in juvenile proceedings. Juvenile court officials now are more aware that their court has many elements of a criminal court; that juveniles are punished by the court, even if such punishment is in their best interests; and that juveniles deserve to have legal rights and protections to ensure that they are treated fairly. Nevertheless, the change is not nearly as broad and sweeping as the Supreme Court intended.

There are various reasons these changes were limited in application, starting with the fact that relatively few juvenile arrests ever result in adjudication hearings.

There Are Few Adjudication Hearings

Studies have found that fewer than 5 percent of all cases originally referred to juvenile courts result in an adjudication hearing.[5] One reason is that, although juveniles have a privilege against self-incrimination, the vast majority of them admit to the offense with which they are charged. Much more than adults, they are influenced by police and court officials, as well as parents who urge them to tell the truth.[6] One study found that, in the face of police questioning, fewer than 10 percent of juveniles asserted their right to remain silent, and that assertion of this right was virtually nonexistent among youth below the age of 15.[7]

To counterbalance this tendency, juveniles may be questioned only in the presence of an "interested" adult, preferably the parent. It is presumed that the adult will ensure that the juvenile's rights are protected. But the above study found that only 20 percent of parents agreed that their children had the right to withhold information from the police or courts. More often, these "interested" adults were interested in having the juvenile admit to the offense, as the parents themselves are looking for help in obtaining services for their children, or perhaps are angry with the child and want him or her institutionalized.

The juvenile court also has a history of heavy reliance on what is called informal processing. Basically, this is a resolution of the case that occurs without any formal hearing before a judge. It typically is offered to the youth at the intake hearing by the probation officer. The youth admits the offense and agrees to be supervised for a period of time on "informal probation." As a condition of this probation, the youth may be required to receive some kinds of "services" or "treatments." If the juvenile successfully completes all the conditions of the informal probation, the charge is dropped so that the youth has no formal record of delinquency.

When offered, this option is often attractive to the juvenile and his or her parents, as it avoids the controversy of a formal hearing, the expense of an attorney, and the consequences of a formal adjudication. However, if the juvenile fails to meet all the conditions, a petition is filed by the probation officer and the youth will go to a formal adjudication hearing before a judge. Since the juvenile has already confessed to the alleged incident (as a condition of receiving the informal probation), an adjudication of delinquency is, therefore, an unavoidable outcome.

Although informal processing varies greatly by jurisdiction, national estimates suggest that in the 1970s and 1980s, about 60 percent of all juvenile cases were handled through some type of informal procedure. Although there has been a trend toward more formal processing of juvenile defendants over the years, in the year 2002, the National Center for Juvenile Justice estimated that still almost 45 percent of all referred cases are handled informally.[8]

The privilege against self-incrimination was only one of five due process protections granted in the *Gault* and *Winship* decisions, but it is largely inoperative in practice. However, once the juvenile has admitted the offense, then there is no occasion to exercise the other four rights in the adjudication hearing: notice, counsel, confront and cross-examine witnesses, and proof beyond a reasonable doubt. Thus, the tendency toward informal processing of juveniles, combined with the frequency with which juveniles openly admit to the alleged offenses, restricts the application of the Supreme Court rulings to only that subset of cases that end in a formal adjudication hearing.

Adjudication Hearings Often Fail to Provide Due Process Protections

Since the time of the *Gault* decision, many studies have been conducted into the actual changes in formal adjudication hearings. A study immediately following the *Gault* decision found that judges rarely informed juveniles of their right to be represented by counsel and were hesitant to assign counsel even when requested.[9] Almost a decade later, things had not improved. A 1977 study found that juvenile court judges often declined to appoint attorneys for indigent juvenile offenders. These offenders make up the vast majority of all youths brought before the system. Furthermore, this study found that when attorneys were appointed, the judges would restrict their ability to make motions and otherwise "curb" their ability to present an adequate defense while in court.[10]

Studies into the 1980s continued to confirm these findings. These studies found that attorneys were present at less than half of eligible adjudication hearings.[11] They also found that rates of representation varied greatly by state, by local jurisdiction, and by type of offense. For example, one study found that in a state with a high rate of representation, such as California or Pennsylvania, over 80 percent of all juveniles received representation; while in a state with a low rate of representation, only around 40 percent of all juvenile defendants were represented by counsel.[12] Another study depicted drastic differences in representation rates *within* a state (Minnesota), with representation ranging from almost 100 percent of all cases in certain urban jurisdictions to less than 5 percent of cases in other, more rural jurisdictions.[13] The presence of defense counsel also differed by type of offense, with juveniles accused of more serious offenses being more likely to be represented by counsel than juveniles charged with status offenses and misdemeanors. Since the majority of juveniles are accused of these more minor types of offenses, this further feeds the problem.

This situation continued into the 1990s. The American Bar Association (ABA) reported in 1995 that defense attorneys were present at less than half of all formal adjudication hearings. Put simply, thirty years after the *Gault* decision, more youth were still facing adjudication hearings without counsel than with counsel.[14] Moreover, through a series of state-wide studies conducted from the late 1990s through the early twenty-first century, the ABA found that, when counsel was provided, it was inadequate owing to a multitude of difficulties, including large caseloads, inexperience, lack of training, and inadequate time to prepare a case. In addition, the ABA found that defense attorneys were frequently pressured by judges to settle quickly while juveniles were also encouraged to move forward without counsel. Juvenile defense attorneys were most often paid considerably less than their counterparts in adult criminal court, and they were paid the same flat rate whether the case went to hearing or settled via plea, thereby further encouraging the defense counsel to settle without a fight.[15]

Additional studies found that when defense counsel is present, counsel may have little impact on the adjudication or may even have a negative impact. That is, when an attorney was present, juveniles were both more likely to be adjudicated and more likely to receive a harsher disposition. These findings apparently hold true even when controlling for the seriousness of the current offense and the juvenile defendant's prior offending and court history.[16]

There may be a variety of reasons for the lack of representation, but one apparent reason is the frequency with which juveniles are persuaded to waive their right to counsel. In most states, juveniles have the right to waive counsel, and in six states (Arizona, California, Massachusetts, Minnesota, South Dakota, and Utah), juveniles actually have the right to self-representation. While most states have some type of regulation requiring the waiver of counsel to be "voluntary and intelligent," there is little specification of how this is to be determined.

Research by the American Bar Association found great disparity in the actual practice of juvenile waiver of counsel, as well as noting that judges often encourage waiver to speed up processing.[17] Other research suggests that parents who are unwilling to pay for representation may also encourage their children to waive the right to counsel.[18] Recent research on adolescent cognitive development suggests that youth understand very little regarding the justice process or the potential long-term consequences of their decisions.[19] This research further brings into question a juveniles ability to *ever* fully understand the potential consequences of waiving the right to be represented by counsel. In addition, research indicates that juveniles, much more so than adults, are easily swayed by outside influence.[20] This finding is of increased importance in light of the previous research discussed, which found judges *and* parents to encourage youth to waive their right to counsel.[21]

In general, then, these studies show that even for the subset of cases that make it to a formal adjudication hearing, representation is often not present; and when it is, counsel is likely to be ineffective in providing an adequate defense.

Adjudication Hearings Are Likely to Result in a Finding of Delinquency

With juveniles rarely informed of their rights, most often unrepresented by counsel, or represented by inadequate counsel, one might assume that outcomes have not changed much, either. That is, if the process has not changed as expected, then the final outcome—adjudicated vs. not adjudicated—should not have changed much as well.

For the decades of the 1970s and the early 1980s, such was the case. However, by the late 1980s and early 1990s, the percentage of cases handled formally, and subsequently the percentage of these cases resulting in a formal adjudication of delinquency actually *increased*.[22] This is the direct opposite of the anticipated outcome of the Supreme Court rulings. While a formal adjudication of delinquency was, and is, somewhat less onerous than an adult criminal conviction, with the further criminalizing of the juvenile court discussed in this and subsequent chapters, such a verdict holds considerable consequence for the bearer.

There are several reasons an adjudication hearing is likely to return a delinquent verdict. One reason relates directly back to the due process movement and the refusal of the Supreme Court to grant juveniles the right to a trial by jury. In adult courts, having a trial before a judge (as opposed to a jury) is sometimes described as a "slow plea of guilty."[23] This phrase suggests that, rather than go through a trial before a judge, the defendant should simply plead guilty and get it over with. Many defense attorneys, therefore, will not allow the defendant to plead "not guilty" unless they also request a jury trial.

But juveniles have no right to jury trials because of the *McKeiver* decision. Defense lawyers (realistically) may advise their juvenile clients to admit the offense even if the juveniles claim they did not commit the offense because the judge is going to find that they committed it anyway.

While the promise of defense counsel for juveniles remains largely unrealized, the role of the state prosecutor has greatly expanded. Prior to *Gault*, the job of a juvenile prosecutor had been fairly easy and routine. As stated by one Montana prosecutor, "it was tough to lose a case when everyone except the defendant sat on one side of the courtroom."[24] The prosecutor often worked close at hand with the judge and probation officer to determine a disposition that was in the best interests of the child. After the *Gault* decision, the presence (or potential presence) of defense counsel led prosecutors to place greater emphasis on representing the best interests of the state rather than those of the juvenile. As one prosecutor advises, "While prosecutors should consider the special interests and needs of a juvenile in their handling of a case, the prosecutor should never lose sight of their primary duty to seek justice and protect the public safety and welfare of the community."[25]

The scenario in a post-*Gault* court room is, then, thus: prosecutors have become more focused on representing the interests of the state rather than the juvenile, while the juvenile is likely to have either no representation at all or inadequate representation. The prosecutor now maintains a more punitive stance, and the juvenile is not entitled to a trial by jury, so the verdict is solely in the hands of the juvenile court judge.

Gone are the informal days when the "benevolent fatherly judge" listened solely to the recommendation of the probation officer who had conducted an investigation into the social history of the youth. Neither have we reached the days foreseen by the Supreme Court when a prosecutor and defense counsel would conduct a fair and unbiased hearing into the facts of the case. What appears to exist instead is a hearing that makes the juvenile court of the past, flawed as it was, appear to be the good old days.

Why Are There So Few Appeals?

With the majority of juveniles referred to juvenile court adjudicated delinquent (either through confession, plea, or formal hearing), it must be assumed that at least some of these juveniles did not commit the offense for which they are charged. That is, some juveniles are actually innocent and would logically attempt to appeal their verdict. Although the *Gault* decision itself did not find that a juvenile has a constitutional right to appeal, most states provide some mechanism for appeal anyway.[26] Yet, for various reasons, appeals from juvenile adjudications are virtually nonexistent.

First, juvenile defense lawyers typically have an extremely heavy workload that simply does not permit the luxury of appealing a case. For example, when Patrick Murphy took over the Juvenile Office of the Legal Aid Society of Chicago in 1970, the first thing he did was to cut the workload to one-third of its former level.[27] This was difficult to do personally because it meant turning away so many cases of children who really needed defense lawyers in court. It was also difficult to do professionally because other people in the juvenile court organization objected to his failure to represent juveniles in court. But Murphy wanted to focus on appeals, which are quite time-consuming, and to do that he had to reduce the number of court cases. Many juvenile defense lawyers are unwilling to take such a drastic step.

Second, there often is less at stake in a juvenile appeal than in an adult appeal. Juveniles frequently are placed on probation, or if they are sent to an institution, they usually get out within one to two years. Appeals can take years, and the juvenile often has been released long before the appeal is settled.

Third, there is organizational pressure against appealing a case because of the treatment orientation of the court. Other court officials more or less say: "Look, we are all acting in this kid's best interests, so why are you messing up the works?"

Fourth, juvenile justice officials can retaliate against the kids involved in the appeal. In many cases that Murphy appealed, the juveniles in the case were held in institutions for as long as the appeal was alive, whereas they would have been released much earlier if no appeal had been filed. Some were even repeatedly placed in solitary confinement, apparently because they were seen as "troublemakers." Defense lawyers who care about kids are often reluctant to expose them to this risk of retaliation.

Fifth, given the informality of juvenile court proceedings, much of what is at issue in an appeal is not on any written record and therefore cannot be considered in an appeal anyway.

Sixth, neither the right to appeal nor the right to a written transcript was provided by the *Gault* decision. Most states, however, provide a mechanism by which juveniles can appeal their cases, but they do not provide transcripts, which can be quite costly. A youth who has the funds to purchase a transcript and hire a lawyer for the appeal probably had the funds to hire a private lawyer in the first place and therefore does not need to appeal the case.

The Lessons of History

If due process rights influence adjudication hearings in actual practice, we would expect to find fewer "innocent" juveniles who are adjudicated and more "guilty" juvenile who are acquitted. Instead, we find that almost all juveniles in juvenile court are adjudicated delinquent or agree to informal sanctions. In addition, we find that there are very few adjudication hearings at all and that the adjudications that are held generally have little exercise of actual due process.

It seems that the due process protections granted to juveniles by the U. S. Supreme Court do not determine the actual practices of the juvenile court. We have tried to explain, at a kind of technical level, why these decisions have had little impact on day-to-day operations. Now we take a broader look at these findings in their historical perspective.

Lesson 1: The Cycle of Juvenile Justice. The widespread perception that juvenile crime rates are unusually high is accompanied by a widespread belief that these rates can be lowered by appropriate juvenile justice policies. This results in a continuous cycle of reform that consists of establishing lenient treatments in a major reform, gradually toughening up those treatments over a long time so that officials end up choosing between harsh punishments and doing nothing at all, and then reestablishing lenient treatments in another major reform.

As noted at the end of the last chapter, granting due process protections in the adjudication hearings did nothing to either toughen up responses to delinquency or provide youth with more lenient treatments. This reform, therefore, fell outside the expected cycle of juvenile justice. One could expect that it therefore would largely fail to be implemented. That appears to be what actually happened.

Lesson 2: Ideas of Juvenile Delinquency. Ideas of delinquency that "sell" (i.e., that succeed in the competition with other possible ideas) propose that delinquents are a subgroup within some larger problem group (e.g., paupers, dependent and neglected children, criminal defendants) with which the public is already familiar. The prevailing idea of delinquency and delinquents thus drives the idea of what juvenile justice should be.

As shown in this chapter, although the Supreme Court proposed that juveniles were indeed a subgroup of criminal defendants and, therefore, entitled to a subset of due process protections, the vision of the Supreme Court never achieved fruition. We propose this is because the provision of such rights would go against some other very important lessons of history, particularly (1) the protection of the economic interests of the rich and powerful and (2) the continued expansion of the power of the state. First, when pitting the interests of the state and the wealthy against the interest of the juvenile delinquent, the latter will necessarily come up short. Second, as we saw after the O'Connell decision limited the state's right to confine juveniles without due process, where there is a will, there is a way. At that time, the way was the invention of the juvenile court as a civil or chancery court. With the juvenile court and its processes already established, the way to circumvent this new rule was even easier: it was embedded in the notion of having a "fatherly" juvenile court judge to whom the juvenile could confess. Once a confession was obtained, the remainder of the due process rights were simply irrelevant.

Lesson 3: Ideas of Juvenile Justice. Responses to delinquency that "sell" (i.e., that succeed in the competition with other possible responses) are slightly modified versions of responses to the larger problem group of which delinquents are thought to be a subgroup (potential paupers, dependent and neglected children, criminal defendants, etc).

Because the idea of the juvenile delinquent as a defendant deserving of due process rights did not sell, the idea of juvenile justice did simply not need to shift to accommodate such due process protections. However, the Court had, perhaps, unwittingly opened up a new window for change in the juvenile court. That is, the redefinition of delinquents as "modified" criminal defendants ultimately undermined the second part of the Supreme Court's decision, which was to maintain the focus on care and treatment as "the best" of the original juvenile court. Indeed, this very redefinition of the juvenile delinquent as a "small criminal defendant" implies that juvenile justice practice should mirror the policies and practice of the adult criminal justice system—ideas that were much more in tune with the political agenda of the 1980s than were the notions of care and treatment.

Lesson 4: Economic Interests of the Rich and Powerful. Responses to delinquency that "sell" focus on the behavior of poor and powerless people but ignore the behavior of rich and powerful people. In particular, responses that focus on poor people's behavior do not harm the economic interests of the rich and powerful—that is, they aim to remove delinquents from the streets rather than change conditions on the streets.

Times do change, at least in some ways. Earlier chapters in this book described the founding of the first House of Refuge and of the first juvenile court. In those chapters, it seemed pretty clear that alternative policies were available that might have been much more effective and appropriate responses to the problems of delinquency. But those policies would have challenged the economic interests of wealthy and powerful people. Policymakers at the time chose to ignore these alternatives and to focus on reforms that left those interests undisturbed.

With the Supreme Court's reform, however, the situation is much less clear. Providing juveniles with due process rights takes money—it makes the juvenile court process more cumbersome and the outcome less certain. Since the vast majority of juvenile defendants are indigent, the money that is spent is usually taxpayer money. Since wealthy people pay the most taxes, one could say that this reform challenged the economic interests of the rich.

As noted at the end of chapter 6, the Supreme Court did not provide the most expensive right to juvenile defendants: the right to a jury trial. Beyond that, in practice the states were very "thrifty" in providing those rights that the Supreme Court did grant to juveniles. Juvenile court judges often encouraged defendants to go without a lawyer. When the defendants requested a lawyer, judges often were hesitant to provide one. When lawyers were provided, they often were poorly trained, poorly paid, and severely overworked, all of which combined to ensure ineffective representation. It would seem, to a considerable extent, that all of these actions reflected concern about the economic interests of the rich and powerful.

Lesson 5: Moral and Intellectual Superiority of Reformers. Responses to delinquency that "sell" imply that delinquents and their parents are morally and intellectually inferior, and that the reformers themselves are morally and intellectually superior.

In general, the Supreme Court's idea that juvenile delinquents were young citizens with rights did not support the sense that the reformers were indeed morally and intellectually superior. Instead, these ideas treated juvenile delinquents as if they were, at least in a political sense, equal to the rest of us. In the end, this idea simply didn't sell. To some extent, the reluctance of judges to provide due process protections to juveniles reflected a rejection of this very idea. These juveniles were not citizens with rights, but instead were young criminals. This alternative view, associated with the "get tough" movement, was much more consistent with a view that the reformers themselves are morally and intellectually superior to the juvenile delinquents.

Lesson 6: The Unfair Comparison. Reformers "sell" their own reforms by an unfair comparison, in which a harsh assessment of actual practices of past policies is compared with an optimistic assessment of reforms, based on good intentions. Because they assume that good intentions directly translate into good practices, reformers promise to solve the problem of juvenile delinquency.

The Supreme Court did provide another example of the unfair comparison in history: they compared an optimistic view of their own good intentions with a harsh appraisal of the actual practices of existing policies. After proclaiming that the juvenile court did, indeed, provide punishment as the basis for the essential provision of due process rights to young offenders, it maintained that the court could provide the "best of both worlds"—due process along with care and treatment. Yet the Supreme Court provided no new mechanism for securing such care and treatment; it simply relied on its optimistic hope that it would happen. Beyond that, the Court did not promise to "solve" the problem of delinquency. It merely asserted that its system would be a better system. Overall, then, the Supreme Court's policy did not really embody the unfair comparison as a technique to "sell" its reform.

Lesson 7: The Power of the State. Reforms that "sell" increase the power of the state, based on optimistic assessments of how effective the reform will be in solving the problem. The power of the state usually continues to expand regardless of the specific content or nature of the reform.

By providing due process protections to juveniles, the Supreme Court's intention was to restrict the power of the state in juvenile court. This simply did not sell. The state found in the decision a loophole by which to expand its power. If the juvenile defendant now has the right to an attorney, then the state will expand the role of its prosecutor, and not to protect the best interests of the child, as was the previous intention of juvenile court officials. Instead, the prosecutor would protect society from this young criminal. The lack of a jury trial and the unavailability of appeals for juveniles further cleared the path for the state to trample the proposed rights of juveniles. In the future, the state would intervene in the lives of these youth in ways the Supreme Court could not have imagined.

As suggested at the end of chapter 6, much of the Supreme Court's attempted reform did not have social or political "appeal." Similar to the good intentions of the juvenile court that were often not found in practice, the good intentions of the Supreme Court did not achieve the desired changes in the juvenile court. Juvenile defendants were not being provided satisfactory due process protections, leading most juveniles petitioned to court to be found delinquent. In sum, the definition of the child as a young citizen in need of protection from the power of the state, for all essential purposes, *did not sell*.

What then did sell? The only portion of the reform that fits well with the lessons of history, and therefore had the potential to sell to the public, was the notion of the juvenile delinquent as a subgroup of adult criminals. Paradoxically, this notion is in direct opposition to the second part of the Supreme Court's attempted reform, which was to allow the juvenile court to maintain its original purpose of providing care and treatment to juvenile offenders. If the juvenile offender is merely a young criminal, then the more punitive responses of the adult criminal justice system form the appropriate response to delinquency. This argument was at the crux of the "get tough" movement of the 1980s and 1990s, to which we now turn our attention.

NOTES

1. Frederic L. Faust and Paul J. Brantingham, *Juvenile Justice Philosophy* (St. Paul, Minn.: West, 1979), 383.
2. See Alexander Volok, *"n Guilty Men," University of Pennsylvania Law Review* 146 (1997): 173.
3. In that sense, Fortas's description was actually one side of an unfair comparison—i.e., it was an excessively pessimistic view of actual practices in the past. Fortas then went on to give the other side of that comparison—an excessively optimistic view of what would happen in the future, based on his own good intentions.
4. Barry Feld, *Bad Kids: Race and the Transformation of the Juvenile Court* (New York: Oxford University Press, 1999), 124.
5. H. Ted Rubin, "The Juvenile Court Landscape," in Albert R. Roberts, *Juvenile Justice* (Chicago: Dorsey, 1989), 129; M. A. Bortner, *Inside a Juvenile Court: The Tarnished Ideal of Individualized Justice* (New York: New York University Press, 1982).
6. James T. Carey and Patrick D. McAnany, *Introduction to Juvenile Delinquency* (Englewood Cliffs, N.J.: Prentice-Hall, 1984), 267–268.
7. Thomas Grisso, *Juveniles' Waiver of Rights* (New York: Plenum, 1981).
8. Howard Snyder and Melissa Sickmund, *Juvenile Offenders and Victims: A National Report 2006* (Washington, D.C.: Office of Juvenile Justice and Delinquency Prevention, U.S. Department of Justice, 2006).
9. Norman Lefstein, Vaughan Stapleton, and Lee Teitelbaum, "In Search of Juvenile Justice: Gault and its Implementation," *Law and Society Review* 3 (1969): 491–562.
10. Steven Scholossman, *Love and the American Delinquent: The Theory and Practice of "Progressive" Juvenile Justice* (Chicago: University of Chicago Press, 1977).
11. Steven H. Clarke and Gary G. Koch, "Juvenile court: Therapy or Crime Control, and Do Lawyers Make a Difference?" *Law and Society Review* 14 (1980): 263–308; James D. Walter and Susan A. Ostrander, "An Observational Study of Juvenile Court," *Juvenile and Family Court* 33 (1982): 53–69.
12. Feld, *Bad Kids*.
13. Ibid.

14. P. Puritz, S. Burrell, R. Schwartz, M. Soler, and L. Warboys, *A Call for Justice: An Assessment of Access to Counsel and Quality of Representation in Delinquency Proceedings* (Washington, D.C.: American Bar Association, Criminal Justice Section, Juvenile Justice Center, 1995).

15. C. E. Stewart, G. Celeste, E. Marrus, I. Picou, P. Puritz, and D. Utter, *Selling Justice Short: Juvenile Indigent Defense in Texas* (Washington, D.C.: American Bar Association, Criminal Justice Section, Juvenile Justice Center, 2000). See also P. Puritz and T. Sun, *Georgia: An Assessment of Access to Counsel and Quality of Representation in Delinquency Proceedings* (Washington, D.C.: American Bar Association, Criminal Justice Section, Juvenile Justice Center, 2001); P. Puritz and K. Brooks, *Kentucky Advancing Justice: An Assessment of Access to Counsel and Quality of Representation in Delinquency Proceedings* (Washington, D.C.: American Bar Association, Criminal Justice Section, Juvenile Justice Center, 2002); P. Puritz, M. A. Scali, and I. Picou, *Virginia: An Assessment of Access to Counsel and Quality of Representation in Delinquency Proceedings* (Washington, D.C.: American Bar Association, Criminal Justice Section, Juvenile Justice Center, 2002); K. Brooks and D. Kamine, *Justice Cut Short: An Assessment of Access to Counsel and Quality of Representation in Delinquency Proceedings in Ohio* (Washington, D.C.: American Bar Association, Criminal Justice Section, Juvenile Justice Center, 2003); American Bar Association, Juvenile Justice Center and New England Juvenile Defender Center, *Maine: An Assessment of Access to Counsel and Quality of Representation in Delinquency Proceedings* (Washington, D.C.: American Bar Association, Criminal Justice Section, Juvenile Justice Center, 2003); E. Cumming, M. Finley, S. Hall, A. Humphrey, and I. P. Picou, *Maryland: An Assessment of Access to Counsel and Quality of Representation in Delinquency Proceedings* (Washington, D.C.: American Bar Association, Criminal Justice Section, Juvenile Justice Center, 2003); B. Albin, M. Albin, E. Gladden, S. Ropelato, and G. Stoll, *Montana: An Assessment of Access to Counsel and Quality of Representation in Delinquency Proceedings* (Washington, D.C.: American Bar Association, Criminal Justice Section, Juvenile Justice Center, 2003); L. Grindell, *North Carolina: An Assessment of Access to Counsel and Quality of Representation in Delinquency Proceedings* (Washington, D.C.: American Bar Association, Criminal Justice Section, Juvenile Justice Center); S. Miller-Wilson, *Pennsylvania: An Assessment of Access to Counsel and Quality of Representation in Delinquency Proceedings* (Washington, D.C.: American Bar Association, Criminal Justice Section, Juvenile Justice Center, 2003); E. M. Calvin, *Washington: An Assessment of Access to Counsel and Quality of Representation in Delinquency Proceedings* (Washington, D.C.: American Bar Association, Criminal Justice Section, Juvenile Justice Center, 2003).

16. Bortner, *Inside a Juvenile Court;* David Duffee, Steven H. Clark, and Gary G. Koch, "1980 Juvenile Court: Therapy or Crime Control, and Do Lawyers Make a Difference?" *Law and Society Review* 14: 263–308; David Duffee and Larry Seigel, "The Organizational Man: Legal Counsel in the Juvenile Court," *Criminal Law Bulletin* 7: 544–553.

17. Puritz et al., *A Call for Justice.*

18. Joseph B. Sanborn Jr. and Anthony W. Salerno, *The Juvenile Justice System Law and Process* (Roxbury, 2005), 321.

19. Thomas Grisso, "What We Know about Youth' Capacities as Trial Defendants," in Thomas Grisso and Robert G. Schwartz, eds., *Youth on Trial* (Chicago: University of Chicago Press, 2000).

20. See Elizabeth S. Scott, "Criminal Responsibility in Adolescence: Lessons from Developmental Psychology," in Grisso and Schwartz, eds., *Youth on Trial*, 291–324; see also "Research Adolescent's Judgment and Culpability," in Grisso and Schwartz, eds., *Youth on Trial*, 325–344.

21. In the case of *Boykin v. Alabama*, the Supreme Court set up a colloquy to ensure that, for adults, the waiver of counsel is indeed voluntary and intelligent. In the colloquy such basic facts are to be determined, such as ensuring that the defendant comprehends the effects of a guilty plea and the resulting conviction and determining that the plea is offered free of outside pressures that may have prompted the plea or overwhelmed the defendant's freedom of choice. We suggest that the above research on juvenile cognition, susceptibility to outside influence, and the nature of juvenile proceedings bring into sincere question that ability of a juvenile to ever meet the requirements of a true *voluntary and intelligent* waiver of counsel.

22. This increase can be documented by comparing juvenile court statistics complied by the National Center for Juvenile Justice and reported semi-annually in Juvenile Court Statistics or in the summary report, Snyder and Sickmund, *Juvenile Offenders and Victims.*

23. Charles Silberman, *Criminal Violence, Criminal Justice* (New York: Random House, 1978), 279–280.

24. Harold F. Hanser, *The Role of the Prosecutor in Juvenile Justice*, manuscript submitted to the Montana Board of Crime Control, 1977, reprinted in H. Ted Rubin, *Juvenile Justice Policy Practice and Law*, 2nd ed. (New York: Random House, 1985), 260.

25. James C. Backstrom, *The Expanding Role of the Prosecutor in Juvenile Justice*, http://www.co.dakota.mn.us/NR/rdonlyres/00000987/qmxaroespdbzrghotrwyasnzjhzkfbou/ExpandingRoleProsecutorJuvenileJustice.pdf, accessed April 2009.

26. Carry and McAnany, *Introduction of Juvenile Delinquency*, 269; see also W. Vaughan Stapleton and Lee E. Teitlebaum, *In Defense of Youth* (New York: Russell Sage, 1972), chap. 5.

27. Patrick Murphy, *Our Kindly Parent, The State* (New York: Viking, 1974).

8

Disposition Hearings Today

The "Get Tough" Movement

From the House of Refuge in the 1820s to the Supreme Court's due process reform in the 1960s, the juvenile justice system has always claimed to provide care and treatment, rather than punishment, to the juveniles who came under its jurisdiction. Yet the reality always has been quite different. Care and treatment were often more the exception than the rule. Even in institutions designed to provide rehabilitation and treatment, conditions of overcrowding, high staff turnover, and limited financial resources have hindered the ability of the system to delivery on this promise. The Illinois Supreme Court acknowledged this reality in the 1870 *O'Connell* case, and nearly one hundred years later the U.S. Supreme Court acknowledged the same thing in the *Kent* and *Gault* cases. Put most simply, there was a great divide between good intentions and actual practice with respect to the care and treatment of juveniles.

In the Supreme Court decisions of the due process movement, however, the provision of care and treatment was not merely an ideal toward which to strive. Rather, it was central to the constitutionality of the juvenile court. The U.S. Constitution requires that all citizens receive the "equal protection of the law." But juveniles receive less protection than adults—for example, juveniles do not have the right to a jury trial. Beginning with the *Kent* decision, the Supreme Court held that this was not unconstitutional because juveniles received a "compensating benefit" in return for this loss of rights: instead of being punished, the state acted in the juvenile's best interests by providing care and treatment.

Thus, the provision of care and treatment was essential to the Supreme Court's finding that the juvenile court itself was constitutional. It was also at the crux of the Court's new conception of the juvenile court as providing juveniles with the "best of both worlds": due process protections in the adjudication hearing, along with care and treatment in the disposition hearing.

Despite the centrality of care and treatment to its constitutional argument, the Supreme Court never ruled that juveniles have a constitutional right to treatment. Nor did the Supreme Court ever suggest a mechanism that would ensure that juveniles actually receive care and treatment rather than punishment. Instead, the Court rested its findings on the ideal system. The potential consequences of this omission should be quite apparent, coming closely on the heels of the Court's finding that the reality of juvenile court had always drastically diverged from the ideal.

In this chapter, we argue that the Supreme Court's new vision was never actually implemented. For example, if the Supreme Court's reform were actually implemented, then we would expect to find a decrease in the rate of adjudications (as the new due process rights enabled juveniles to fight the allegations against them) and an increase in the care and treatment given to the juveniles who were adjudicated (instead of the punishment that the Supreme Court said juveniles had been receiving all along). In fact, neither of these things happened. Instead, we find that the Supreme Court's ideas of juvenile delinquency and juvenile justice were replaced by very different ideas: those of the "get tough" movement.

The "Get Tough" Idea of the Juvenile Delinquent: Small Criminals

To understand the actual changes to the juvenile court disposition that came after the Supreme Court decisions, we must first understand how these decisions were interpreted and how they fit into the historical context. History shows that, at any given time, people hold a predominant belief about what juvenile delinquency is and what kinds of youths commit these acts. These beliefs are important because they shape our notion of what juvenile justice should be.

The founders of the original juvenile court had defined juvenile delinquency as wayward behavior by misguided youths. They, therefore, defined juvenile delinquents as needy and dependent children who were not receiving proper care and protection from adults. This belief then led directly to their conception of juvenile justice: the state should step in as the parent upon whom they can depend for care and treatment. Thus,

this particular belief about juvenile delinquency and the juvenile delinquent is the premise behind the *parens patriae* doctrine and at the heart
of the provision of lenient treatment for juveniles.

The Supreme Court had now proposed a very different idea: juvenile
delinquents were citizens to be presumed innocent until proven guilty,
and they were entitled to the rights and protections provided in the U.S.
Constitution. Implicit in this definition was the notion that the rights
entitled to youths in juvenile courts were similar to those granted to
criminal defendants in criminal courts. In that sense, the Supreme Court
defined juvenile delinquents as a slightly modified version of a group
with which we are all quite familiar: criminal defendants.

While not directly supposed, it was only a short deductive step from
the idea that juvenile defendants are "small" criminal defendants to the
idea that juvenile delinquents are "small" criminals. This was the step
taken by the "get tough" movement.

If juvenile delinquents merely are small criminals, then juvenile delinquency is made up of criminal acts. On the surface, this seems like an
obvious statement, but think back to the beginnings of the juvenile court,
when officials were concerned with juveniles' begging on street corners.
Juvenile delinquents were defined as "potential paupers." This proposed
new juvenile criminal is not merely at risk of growing up to be a pauper
and a financial drain on society but he or she is also an immediate risk to
the average law-abiding citizen. These juveniles rob, rape, and murder.

So despite their good intentions, the Supreme Court's due process
reforms laid the foundation for the "get tough" movement in juvenile
justice. Whereas the Supreme Court's idea fell outside the expected cycle
of juvenile justice, the notion that delinquents are small criminals fits
well within the lessons from history. It upholds the moral superiority of
the reformers—after all, criminals are low-life scum and those who
fight crime are heroes. It protects the economic interests of the rich and
powerful—it attempts to change or confine the "criminal" and does not
expect any changes in the behavior of those with power. It increases the
power of the state to intervene in the lives of these children, but it lifts
the requirement to provide them care and rehabilitation. It suggests
"new" and "better" juvenile justice policies that promise to "solve" the
problem of juvenile delinquency. But in fact, those policies aren't so new
and different after all–rather, they are a modified version of policies with
which we all are quite familiar and comfortable: the policies of the adult
criminal justice system.

This new conception of the juvenile delinquent "sold" in part because
it arrived on the scene at the same time as a major increase in the arrests
of juveniles for violent crimes. From 1988 to 1994, juvenile arrests for

violent crimes in general increased 61 percent.[1] Even more disturbing, homicides committed by youths under the age of 18 began to increase in the late 1980s, and by 1994, they had increased 110 percent from the level just a decade before.[2] These alarming figures were used to justify the wholesale transformation of juvenile justice across the nation.

Most examiners of these statistics came to the conclusion that it was not, after all, a national wave of violent juvenile crime. Rather, the increases occurred entirely within very limited geographic areas of the country—inner-city neighborhoods. Some studies attributed this to the crack cocaine epidemic of the late 1980s. Crack and powdered cocaine are identical in many ways, but crack is in a form (rocks) that can be sold in much smaller quantities and is often mixed with other substances to reduce its purity. Thus, crack cocaine was popular in poor neighborhoods because it was more affordable for those who did not have much money. In these neighborhoods, drug dealers often recruited juveniles to sell crack because juvenile labor is cheap and because individual sales of such small quantities did not produce much profit. Juveniles in these neighborhoods, therefore, started carrying both drugs and cash on their person, and they started carrying guns as protection. This led to large increases in the use of guns in conflicts over the drug markets, and these conflicts subsequently resulted in a greater use of guns in the normal fights and conflicts in which juveniles are typically involved.[3]

At the same time this was happening in the inner cities, all other juvenile crime, including violent crime by juveniles in non-inner-city areas and non-gun violent crime by juveniles, was declining. Nevertheless, these increases in violent juvenile crime were used to justify a nationwide transformation of the juvenile justice system. The reasons for this were fairly straightforward. When a firearm is involved in a crime, the potential for physical harm and the extent of that harm are much higher.

The commission of such violent acts by youngsters betrayed the notion of a juvenile delinquent as merely a needy child. Certainly, anyone who could yield and fire a weapon possessed a greater resemblance to a criminal than to a wayward youth. And although the events were restrained to a very limited geographical area, they made national headlines that resulted in an unprecedented campaign of fear. While earlier reports of delinquency were confined to the written press, the widespread popularity of television and the visual news media brought these violent youth and their crimes right into people's living rooms. From the Midwest farmer to the suburban housewife, we were all suddenly in danger of a stray bullet or drive-by shooting by these vicious youngsters, who committed senseless violence without remorse.

Building on a media campaign of fear, politicians across the nation competed to "get tough" on juvenile crime. Just as the lines between delinquency and crime and between the delinquent and the criminal were becoming blurred, so would the distinction between the juvenile civil court and the adult criminal court.

The "Get Tough" Idea of Juvenile Justice: Modified Criminal Court

The series of changes that occurred during the 1980s and 1990s has since been deemed the "get tough" movement. This movement led to the most substantive changes to the juvenile justice system since its inception. Unlike the due process movement, which consisted of a small number of court cases that had national impact, thereby unifying practices across states, the "get tough" changes occurred primarily in the states, where each state legislature passed its own version of "get tough" policies.

For the ease of discussion we group these changes into four general categories, as follows: (1) changes to the purpose of the juvenile justice system, (2) changes to the process of the juvenile courts; (3) changes to the dispositional outcomes of the juvenile system, and (4) changes to the jurisdiction of the juvenile courts. We discuss the first three of these categories below, as they directly impacted the day-to-day functioning and dispositional outcomes of juvenile courts across the nation. The fourth, jurisdictional authority, will be discussed in the following chapter, as it involves the processing of juveniles in an entirely separate system of justice—the adult criminal court. Throughout both of these chapters, our focus remains on trends across states, as it has been duly noted that America does not have *a* juvenile justice system but, rather, fifty-one juvenile justice "systems" (the fifty states plus the District of Columbia), with a full comparison of differences across states being well beyond the scope and focus of the current endeavor.[4]

The Purpose of Juvenile Justice

Since the inception of the first juvenile court in Cook County, Illinois, in 1899, the court was premised on a civil court model and the *parens patriae* philosophy. While each state passed its unique version of a juvenile court act, the Standard Juvenile Court Act, proposed by the National Council of Juvenile Court Judges, the National Probation and Parole Association, and the U.S Children's Bureau in 1959, encompasses the basic sentiment of juvenile courts at the time. According to this act, the juvenile court was to ensure that:

> Each child coming within the jurisdiction of the court shall receive. . the care, guidance and control that will conduce to his welfare and the best interests of the state, and that when he is removed from the control of his parents the court shall secure for him care as nearly as possible equivalent to that which they should have given him.[5]

In addition, in defining the jurisdiction of the juvenile court, the act, as well as later standards promoted by the American Bar Association (1980), recommended that the court have jurisdiction over "such conduct as would be designated a crime if committed by an adult."[6]

If the act would be designated a crime if committed by an adult, then the suggestion here is that it isn't the crime but, rather, the behavior that is *different from* that of an adult criminal. The juvenile delinquent is *not* an adult criminal; he or she is only a *potential criminal* who, with proper care and treatment, can be diverted from such a dismal fate. However, with juvenile delinquency perceived to be at an all-time high, and more serious than ever, such lenient treatment and care provided by a "kiddie court" was not an acceptable policy response. Juveniles were no longer committing acts that *would be crimes* if they were adults—they were committing *crimes*, and the juveniles should be punished.

If the juvenile court, however, were simply to adopt adult punishments, then there would be no need for a separate system of justice, and the juvenile court would cease to exist. If the juvenile court were to survive as a separate entity, then a middle ground must be found. The first steps toward finding this middle ground had already been forged in the expanded role of the prosecutor in the adjudication hearing.

Remember, the prosecutor was present to represent the best interests of the state and the victim, and to promote public protection. These interests were in direct competition with the focus of the original juvenile court and with the "theoretical" defense counsel, which was to promote the best interests of the child. Not willing to fully convert to an adult criminal court model, in which the individual juvenile's treatment needs were dismissed in lieu of pure punishment, yet unable to maintain a model based solely on the best interests of the juvenile, court officials sought a model that would blend the interests into a new mission for the juvenile court.

Juvenile court officials found just such a model in a relatively simple juvenile probation practice that was being promoted in Deschutes

County, Oregon. This model proposed a "balanced approach" to juvenile probation that weighed the need to hold juveniles accountable for their actions against the need to help juveniles develop into competent adults, while protecting the public from dangerous offenders.[7] These forces would not compete with each other as the primary focus of juvenile court but, rather, would unite and balance each other to provide a more complete and effective juvenile justice strategy.

Reviews of legislation regulating juvenile courts across the states estimate that from seventeen to twenty-five states have specifically redefined their purpose clause to incorporate these principles. The following example from Pennsylvania's revised juvenile justice act (Act 33 of the 1995 Special Legislative Session on Crime) provides an example of this revised "purpose of justice":

> Consistent with the protection of the public interest, to provide for children committing delinquent acts programs of supervision, care and rehabilitation which provide balanced attention to the protection of the community, the imposition of accountability for offenses committed and the development of competencies to enable children to become responsible and productive members of the community.[8]

This language articulates the role of the state as no longer to merely provide for the best interests of the child but also that the juvenile court is to provide justice for the victim, the community, and the state. The state is no longer simply to remove consequences from a juvenile but must also hold him or her accountable for the crime. It should be noted, however, that in the original language of the balanced-approach philosophy, to be held accountable is not equivalent to being punished.[9] Rather, it is assumed that many young juveniles simply do not understand the consequences of their actions and that by holding them accountable to the victim or community harmed, they will realize the error of their ways. In this regard, holding a juvenile accountable is still similar to the actions of the "kindly parent" who, for example, might make his or her child pay for a window that the child has broken or return a stolen item to a store and apologize to the clerk. On the surface, at least, accountability is a middle ground, in that it provides some level of justice for the victim and community without promoting a pure punishment philosophy.

However, other states have gone even further toward "criminalizing" the juvenile court by redefining the sole purpose of the juvenile court as handing out punishment for offenses. This "get tough" language, while not as popular as the balanced and restorative justice language noted above, can be found in the purpose clause of at least six states. For example, in

Texas, the primary purpose of the juvenile justice system is "to protect the public and public safety." The act then goes on to note that "consistent with the protection of the public and public safety," the court is "to promote the concept of punishment for criminal acts."[10]

In a slightly softer approach, the Wyoming statute first states that the purpose of the juvenile court is to provide for the best interests of the child and the protection of the public, while still promoting "the concept of punishment for criminal acts." Still more confusing, the court is also directed to somehow distinguish "the behavior of children who have been victimized or have disabilities such as serious mental illness that requires treatment."[11] For this particular subset of children, the court is then to provide protection and care instead of punishment.

According to the National Center for Juvenile Justice, as of 2006, only *one state* currently maintains language that fully preserves the original juvenile court's focus on child welfare.[12] The Massachusetts Juvenile Court Act *alone* maintains that accused juvenile delinquents should be treated "not as criminals, but as children in need" and that proceedings in juvenile court "shall not be deemed criminal proceedings."[13]

Changes to the Process of Juvenile Justice

In addition to redefining the purpose of justice, the "get tough" movement involved the passage of legislation that altered the process of juvenile justice leading up to a disposition hearing, as well. The experience for a youth brought into the system, from start to finish, would now be more formal and adversarial; in short, it would in many ways begin to resemble the adult criminal justice system more than a social welfare agency.

Initial Processing

The juvenile court had traditionally referred to a youth as "being taken into custody," not as arrested. When a youth was taken into custody, it was not customary to photograph and fingerprint the juvenile, as an officer would do with an adult criminal. The juvenile's name would not appear in the paper or on television. And while pre-adjudicatory detention was an option, it was more the exception than the rule. Additionally, most often, the juvenile would be released to his or her parents and undergo an intake evaluation by a probation officer. These procedures were designed to be in the best interests of the child, protecting him or her from suffering stigmatization.

Legislation passed during the "get tough" era not only allowed for the fingerprinting and photographing of youth but also, in some states, actually required the fingerprinting of all arrested youths, or at least for youths arrested for certain types or levels of offenses. Some jurisdictions also required that the police department release the juvenile's information to the press, as it would for an adult criminal. In fact, at the time of the writing of this book, all states except Vermont and Alabama specifically *require* the release of a juvenile's name under certain circumstances, although these circumstances vary from state to state, based on the age of the alleged offender, the nature of the offense, and whether or not the case is eligible for transfer to adult court.[14]

As we have seen before, it is also common for laws to be developed that apply only to juveniles. Here, one such law has evolved, with forty-five states adopting legislation that required law enforcement or the juvenile court to notify a student's school if the student is charged with a delinquent act.[15]

Other changes that impact this process include the forwarding of a juvenile offender's information to the state repository, which makes the juvenile's arrest record more accessible for criminal background checks. In addition, juvenile court records are now often officially released, and most states have made it more difficult to have a juvenile record expunged.[16] Juveniles convicted of sex offenses must register on state sex offender registries. Adult courts have expanded the use juvenile records as a measure of any prior record, so as to enhance adult court sentencing; and in at least one state, California, a juvenile felony counts as a "first strike" in the newly passed "three strikes and you're out" legislation.

Although these changes do not necessarily impact the outcome of the juvenile court case (adjudicated or not, and type of disposition), they do have significant symbolic and real consequences for the juveniles involved. A youth is no longer viewed or treated as a needy child. The fingerprinting and mug-shot processes in and of themselves send a message to the juvenile that he or she is a criminal. Police and court officials have all but done away with the language of merely "taking a juvenile into custody." In fact, juvenile justice reports and textbooks routinely talk about juvenile arrests, forgoing the original civil court language of the juvenile system.

With fingerprints and photographs on file, offender names and court records released, and juvenile sex offenders' names and faces plastered on state sex offender registries, the confidentiality of the juvenile proceeding has also been changed. The young offender is now more open to public scrutiny; and depending on individual state law, his or her juvenile arrest record can impact future education and employment opportunities in much the same way as arrest records affect adults' lives. For juveniles charged with eligible sex offenses, the consequences are even more far-reaching, impacting their ability to attend school, or even live within a given radius of a school. In short, the stakes associated with a juvenile "arrest" have been raised.

Confidentiality of Proceedings

Another factor that had distinguished a juvenile court proceeding from an adult court proceeding was that the juvenile court was closed to the media and general public. According to the Standard Juvenile Court Act of 1959, the purpose of confidentiality was to contribute to the casework relationship of the proceeding. However, the Supreme Court has never ruled that such confidentiality was an essential part of the juvenile justice process. With the public panicked about juvenile delinquency at the time, and the increased criticism of the courts, many saw opening up the juvenile court to the public and/or media as a self-defense mechanism. That is, making the proceedings public would show people that the court was not a "kiddie court" and that it handled cases seriously, meting out serious consequences for young law violators.

Again, the changes happened at the state level, so there is no national consensus on the opening of the juvenile court room; but almost half of all states now allow the public or media into the court room under certain circumstances. The "open" courtroom is sometimes restricted to youth over a certain age or to those who have committed certain types of felonies or violent offenses; however, some states allow the public to attend any and all proceedings.[17]

The Expanding Role of the Prosecutor

While defense attorneys still struggle to gain an active presence in juvenile proceedings, it was noted in the previous chapter that states responded to *Gault* by expanding the role of the prosecutor in juvenile court. In addition to their role in the court room, the prosecutors in many states have assumed greater authority in the charging, intake, and detention decisions.

For example, in many jurisdictions, while charging and diversion decisions were historically handled by juvenile court intake workers (usually probation officers), the prosecutor now has increased input and responsibility for these decisions. In fact, in South Dakota, Washington, and Wyoming, prosecutors are responsible for *all* decisions at the intake stage. In addition, many more states have passed legislation requiring prosecutors to concur or have input into intake decisions regarding certain types of offenses or certain types of juveniles, based primarily on prior record.[18]

Examined from a different angle, what this expansion of authority means in reverse is that the decision to offer an informal diversion, rather than a formal petition to court, is removed from the intake workers and placed solely in the hands of the prosecutor. The prosecutor, not the probation worker, decides who is processed formally or informally. This change might well help to explain the previously noted trend toward more formal processing in juvenile court.

The prosecutors are also enjoying greater say and flexibility in determining which juveniles are placed in pre-adjudicatory detention.[19] This particular decision stage is deemed one of the most crucial, owing to its far-reaching consequences. First, unlike adult offenders who enjoy a right to bail, juvenile defendants historically have been given no such right; currently only twenty-one states have any provision for juveniles to be able to post bail or to be released to parents under bond.[20] Second, although the detention decision is reviewed by a juvenile court judge at a detention hearing, a juvenile does not have a constitutional right to defense counsel at this stage. Even in states that allow for defense counsel at the detention hearing, representation is seldom present.[21] As might be assumed, then, the juvenile court judge rarely reverses the detention decision; to do so would be to question the decision-making capabilities of a fellow justice official. Moreover, the difficult decision to separate a juvenile from his or her home has already been made.

Finally, studies have found that juveniles held in pre-adjudicatory detention are more likely to receive a disposition of residential placement, and to be confined in such placement for a longer period of time, than juveniles released to their parents to await processing.[22] There are several proposed reasons that detention holding may influence the disposition stage. For instance, it may be that by detaining the juvenile, the prosecutor is sending an unwritten message to the judge that this particular youth is a greater threat to society than others. Certainly, the youth's appearance at court does not help the situation. For example, while the youth who returns home to await trial usually arrives at court with his or her parent or guardian, and is dressed in his or her Sunday best, the juvenile in detention arrives in a nicely tailored state-issued jumpsuit, often in handcuffs and with feet shackled together. Thus, one youth looks like a child while the other looks like a criminal. Moreover, for the youth in detention, the difficult decision to remove the child from the home environment has already been made; therefore, ordering the youth to residential placement is simply maintaining the status quo.

Victim Inclusion

The new, balanced purpose of juvenile justice proposed in many states required the juvenile to be held accountable—but accountable to whom? While the adult criminal justice system holds the offender accountable to the state, the juvenile system adopted a more restorative justice philosophy, proposing to hold the juvenile accountable directly to the victim or community harmed.

As previously noted, in rhetoric this philosophy assumes that the juvenile did not truly understand the full consequences of his or her actions, and that by making the juvenile pay amends to the victim or community harmed, he or she will gain a better understanding of the hurt created by that crime. Practices such as victim offender medication, arbitration, and community restitution boards exemplify this type of thinking, and they have been promoted as some of the current best practices in juvenile justice.[23]

However, other interpretations of accountability have emerged as well. Victim advocacy groups have promoted the passage of a specific "Victim's Bill of Rights" to be applicable in juvenile courts; this legislation would extend to the crime victim privileges such as the right to be present at all hearings, the right to give a written or oral victim impact statement, and the right to be informed of a juvenile's home visits or release back into the community. Of these rights, it is perhaps the victim impact statement that has the greatest potential to advance the adversarial nature of the dispositional stages of processing. Remember, in the *Gault* decision, the right to an attorney was granted at the adjudication hearing, as this stage was primarily driven by fact finding. However, a bifurcated proceeding was established in which the disposition hearing would be held at a later stage, so as to ensure that the focus at this stage was on care and treatment—the "best of both worlds" argument of due process protections at adjudication, and care and treatment at disposition.

While we have not been able to identify any studies that directly assess the role of the victim at the dispositional hearing, it seems obvious that having a victim impact statement read or presented at this stage may, indeed, refocus attention on the facts and consequences of the crime rather than on the child's needs. While many victims of juvenile crime are sympathetic to the fact that their perpetrator is young and may not be fully culpable or blameworthy for his or her actions, certainly not all victims feel this condition warrants mitigation of consequences, and they will ask the court for confinement of a juvenile to satisfy their needs for justice or to promote their sense of personal safety.

This effect may be magnified by the lack of defense counsel to promote the juvenile's best interests. An attorney was not a constitutional guarantee at the disposition hearing, as the focus at this stage was to remain on the child and not on the facts of the crime. If the facts presented in the previous chapter regarding the lack of counsel at the adjudication stage remain true, then we can only assume that a similar, if not greater, lack of representation will exist at the disposition stage, where it is not constitutionally guaranteed.

Changes to the Dispositional Outcome

The purpose of the disposition in traditional juvenile court was to treat and rehabilitate the individual offender. Therefore, a disposition determined by a juvenile court judge was to focus on the social history of the juvenile, prepared by the probation officer or social worker. Unlike in adult court, where the punishment is to be proportionate with the crime, the juvenile disposition was to address the specific needs of the child. According to the changes being made to the purpose of juvenile justice, however, the focus was no longer to be only on the juvenile but, rather, also to ensure public safety and, as noted above, accountability to the victim. Moreover, "rehabilitation," a term that has been plagued by reports that "nothing works," was replaced with terms such as "redemption" and "competency development."[24] But what exactly do those terms mean? What would the new juvenile disposition truly look like, and would it truly reflect the good intentions of the court and the best interests of the child?

The Disposition Hearing

The disposition hearing, according to *Gault*, was to refocus on the needs of the juvenile, rather than the facts of the case; therefore, an attorney was not needed at this stage. In many states, the disposition hearing is held immediately following adjudication. In other jurisdictions, the disposition hearing is held at a later date, it is hoped after some initial assessment of treatment needs is conducted.

However, similar to what has happened with the adjudication hearing, such a formal disposition hearing rarely occurs, as plea bargaining is also becoming more and more popular in juvenile court. While there are two specific types of plea bargaining—charge bargaining and sentence bargaining—in truth, the two are usually intertwined. For example, if charged with felony possession with intent to deliver marijuana, which may incur a possible three-year placement in a residential facility in a given state, the juvenile may plea to a charge of simple possession with thirty days' confinement in a detention center. Thus, the adjudication and disposition hearing become one process. The probation officer is usually nonexistent in these proceedings, and the negotiations occur in a hallway or behind closed doors, between the prosecutor and defense counsel, or prosecutor and parents when present. While the judge ultimately retains power to reject or accept a plea agreement, in recognition of court caseloads and the intricacies of the court room workgroup, a judge will usually accept such a plea without question.

Not surprisingly, whether the process involves the plea agreement or a formal hearing, the tendency of the disposition to be focused on punishment rather than treatment has been increasing. In a 1995 report, the National Center for Juvenile Justice specifically noted "a trend by legislatures to make dispositions more offense-based as opposed to the more traditional offender-based sanction, with the goal of punishment or incapacitation rather than rehabilitation."[25] Some states have gone so far as to approve mandatory sentences for particular kinds of crimes or sentencing guidelines for juvenile court judges to follow.[26] In some states, a compromise was made that awarded juvenile court judges the authority to hand down "blended sentences" that combine elements of the juvenile justice system with adult punishments, including terms of confinement in adult prisons.

Blended Sentencing

Blended sentencing practices present a unique and troublesome approach to determining the juvenile disposition. In states that allow blended sentencing in juvenile courts, there are three specific approaches this method can take: (1) a juvenile inclusive sentence, (2) a juvenile exclusive sentence, or (3) a juvenile contiguous sentence. Notice that for each approach, the outcome is deemed a sentence and not a disposition.

In the first approach, a juvenile inclusive sentence, the juvenile court judge is awarded the authority to devise a sentence that includes elements of both the juvenile and the adult justice systems. How such a sentence is crafted obviously differs from judge to judge, but the sentiment appears to be to use the carrot-and-stick approach. That is, the judge offers a sentence of juvenile probation as the carrot; however, if the juvenile does not satisfactorily meet all conditions of probation, the stick is placement in an adult correctional facility.

For example, in Arkansas, the Extended Juvenile Justice Jurisdiction Act of 1999 (EJJ) allows the prosecutor to decide if a case, based on age and offense seriousness, should be tried under this act.[27] If tried under EJJ, the juvenile has full constitutional rights, including a trial by jury. Then, at the disposition stage, the juvenile court judge may order a "suspended adult sentence," which is held at bay while the juvenile completes conditions of a juvenile disposition. The juvenile's case is then reviewed at a hearing and if it is found that the juvenile (1) has not completed all components of the ordered treatment, (2) or has been adjudicated on a new offense, or (3) is not otherwise amenable to treatment as a juvenile, the adult sentence is imposed. The legislation applies no general limits on the length of the adult sentence.

In the second approach, a juvenile exclusive sentence, the juvenile court judge has the authority to devise a sentence that makes use of *either* juvenile sanctions or adult sanctions, but not both. That is, after processing a juvenile in juvenile court, if the juvenile court judge does not feel the youth is amenable to treatment in the juvenile system, instead of retrying the juvenile as an adult, the judge may simply order an adult criminal sanction.

New Mexico, the first state to enact a blended sentencing provision, took this approach. According to the Youthful Offender Act of 1993, a juvenile 14 years or older (previously 15 or older) can be tried under this act.[28] If found guilty, the juvenile court judge selects either a juvenile disposition of treatment or an adult sentence of confinement. In all cases tried under the Youthful Offender Act, however, the juvenile is allowed to request a trial by jury.

In the third approach, a juvenile contiguous sentence, the typical model is that the juvenile court judge can order a sentence that continues far beyond the maximum age of juvenile court jurisdiction. In such an instance, the youth is placed in a juvenile residential facility until a certain age (typically the 18th or 21st birthday). On this birthday, the youth is then transferred to an adult facility to serve the remainder of this sentence. For example, in Texas, a juvenile court judge may order a sentence of up to forty years for a "serious" offender, as defined by state law.[29]

In regard to the constitutionality of such sentences, it should be noted that in almost all states enacting blended sentencing laws, provisions have been enacted that specifically require or allow for trial by jury and other adult due process protections in juvenile court.

While these statutes vary so vastly by state that it is impossible to effectively summarize each in this forum, the general intent is to allow a juvenile court judge to order adult sanctions when deemed appropriate. It is the opinion of some that this approach was a fail-safe mechanism to prevent state legislatures from transferring even more juveniles to adult court by introducing greater flexibility in the juvenile court.[30] However, whatever the purpose behind the legislation, the undeniable outcome is certainly a further blurring of the boundary between the juvenile and adult courts.

Despite the introduction of blended sentencing, it remains the fact that most juveniles brought before the juvenile justice system are subject to dispositions that remain within the jurisdiction of juvenile justice system.

As with previous assessments of the institutions and options, some courts continue to focus on care and treatment, while many others have turned their focus onto punishment, and still others provide punishment even though their original intent was to provide care and treatment. Thus, for a juvenile adjudicated delinquent, the prospects of receiving a program of care and treatment truly fitted to the youth's best interests remains, at best, a gamble.

Lessons from History

The U.S. Supreme Court argued that the juvenile justice system of its time did not provide the promised care and treatment to juveniles, and simply punished them instead. Yet this same Supreme Court had an optimistic view that its own good intentions—providing juveniles with the "best of both worlds"—would be realized in actual practice. In reality, however, the juvenile justice system moved in a different direction. Although the emphasis on punishment versus treatment varies greatly from jurisdiction to jurisdiction, and even from judge to judge, the overall effect of the "get tough" movement was to adjust the focus at disposition away from the offender and onto the offense. The expanded role of the state prosecutor at many important decision stages ensures this focus on the seriousness of the offense throughout the juvenile justice process, from initial intake decisions to decisions to prosecute in the adult court or in the juvenile court under blended sentencing provisions.

In the adjudication phase, as we argued in the conclusion to the last chapter, the Supreme Court's ideal of providing juveniles with most due process rights has not been fully realized in practice. But the ideal itself remains. In the disposition phase, however, the situation is much worse. To a considerable extent, the very ideal itself (of providing care and treatment to juveniles in the disposition stage) has been abandoned.

The "criminalization" of juvenile proceedings has altered the process experienced by juveniles, as well as their dispositional outcomes. The juvenile offender is fingerprinted and photographed, he or she is subject to public scrutiny, is more likely to be held in pre-adjudicatory detention, and is more likely to appear in court in handcuffs and shackles. The juvenile offender, in short, looks and feels more like an adult criminal than like a needy child. Unlike juvenile dispositions of the past—which upheld the mission, if not the actual practice, of treatment—the dispositions in the new juvenile court have forgone the facade of treatment and have embraced the notions of accountability and punishment. Perhaps most disturbing are the extended publication and use of juvenile court records to enhance adult sentences and to limit future opportunities for youth—opportunities such as education and employment that are *crucial* to becoming productive adult citizens rather than adult criminals.

Lesson 1: The Cycle of Juvenile Justice. The widespread perception that juvenile crime rates are unusually high is accompanied by a widespread belief that these rates can be lowered by appropriate juvenile justice policies. This results in a continuous cycle of reform that consists of establishing lenient treatments in a major reform, gradually toughening up those treatments over a long time so that officials end up choosing between harsh punishments and doing nothing at all, and then reestablishing lenient treatments in another major reform.

Certainly, in the late 1980s and early 1990s, there was widespread alarm that rates of juvenile crime were unusually high and that they could be lowered by providing "get tough" punishments for juvenile offenders. Those punishments fit well within the projected cycle of juvenile justice. As society became increasingly alarmed with the proposed increases in juvenile crime, blame for the problem was laid solely on the existing juvenile justice system. Defined as a "kiddie court" that provided nothing more than a slap on the wrist to offenders, the juvenile courts were transformed by measure after measure to toughen up the sanctions for juvenile delinquency. One could expect that, at some time in the future, these tough sanctions would result in criminal justice officials being forced to choose between imposing sanctions that seem much too harsh for the particular offenders and doing nothing at all. The rate of juvenile crime, which will again be perceived as increasing, will be blamed on this forced choice, and lenient treatments will be reintroduced into the system.

Lesson 2: Ideas of Juvenile Delinquency. Ideas of delinquency that "sell" (i.e., that succeed in the competition with other possible ideas) propose that delinquents are a subgroup within some larger problem group (e.g., paupers, dependent and neglected children, criminal defendants) with which the public is already familiar. The prevailing idea of delinquency and delinquents thus drives the idea of what juvenile justice should be.

In their own reform, the U.S. Supreme Court had proposed the idea of juvenile delinquents as criminal defendants—that is, citizens who are presumed innocent until proven guilty and who therefore are entitled to the rights and protections embedded in the Constitution. This idea certainly didn't sell very well, but it was only a short step from juveniles as "criminal defendants" to juveniles as "criminal offenders," and this idea sold quite well.

Lesson 3: Ideas of Juvenile Justice. Responses to delinquency that "sell" (i.e., that succeed in the competition with other possible responses) are slightly

*modified versions of responses to the larger problem group of which delin-
quents are thought to be a subgroup (potential paupers, dependent and
neglected children, criminal defendants, etc).*

The idea of juvenile delinquency that took hold in the "get tough"
movement was a modified version of the adult criminal offender: juvenile offenders were smaller than adult offenders but otherwise they were
pretty much the same. Once this "new" idea of juvenile delinquency
emerged, the "new" idea of juvenile justice quickly followed: juvenile
delinquents should be treated pretty much the same as adult criminals. A
saying associated with this movement expressed it well: "If you are old
enough to do the crime, you are old enough to do the time." That is, you
get the same punishment for the same offense, regardless of your age.

Thus, the juvenile justice system began to take on more and more
characteristics of the adult criminal justice system. The civil court language of the juvenile court would be replaced by criminal terms such as
arrest, arraignment, sentencing, and *incarceration.* More and more youths
would be tried in adult criminal court, and the line between juvenile
"residential placement" and adult "incarceration" would blur.

*Lesson 4: Economic Interests of the Rich and Powerful. Responses to delin-
quency that "sell" focus on the behavior of poor and powerless people but ignore
the behavior of rich and powerful people. In particular, responses that focus
on poor people's behavior do not harm the economic interests of the rich and
powerful—that is, they aim to remove delinquents from the streets rather
than change conditions on the streets.*

The prosecutor is assigned the task of protecting the public interest,
and the public interest includes the interests of those who are rich and
powerful. Youths who threatened the safety of society previously would
be locked away for long periods of time instead of investing public dollars
in their care and treatment. Politicians of the day would also capitalize on
public fear, and propel themselves to power through promises of tougher
sanctions for juvenile criminals. Those defined as juvenile delinquents in
these earlier days tended to come from families of poor socioeconomic
resources. During this era, it was particularly African American youths
living in stagnant urban communities that bore the brunt of the
"reform."

One important element of the more recent "get tough" movement
that cannot be overlooked is its immediate inauguration on the heels of
the biggest civil rights movement in American history, since the Civil
War itself. The civil rights movement of the 1960s and 1970s resulted in
extended opportunities for education, employment, and civic participation for African Americans. But just as many of the due process rights
extended to juvenile and adult offenders during the liberal Warren

Court were not readily embraced or implemented by the conservative regime that followed, so, too, conservative white America was not ready to give up its economic and political foothold to African Americans in later years.

While we would not go so far as to suggest that the "get tough" era itself was a result of overt racism, one cannot help but notice its impact on today's poor African American families. The media have sold fear of the young, African American male as a commodity. Films such as *Boys 'n the Hood* etched in the collective psyche of America the vision of the black gang-banger who sold drugs, particularly, crack cocaine, and carried a gun to kill anyone who got in his way. Juvenile and adult correctional facilities became holding grounds for young African American males, much in the way colleges served as launching pads for affluent white youths. Laws that provided harsher penalties for possession of emerging crack cocaine (a less expensive version of cocaine used in poor black communities) than for powder cocaine (the more expensive drug of choice of white college youth) provided one example of how these disparities became institutionalized. Laws that followed, then, actually "limited" education, employment, and opportunities for civic participation for those with certain types of criminal records (most prominently drug offenses), thus stripping from many African American males the rights granted via the Civil Rights Act.[31]

Lesson 5: Moral and Intellectual Superiority of Reformers. Responses to delinquency that "sell" imply that delinquents and their parents are morally and intellectually inferior, and that the reformers themselves are morally and intellectually superior.

As previously noted, it is with ease that society defines the criminal as devoid of moral character. Now, young juvenile offenders not only come from families that were not providing them with proper care and instruction (morally inferior), but they themselves are devoid of human emotions such as empathy and remorse. In short, something is wrong with the juvenile who can commit these acts.

What is wrong is that he or she is criminal. As suggested above, the African American community was particularly targeted in this most recent reform. The media and politicians painted a picture of the criminal to be most feared as the young black male emanating from the urban ghetto. His father was in prison, his mother was on drugs and/or on welfare, and he had been raised with no respect for humanity. Unlike juveniles of the past, however, who could be saved by removing them from these negative home influences, there was no hope for reforming this violent super-predator. He must be confined to protect the morality of the rest of society.

Lesson 6: The Unfair Comparison. Reformers "sell" their own reforms by an unfair comparison, in which a harsh assessment of actual practices of past policies is compared with an optimistic assessment of reforms, based on good intentions. Because they assume that good intentions directly translate into good practices, reformers promise to solve the problem of juvenile delinquency.

The Supreme Court had provided a good example of the unfair comparison in its decisions, comparing the actual practices of the existing juvenile court with its potential to perform in the future. Care and treatment were the exceptions rather than the rule in the juvenile court, argued the Supreme Court, despite the good intentions of the founders. But then the Supreme Court simply assumed that the new constitutional juvenile court would fulfill those same good intentions in the future.

What the Supreme Court did not foresee was that the "get tough" movement would abandon care and treatment even as just the intention of the juvenile court. Instead, the new purpose clauses for the juvenile courts included language that ranged from "increased accountability" to outright "punishment" of juvenile offenders. Care and treatment largely ceased to be the mission of the juvenile court. The new mission looked to the juvenile court to protect victims and society from young offenders, by providing dispositions (sentences) based on the offenses rather than the offenders' needs. These harsher dispositions took many forms, but for the most part they mirrored, or actually were, punishments already in practice in the adult criminal justice system.

Of course, "get tough" advocates did exactly what the Supreme Court had done before them—and what the founders of the original juvenile court had done: they based their reforms on the "unfair comparison." They harshly assessed the effectiveness of the existing juvenile justice system in actual practice, and then provided a very optimistic assessment of the effectiveness of their own reforms, based on their own good intentions. Their good intentions were to deter juvenile offenders by harshly punishing them for their offenses, and to prevent them from pursuing lives of crime by confining them in adult facilities for extended periods of time. However, research at the time already strongly indicated that, contrary to their stated good intentions, these practices had a strong tendency to produce higher rates of recidivism and more serious offending than did treatments determined in the traditional juvenile court. "Get tough" advocates ignored this research, and simply assumed that their own intentions would be achieved in actual practice. As the cycle of juvenile justice turned once again, that assumption became increasingly difficult to maintain.

Lesson 7: The Power of the State. Reforms that "sell" increase the power of the state, based on optimistic assessments of how effective the reform will be in solving the problem. The power of the state usually continues to expand regardless of the specific content or nature of the reform.

While the act establishing the original juvenile court extended the possibility of court intervention to almost all poor youths or youths of immigrant parents, the "get tough" movement saw unprecedented expansion of the state's authority to remove juveniles from their homes and to place them, not in the "care" of the state but in the "custody" of the state. The state gained a greater say in charging and detention decisions, as well as in prosecuting the young offenders as adult criminals. The juvenile court enjoyed expanded jurisdiction that allowed it to invoke sentences both outside of the traditional age range for juvenile court jurisdiction and outside of the traditional dispositional options available to a juvenile court (e.g., blended sentencing). With the state's newfound power built on public fear and media hype, the self-perpetuating nature of the cycle of juvenile justice was guaranteed: the media report on juvenile crime, the public becomes concerned about juvenile crime, reforms are instituted, and so on. And if there is one thing we have learned about state power in history, it is that once power is gained, it is not easily relinquished.

The Supreme Court's due process reform seemed strangely out of place with respect to the lessons of history, and it turns out that these reforms simply were not implemented. For instance, in the adjudication hearing, the ideal of providing juveniles with most of the due process rights of adults was never fully realized. In the disposition hearing, the ideal was to provide juveniles with the care and treatment proposed by the original juvenile court; not only was this not fully realized but also it was largely abandoned, in favor of a "get tough" focus on punishment.

The principles and policies of the "get tough" movement provide a much better fit with the lessons of history and the proposed cycle of juvenile justice. As noted above, it is consistent with the lessons of history and it sold extremely well with the general public. However, the full range of this movement's effect was not felt within the juvenile justice system itself. Rather, one of its major impacts was on the boundary between the juvenile and the criminal courts. It is that boundary that we explore in the following chapter.

NOTES

1. Howard Snyder and Melissa Sickmund, *Juvenile Offenders and Victims: A National Report* (Washington, D.C.: Office of Juvenile Justice and Delinquency Prevention, U.S. Department of Justice, 2006), 132–133.

2. Ibid., 133. See also Patricia Torbet and Linda Szymanski, *Juvenile Offenders and Victims: 1996 Update on Violence* (Washington, D.C.: Office of Juvenile Justice and Delinquency Prevention, U.S. Department of Justice, 1996).

3. For discussions of the proposed juvenile crime wave, see Thomas J. Bernard, "Juvenile Crime and the Transformation of Juvenile Justice: Was There a Juvenile Crime Wave?" *Justice Quarterly* 16, no. 2 (1999): 337–356; Alfred Blumstein, "Youth Violence, Guns, and the Illicit-Drug Industry," *Journal of Criminal Law and Criminology* 86 (1995): 10–36; Franklin Zimring, "Kids, Guns, and Homicide: Policy Notes on an Age-Specific Epidemic," *Law and Contemporary Problems* 59 (1996): 25–37; and Franklin Zimring, *American Youth Violence* (New York: Oxford University Press, 1998).

4. For further comparisons and specifications of state laws, see Joseph B. Sanborn Jr. and Anthony W. Salerno, *The Juvenile Justice System Law and Process* (Los Angeles: Roxbury, 2005). Also, at the time of publication of this book, the National Center for Juvenile Justice has provided summaries of each state's juvenile justice system and links to statutes at *ncjj.org/stateprofiles*.

5. Monroe J. Paxman, "Evolution of the Standard Juvenile Court Act," *Crime and Delinquency* 5 (1959): 392–403.

6. Institute of Judicial Administration, American Bar Association, Juvenile Justice Standards, recommended by the Joint Commission on Juvenile Justice Standards and approved by the House of Delegates of the American Bar Association, 1980, as reported by John M. Junker, http://library.mssc.state.ms.us/FullDisp?itemid=00007035, accessed May 2009.

7. The concept of a balanced approach was first brought to national attention by Dennis Maloney, Dennis Roming, and Troy Armstrong, "Juvenile Probation: The Balanced Approach," *Juvenile and Family Court* 39, no. 3 (1988): 1–57. For examples of states adopting the language of balanced approach, see also Patricia Torbet and Douglas Thomas, "Balanced and Restorative Justice: Implementing the Philosophy," *Pennsylvania Progress* 4, no. 3 (October 1997).

8. *42 Pennsylvania Consolidated Statutes*, §6301 (b)(2).

9. Maloney, Armstrong, and Romig, "The Balanced Approach," 1–57. For further elaboration of approaches to accountability, see also Megan Kurlychek, Patricia M. Torbet, and Melanie Bozynski, "Focus on Accountability: Best Practices for Juvenile Court and Probation," bulletin of the U. S. Department of Justice, Office of Justice Programs, Office of Juvenile Justice and Delinquency Prevention, Juvenile Accountability Incentive Block Grants Program, August 1999.

10. *Texas Family Code*, Title 3, ch. 51–60.

11. *Wyoming Statues*, Title 14, ch. 6, juv. art. 2.

12. Patrick Griffin, "State Juvenile Justice Profiles, Pittsburgh, Pennsylvania," National Center for Juvenile Justice, http://www.ncjj.org/stateprofiles, accessed March 2009.

13. *General Laws of Massachusetts*, Part 1, Title XVII, ch. 119.

14. Griffin, "State Juvenile Justice Profiles."

15. Patricia Torbet, Richard Gable, Hunter Hurst, Imogene Montgomery, Linda Szymanski, and Douglas Thomas, *State Responses to Serious and Violent Juvenile Crime*, (Washington, D.C.: Office of Juvenile Justice and Delinquency Prevention, U.S. Department of Justice, 1996).

16. Ibid.

17. For useful comparisons of state laws regarding the intake process, see Sanborn and Salerno, *Juvenile Justice System Law and Process.*

18. Ibid.

19. Ibid.

20. Ibid.

21. Owing to the importance of a detention decision, most states have timelines in place that require a detention hearing to be held within 24 to 72 hours. This is a double-edged sword, because this deadline makes it difficult for states to assign an attorney and/or for the attorney to properly prepare for this important hearing. For further discussion on the importance of counsel at the detention hearing, see Publication Development Committee, Juvenile Delinquency Guidelines Project, *Juvenile Delinquency Guidelines: Improving Court Practice in Juvenile Delinquency Cases* (Reno: National Council of Juvenile and Family Court Judges, 2005).

22. P. Puritz, S. Burrell, R. Schwartz, M. Soler, and L. Warboys, *A Call for Justice: An Assessment of Access to Counsel and Quality of Representation in Delinquency Proceedings* (Washington, D.C.: American Bar Association, Criminal Justice Section, Juvenile Justice Center, 1995), 32. For a discussion of similar issues dealing with rates of detention by race, see E. Poe-Yamagata and M. A. Jones, "And Justice for Some: Differential Treatment of Minority Youth in the Justice System," *Building Blocks for Youth*, April 2000.

23. Patricia Torbet and Valerie Bender, "Advancing Accountability: Moving Towards Victim Restoration: A White Paper for Pennsylvania," National Center for Juvenile Justice. Pittsburgh, Pennsylvania, 2006. See also Peter Freivalds, "Fact Sheet #42: Balanced and Restorative Justice Project" (Washington, D.C.: Office of Juvenile Justice and Delinquency Prevention, U.S. Department of Justice, 2006).

24. Starting with a report by Robert Martinson, "What Works? Questions and Answers about Prison Reform," *Public Interest* 35 (1974): 22–54, officials and the public began to question our ability to reform offenders in either the adult or the juvenile justice system. Since that report, much research has been done on further documenting what does or doesn't work. For further discussion of this issue, see also Lawrence Sherman, Denise Gottfredson, Doris MacKenzie, J. Eck, P. Reuter, and Shawn Bushway, eds., *Preventing Crime: What Works, What Doesn't, What's Promising* (Washington, D.C.: National Institute of Justice, 1997); and James C. Howell, *Preventing and Reducing Juvenile Delinquency: A Comprehensive Framework* (Thousand Oaks, Calif.: Sage, 2003).

25. Torbet et al., *State Responses.*

26. Ibid.

27. Griffin, "State Juvenile Justice Profiles."

28. New Mexico Statutes Annotate §532 A-2-20(b)(1)

29. Texas Family Code Annotated §54.04(3)

30. Patrick Griffin, "Different from Adults: An Updated Analysis of Juvenile Transfer and Blended Sentencing Laws, with Recommendations for Reform:

Models for Change, Systems Reform in Juvenile Justice," National Center for Juvenile Justice, Pittsburgh, Pennsylvania, November 2008.

31. H. J. Holzer, S. Raphael, and M. A. Stoll, "Will Employers Hire Former Offenders? Employer Preferences, Background Checks and Their Determinants," in D. Weiman, B. Western, and M. Patillo, eds., *Imprisoning America: The Social Effects of Mass Incarceration* (New York: Russell Sage, 2004), 205–246. See also A. Zimmerman and K. Stringer, "As Background Checks Proliferate, Ex-cons Face a Lock on Jobs," *Wall Street Journal*, August 26, 2004, B1; T. M. Hammett, C. Roberts, and S. Kennedy, "Health-Related Issues in Prisoner Reenter," *Crime and Delinquency* 47 (July 2001): 390–409; C. Uggen, "Barriers to Democratic Participation," paper presented at Prisoner Reentry and the Institutions of Civil Society: Bridges and Barriers to Successful Reintegration Roundtable, Urban Institute, Washington, D.C., March 20–21, 2002.

9

Youths in the Adult System

The "get tough" philosophy conceived of the juvenile court as a modified version of the adult criminal court. As the "get tough" changes were implemented in juvenile courts across the country, these juvenile courts increasingly looked like criminal courts. If this trend were to continue, there would be fewer and fewer reasons for a separate juvenile court at all. Instead, juveniles could be processed, under slightly modified rules, in the same criminal courts as were adults. Thus, when the "get tough" movement was in full bloom, it looked as if the juvenile court, and the juvenile justice system along with it, was on the road to extinction.

Many people who actually worked with delinquents, however, wanted to keep a separate juvenile justice system. These people often favored efforts to "toughen up" the juvenile court as an attempt to salvage public support for it. So, for example, the legal statutes that defined the purposes of juvenile courts in most jurisdictions were changed to include steps like holding juveniles accountable for their actions, ensuring public safety, and even punishing juveniles for their offenses. But these same legal statutes still allowed much more room for rehabilitation in juvenile courts than could be found in criminal courts, even though rehabilitation was often camouflaged under new terms such as "competency development." Even more important, a separate juvenile system allowed juveniles to be held in separate facilities from adults, a practice going back to the original early House of Refuge.

Unfortunately, the sentiment in favor of retaining a separate juvenile system was not shared by the general public at the time, and that public sentiment was reflected in the opinions of public officials. No matter how tough the juvenile system claimed to be, the public was still suspicious of its ability to deal with the "violent new breed" of young offender. The public more or less took the view that youths who committed serious violent crimes were mature enough to be processed and treated in the adult system—the crime itself was proof of their maturity.[1] These youths, in the view of the public, should not be afforded the special protections and special treatments of a separate juvenile system.

As a result of this sentiment, there was considerable effort in the 1990s to reduce the jurisdiction of the juvenile courts and to process more and more juveniles in the adult criminal court system. In the previous chapter, we discussed how the "get tough" changes in the juvenile court made it more and more like the criminal court. In this chapter, we discuss an additional effect of the "get tough" movement: more and more juveniles being taken out of the juvenile court and transferred to the criminal court for full criminal processing.

Reducing Juvenile Court Jurisdiction

The juvenile court was originally designed to deal with youths whose criminal responsibility for their actions was seen as being somewhere between the innocence of an infant and the full criminal responsibility of a mature adult. As detailed in chapter 2, this view of youthful criminal responsibility has been a common thread through human history and across civilizations. In English common law, for example, youths below the age of 7 were said to have no criminal responsibility for their actions; youths between 7 and 14 were presumed to lack criminal responsibility, although the prosecution could argue otherwise; youths between the ages of 14 and 21 were presumed to be criminally responsible, although the defense could argue otherwise; and on the 21st birthday, everyone assumed full criminal responsibility.

Age of Juvenile Court Jurisdiction

When the first juvenile court was founded in Chicago in 1899, the upper boundary of its jurisdiction was set at the 16th birthday. That is, youths who were 15 and under were to be handled in the new juvenile court, although prosecution could argue that some youths under this age should appropriately be tried in criminal court. This arrangement was directly comparable to the way English common law had handled youths between the ages of 7 and 14.

Legally, this meant that the juvenile court had *original jurisdiction* over all youths under the age limit—that is, when they committed an offense, all of these youths would go directly to juvenile court. But the prosecutor could argue that it was inappropriate for a particular youth to be handled there. If the juvenile court judge agreed with the prosecutor, then the judge would *waive* (i.e., give up) jurisdiction over this youth and transfer the youth to the (adult) criminal court.

The Illinois juvenile court jurisdiction was later extended to the 18th birthday, and in the 1990s, that date remained the upper limit of juvenile court jurisdiction in thirty-seven states. Ten states had the upper age limit on the 17th birthday, and three states (New York, Connecticut, and North Carolina) maintained a maximum age of the 16th birthday.[2] As part of the "get tough" movement, however, many people began questioning the age limit of juvenile court jurisdiction, especially for serious violent crimes. Didn't 15-year-olds really know what they were doing when they committed rape or murder? Don't even young children know that murder is wrong? And if that is true, then shouldn't they be held responsible for their actions despite their age?

These questions were widely asked in the 1990s, but only three states actually reduced the upper age limit of juvenile court jurisdiction as a consequence: Wyoming lowered its upper limit from the 18th birthday to the 17th in 1993, while New Hampshire and Wisconsin lowered their upper age limit from 17th to the 16th birthday in 1996. Other states, however, found additional ways to remove large numbers of youths from juvenile court, based not solely on age but, rather, on offense or age/offense combinations, as described below.

Statutory Exclusion of Offenses from Juvenile Court Jurisdiction

While only three states reduced the maximum age of juvenile court jurisdiction during the 1990s, many states passed laws that excluded from juvenile court jurisdiction certain classes of juveniles based on a combination of age and offense. When laws are passed that exclude certain offenses or offenders from juvenile court jurisdiction, it is referred to as either *statutory exclusion* or *legislative exclusion*.

For example, in California, youths under the age of 18 fall within the original jurisdiction of the juvenile court. However, if the juvenile is at least age 14 *and* is accused of one of several specific offenses, he or she is prosecuted "under the general law in a court of criminal jurisdiction." The offenses that are listed are those that impose a mandatory life without parole or death sentence.[3] In Delaware, the statutory exclusion provision reflects the public fear of juvenile firearm violence, indicating that offenders 15 years or older who possessed and/or used a firearm in the commission of certain felonies are excluded from the original jurisdiction of the juvenile court.[4]

Other statutory exclusion laws consider only the offense itself and do not consider the age of the offender. Certain crimes may be considered so heinous that only someone with an adult mind and adult culpabilities could commit them; the offense is thus excluded from the definition of a "delinquent act." For example, in Pennsylvania, the juvenile act excludes the crime of murder from the definition of "delinquent act." Thus, any youth charged with murder, regardless of age, falls within the original jurisdiction of adult criminal court.[5]

Statutory exclusion laws ignore the traditional age boundaries of the juvenile court, with its concept of diminished responsibility and mitigated punishments for those below the specified age. These laws focus on the severity of the offense itself, rather than the age, maturity, and culpability of the offender, and they impose the adult system's "offense-based" punishments on youths who otherwise would be defined as juveniles.

Legally, these laws give *original jurisdiction* over certain youths to the criminal courts, rather than to the juvenile courts. That is, these youths go directly to criminal court and do not pass through the juvenile court on their way there. In this manner, statutory exclusion laws also eliminate the need for waiver hearings as set forth by the *Kent* decision, in which all factors (offense, age, maturity, amenability to treatment, etc.) must be considered. Currently, thirty-seven states maintain some form of statutory exclusion.[6]

Most states with statutory exclusion laws also retain judicial waiver hearings. That is, some youths are statutorily excluded from juvenile court jurisdiction and go directly to criminal court without passing through juvenile court. Youths who are not statutorily excluded will first go to juvenile court, but the juvenile court judge may still conduct a waiver hearing and decide to waive jurisdiction and send them to criminal court.

Concurrent Jurisdiction and Prosecutorial Discretion

Another mechanism for reducing juvenile court jurisdiction falls within the venue of the state prosecutor. Rather than providing original jurisdiction over certain offenses to either the juvenile court or the criminal court, fifteen states have passed laws that provide both the juvenile court and the adult criminal court with *concurrent jurisdiction* over certain offenses. This term literally means that both courts have original jurisdiction over the same offenses at the same time. The prosecutor, then, is awarded the authority to decide whether to process the case in juvenile court or in criminal court. Since it is the prosecutor who actually decides whether to directly file the case in adult court, this type of transfer is often described as prosecutorial discretion, or a "direct file."

As with statutory exclusion, this type of transfer does not involve a waiver hearing. The juvenile never goes to juvenile court at all, and so there is no opportunity for the juvenile court to waive jurisdiction. Another trait of prosecutorial-based charging decisions relates to the previous discussion regarding a juvenile's waiver of *Miranda* rights. As noted, most youths are encouraged to cooperate with police and other officials. Parents often assume that their child, because of his or her age, will be handled in the juvenile court. It is only *after* waiving the right to remain silent and/or the right to an attorney that the juvenile and the family become aware of the prosecutor's decision to try the child as an adult. The police have, at this point, already obtained a confession from the juvenile, so the due process protections of the adult criminal justice system are, for all practical purposes, not applicable, either. In other words, the prosecutor has a slam dunk.

In practice, then, states with such concurrent jurisdiction laws have substantially limited the jurisdiction of the juvenile court, extinguished the decision-making power of juvenile court personnel in potential waiver cases, and reduced or almost eliminated the need for waiver hearings.

While relatively few states have these laws, in those states that do, there have been very large increases in the numbers of juveniles processed in adult court. This would naturally be expected, since the focus of the prosecutor is on the seriousness of the present offense and the prior offending. In comparison, a waiver hearing held before a juvenile court judge focuses on a broad range of factors besides the present and prior offenses, including assessments of the juvenile's maturity, culpability, and amenability to treatment.

The Evolving Waiver Hearing

At the time of the *Kent* decision, the Supreme Court did not require states to maintain a separate system of juvenile justice, but it declared that if they did, every youth falling within their original jurisdiction must be afforded a formal waiver hearing with an attorney present before the youths could be waived to adult court for criminal prosecution. Factors to be considered at such hearings were to include not only the seriousness of the offense but, as per the rehabilitative tradition of the juvenile court, also indicators of the youth's maturity, culpability, and amenability to treatment. Such a waiver hearing is usually referred to as a *discretionary waiver hearing*. Similar to English common law, the youth is presumed to lack responsibility, and it is up to the prosecutor to convince the juvenile court judge otherwise.

During the "get tough" movement, legislatures across the country developed variations on this theme, most notably the presumptive waiver and the mandatory waiver. Although, as with other changes described in this section, specifications of such waiver processes vary from state to state, we attempt to provide a basic description of the main focus of these new policies as they compare to the traditional *Kent* waiver hearing.

A *presumptive waiver* can be visualized as most closely related to that which was assumed for juveniles aged 14 to 21 in English common law. The presumption is that the youth is responsible for his or her actions, but the defense attorney has the opportunity to argue otherwise before the juvenile court judge. Similar to the statutory exclusion provisions described above, most states establishing this type of hearing base the presumption of responsibility on a combination of the age of the juvenile and the seriousness of the offense.

For example, New Hampshire law states that when the age, current offense, and prior record of a juvenile offender meet certain criteria, "the law creates a presumption that the factors that must be considered by the juvenile court judge in ruling on a transfer petition support a transfer."[7] In Nevada, the language is a bit stronger, stating that under certain legislatively set age/offense combinations, the juvenile court judge *must* certify the case to adult court unless the court finds the juvenile is "developmentally or mentally incompetent" or that the child's actions were the result of an emotional, behavioral, or substance-abuse problem that can be "treated" through the juvenile court.[8] Overall, fifteen states have presumptive waiver language on the books.

A *mandatory waiver* hearing is generally defined as one that goes one step further—it eliminates from consideration any individualized assessment of these criteria. There is no argument in court about whether the juvenile is or isn't responsible for his or her actions. Rather, the waiver to adult court is mandatory if the judge finds that the youth is of the minimum age limit set by statute and if the prosecutor has rightfully charged the youth with one of the offenses specified in the law.[9]

A mandatory waiver is best conceived of as a formal hearing before the juvenile court judge in which the only issues are whether the age of the juvenile and the charges brought by the prosecutor meet the criteria established by the legislature. If they do, then the law states that the judge "shall" transfer the case to adult court. In this type of hearing, the *Kent* criteria are removed from the hearing and the discretionary decision making is removed from the judge. Thus, this type of waiver hearing is basically an added procedural step to a statutory exclusion, rather than an actual waiver hearing. For example, Virginia law mandates that the juvenile court judge certify for adult prosecution a juvenile who is at least 14 years of age when there is probable cause to believe that the juvenile committed a certain offense, such as murder and aggravated wounding.[10]

Youths in Criminal Court

The "get tough" movement created a range of new mechanisms by which youths under the age of juvenile court jurisdiction could end up in criminal court. With these newly forged roads leading to adult court, one might assume that many more youths were finding themselves on this course. That assumption would be correct.

Judicial waiver, the traditional mechanism for transferring youths to criminal court, remained on the books in almost all states, with forty-five states and the District of Columbia maintaining this mechanism.[11] During the "get tough" movement, the number of waivers nationwide increased, from 7,200 in 1985 to a peak of 13,200 in 1994. Since that time, the number has again been declining, with the most recent national estimate reporting 6,300 waivers in 2001.[12] This decline could be interpreted either in terms of the nationwide decline in juvenile crime that occurred at the same time or it might suggest a movement in the direction of leniency for juvenile offenders. Before jumping to such a conclusion, however, we must remember that judicial waiver is being augmented by two new mechanisms for transferring juveniles: statutory exclusion and concurrent jurisdiction (e.g., prosecutorial waiver and/or direct file).

Prosecutorial discretion is the least common method for transferring juveniles; in 2004, it was available in only fifteen states. While there are no national figures for this method of transferring juveniles, state statistics suggest that, where it is available, it generally accounts for a large majority of transfers. For example, both prosecutorial discretion and judicial waiver are available in Florida, but in the year 2000, 95 percent of transfers were accomplished by prosecutorial discretion and only 5 percent by waiver.[13] In 2001, a year during which there were 6,300 judicial waivers nationwide, Florida alone transferred over 2,000 juveniles to criminal court by prosecutorial discretion.[14]

Finally, a large number of juveniles are transferred to criminal court by means of statutory exclusion. Unfortunately, again, we find no precise nationwide figures on the number of juveniles reaching adult court by this particular mechanism. In 2004, twenty-nine states had laws that specify some combination of age and offense for placing original jurisdiction in criminal court for offenders who are under the age of juvenile court jurisdiction.[15] In addition, thirteen states set the age of juvenile court jurisdiction below 18 years—in those states, 16- and 17-year-olds may be tried in criminal court regardless of their offenses. In total, it is estimated that, in a given year, 200,000 to 300,000 youths under the age of 18 are processed as adults in criminal courts.[16]

Youths in Adult Correctional Facilities

The ramifications of the increased processing of youths in criminal courts are felt subsequently in the adult correctional system. The number of youths held in adult jails grew steadily, from an estimated 1,700 in 1983 to a peak of over 14,400 by 1999.[17] The number of youths in state prisons reached a peak in 1997, at about 5,400. Recent estimates show that these numbers are again decreasing, where on the average day in 2004, adult correctional facilities housed about 9,500 youths under the age of 18. About 7,000 of these youths were being held in adult jails nationwide, and the remaining 2,500 were being held in state prisons.[18]

Because the focus of the adult correctional system is not on treatment and rehabilitation but, rather, on punishment, it might be assumed that outcomes for these youths are much more severe than for their counterparts processed in a juvenile court. However, history also suggests that adult juries and criminal court judges are hesitant to convict juveniles and to place them in adult penitentiaries, which suggests an alternate outcome: that when faced with the forced choice of placing these youths in adult prisons or doing nothing, the system frequently will opt to do nothing.

Early studies of juveniles tried in adult court suggest that this, in fact, was what was happening. Judges, for various reasons, seemed to be hesitant to place juveniles in adult incarceration settings.[19] For example, studies suggest that juveniles incarcerated in adult facilities are more likely to be physically and/or sexually assaulted, and they are more likely to gain further criminogenic attitudes and skills rather than being "reformed."[20] Indeed, these were the original concerns of the child-savers that proved the catalyst in 1825 for the design of the first House of Refuge for young offenders.

However, more recent studies are emerging that suggest that this hesitancy may have been overcome by the public fear of juvenile violence that fueled the "get tough" movement itself. Recent work suggests that juveniles processed as adults are likely to be convicted, receive a sentence of incarceration, and be incarcerated for increasingly lengthy periods of time. In fact, some studies even suggest that these juveniles are receiving more severe sentences than would an offender over the age of 18 if convicted on the same charge.[21] Other studies show these youths to have less favorable long-term outcomes, being more likely than youths processed in the juvenile system to recidivate and to recidivate with more serious offenses.[22]

In addition, juveniles processed in adult court historically have faced two possible outcomes not available to the juvenile court, even through blended-sentencing provisions: life without parole, and death. In the next two sections, we discuss these two sentences as applied to those who committed their offenses while under the age of 18.

Youths Serving Life without Parole

In 2007, there were 2,387 youths who were serving life without the possibility of parole (LWOP) in American prisons for crimes committed while they were under the age of 18.[23] These youths can be sentenced for various crimes, but about 93 percent of them receive this sentence for the crime of murder.

For over half of these youths, the offense for which they serve this sentence was their first offense—as either a juvenile or an adult. For over one-fourth of the cases, the juveniles fell under a state's "felony murder" law, which holds that if a death occurs during the commission of a felony, everyone involved in the felony is equally responsible for the death. A common situation is that these juveniles were brought into the crime by older offenders, such as when they are tagging along with a group or doing the driving. For example, in 2001, a 14-year-old boy in California got a ride home from a party from a 27-year-old man. On the way, the man kidnapped another man and negotiated with the victim's brother for ransom. The victim was eventually released without injury, but the boy was sentenced to life imprisonment without parole for his participation in the crime.[24] This case was one of the relatively few nationwide in which a juvenile received a life sentence for a crime other than murder.

Thirty-nine states and the federal government provide LWOP for those who commit their offenses while under the age of 18. In 2003, Pennsylvania, which has a strict felony murder law, had the largest number of youthful offenders serving that sentence (332), and Pennsylvania was followed rather closely by Michigan, Louisiana, and Florida. That same year, California had 180 and Illinois a little over 100 youthful offenders on LWOP; all the other states had fewer than 100. Three states—New Jersey, Utah, and Vermont—allow the LWOP sentence but reportedly have no juveniles who have received it.[25]

Amnesty International argues that race plays a role in the distribution of LWOP sentences.[26] African American youths are ten times more likely to receive a sentence of LWOP than are white youths. This exceeds the ratio between the black and white rates of arrest for murder. The ratio between these two rates peaked in 1993, when the arrest rate of black juveniles for murder was more than nine times that of the white rate. This ratio declined during the late 1990s and early 2000s, falling to below five to one in 2003. However, between 2003 and 2006, the racial disparity in the rates increased, reaching seven to one in 2006.[27] The excess sentencing of black juveniles to LWOP might reflect a consideration of race per se, or it might be a result of the murders committed by black youths being more "serious" than the murders committed by white youths. Amnesty recommends that this question be studied to determine whether race itself is the cause of this discrepancy.

Youths and the Death Penalty

Another sentence that is a potential outcome of adult court processing is the death penalty. While several state legislatures had set a minimum age that an offender must have been when committing an offense for the prosecutor to call for the death penalty, there was no national consensus on the issue until two cases reached the Supreme Court in the 1980s. These cases served as the law of the land until a third case reached a reconstituted Supreme Court in 2002. We present these three cases in a similar way as the previous Supreme Court cases were presented in chapter 6, regarding the due process movement.

Thompson v. Oklahoma (1988)

Facts. On the evening of January 22, 1983, William Wayne Thompson, then 15 years old, and three older friends left his house, declaring they were going to kill Charles Keene. Mr. Keen had been married to Thompson's older sister, and he had been suspected of physically abusing her. According to Thompson's recollection of the events, he said that he "shot him in the head and cut his throat in the river." According to the older companions, Thompson had shot Mr. Keen in the head twice, and then cut his head, abdomen, and chest before throwing him into the river. When Keene's body was recovered from the river, the medical examiner confirmed that the injuries did indeed match this description.

The three older accomplices, all of whom were over 18, were convicted of murder and sentenced to death. The prosecutor requested a waiver hearing, at which time Thompson's case was certified to adult court by the juvenile court judge. Thompson had a long history of juvenile offenses, and workers from the juvenile system testified at the waiver hearing that he was not "amenable to rehabilitation." Thompson had also been diagnosed with antisocial personality disorder, and psychological reports indicated that he did not possess the potential for change or rehabilitation. Thompson was convicted of first-degree murder in adult court and sentenced to death.

Issue. Does the execution of a youth who was 15 at the time he committed the offense in question violate the Eighth Amendment's prohibition against "cruel and unusual punishment"?

Decision. The Supreme Court ruled that the execution of a person who was under 16 at the time of the offense violated the Eighth Amendment's prohibition against cruel and unusual punishment.

Reasons. In drafting the decision, Justice Stevens, joined by Justice Brennan, Justice Marshall, and Justice Blackmun, evaluated the meaning of cruel and unusual punishment according to "evolving standards of decency that mark the progress of a maturing society." In applying this standard to the given case, the Court first reviewed the history of laws that set different standards, rights, and responsibilities for children and adults. Although the Court recognized that "the line between childhood and adulthood is drawn in different ways by various states . . . [t]here is, however, complete or near unanimity among all 50 states and the District of Columbia in treating a person under 16 as a minor for several important purposes." The Court cited age restrictions on voting, driving, marrying without parental consent, and gambling, among others in the argument. Most persuasive, perhaps, was the argument that no state at that time set the maximum age for juvenile court jurisdiction at lower than 16.

While the Court acknowledged that most states had not set a minimum age at which an offender could be sentenced to death, of the eighteen states that had explicitly addressed the question, all had set the minimum age at 16 or higher.

The Court also considered policies in other western nations of similar heritage that did not allow for the execution of juveniles; the positions of professional organizations such as the American Bar Association and the America Law Institute, which had formally opposed the imposition of the death penalty on offenders who were juveniles at the time of their offense; and the behavior of juries. Regarding the latter, the Court relied on Department of Justice Statistics that showed, of the 1,393 persons sentenced to death between 1982 and 1986, only 5 were under the age of 16 at the time of the offense.

In a concurrent line of reasoning, the Court also addressed the proposed culpability of a juvenile, and it declared that "less culpability should attach to a crime committed by a juvenile than to a comparable crime committed by an adult" and that "the reasons why juveniles are not trusted with the privileges and responsibilities of an adult also explain why their irresponsible conduct is not as morally reprehensible as that of an adult." In one final line of reasoning, the Court also shot down the deterrence effect, or purpose of imposing the death penalty on a juvenile under 16, noting that youth under this age account for less than 2 percent of all such crimes.

Dissent. Justices Scalia, Rehnquist, and White dissented from the majority opinion in this case. In writing the dissent, Justice Scalia focused primarily on the notion that the Court used too broad a brush in painting the immaturity of youth, by suggesting that no juvenile, even one day before his or her 16th birthday, could be fully culpable and responsible for his or her crime. In his opinion, Scalia appeared to lean on some of the principles of English common law, discussed earlier in this text; he believed that, while it might be appropriate to grant such a youth the "rebuttable presumption" that he is not mature and responsible enough to be punished as an adult, such a case should still be left to the courts to decide on an individual basis. That is, the prosecution could prove that, for this particular juvenile, in this particular crime, he or she did possess *mens rae* and should be punished in the same manner as an adult who committed a similar crime. In support of his position, Scalia posited that:

William Wayne Thompson is not a juvenile caught up in a legislative scheme that unthinkingly lumped him together with adults for purposes of determining that death was an appropriate penalty for him and for his crime. To the contrary, Oklahoma first gave careful consideration to whether, in light of his young age, he should be subjected to the normal criminal system at all. That question having been answered affirmatively, a jury then considered whether, despite his young age, his maturity and moral responsibility were sufficiently developed to justify the sentence of death.

The dissent, therefore, rests that, in this particular case, the facts were weighed appropriately; and furthermore, that there may exist other juveniles under the age of 16 who are fully culpable for their crimes and who, upon careful consideration of the circumstances of the case by a judge and jury, should be sentenced to death.

Comments. Although the 1980s and 1990s were a time of getting tough on juveniles, we see here, in the reasoning of the Supreme Court, the retention of some of the original ideas about juveniles and juvenile delinquency proposed by the child-savers. Primarily, this viewpoint is that juveniles are not yet fully mature, therefore they are not fully responsible for their actions and should receive mitigated punishments. However, the Court falls short of suggesting that all youths can be rehabilitated, and instead it focuses on the fact that imposing the death penalty, rather than life without parole, would not have a deterrence effect that would increase public safety. Also, it should be noted that counsel in this case, as well as various *amici curiae*, asked the Court to set the bar higher, drawing the line for execution at age 18. The Court rejected this proposal, choosing instead to "decide the case before us."

Stanford v. Kentucky (1989)

Facts. On January 17, 1981, Kevin Stanford and an accomplice robbed a gas station at which Baerbel Poore was working as an attendant. During the course of the robbery, 20-year-old Poore was raped, sodomized, and finally shot to death. In justifying the shooting, Stanford told the police that he had to shoot her because she lived next door to him and could have identified him. Stanford was tried in adult court, convicted of first-degree murder, and sentenced to death. At the federal level, this case was combined with a similar case, *Wilkins v. Missouri* (1989), in which 16-year-old Heath Wilkins stabbed to death an attendant at a convenience store he was robbing. In this brutal murder, Wilkins and his accomplice immediately stabbed the attendant upon entering the store. Not yet dead, the attendant, 26-year-old Nancy Moore, offered to help Stevens when he had trouble opening the cash register. Wilkins responded by stabbing her in the chest three more times. As she begged for her life, he stabbed her an additional four times in the neck, opening her carotid artery and causing her death. Wilkins was convicted of first-degree murder and sentenced to death.

Issue. Does the imposition of the death penalty on an individual for a crime committed at the ages of 16 or 17 years of age constitute "cruel and unusual punishment" under the Eighth Amendment?

Decision. The Court concluded that capital punishment imposed on offenders who had reached the age of 16 or 17 at the time of the offense "does not offend the Eighth Amendment's prohibition against cruel and unusual punishment."

Reasons. In this decision, Justice Scalia was in the position of writing for the plurality rather than for the dissent. He began, however, with relatively the same argument regarding the importance of individualized consideration of factors related to maturity and judgment, stating that:

> There is no relevance to the state laws cited by petitioners which set 18 or more as the legal age for engaging in various activities, ranging from driving to drinking alcoholic beverages to voting. Those laws operate in gross, and do not conduct individualized maturity tests for each driver, drinker, or voter; an age appropriate in the vast majority of cases must therefore be selected. In the realm of capital punishment, however, individualized consideration is a constitutional requirement.

In this decision, the Court again addressed the notion of a national consensus regarding evolving standards of decency. Looking to the eighteen states that had set a minimum age for the death penalty, they noted that fifteen of the eighteen states prohibited its imposition in cases in which the defendant was 16 years old at the time of the offense, and twelve states prohibited its use in cases against 17-year-old defendants. More important, however, they conferred upon those states that have set no minimum age the status of having approved the execution of minors, since they do not directly prohibit such a practice. Overall, these differences are interpreted to represent a general lack of national consensus regarding the appropriateness of capital punishment for youths of 16 and 17 years of age.

Interestingly, the Court again looked to Department of Justice statistics to note that of the 2,106 death sentences imposed between 1982 and 1988, only 15 were on youths 16 and under, and only 30 on youths 17 and under. However, in this instance, the Court then turned to the fact that juveniles are much less likely to commit homicide than adults, in order to account for this difference and to declare that these statistics "are of little significance."

Finding no national consensus on the issue and the statistics unconvincing, the Court rejected arguments by outside professional agencies and public-opinion polls, saying that "a revised national consensus so broad, so clear and so enduring as to justify a permanent prohibition upon all units of democratic government must appear in the operative acts (laws and the application of laws) that the people have approved."

In the final portions of the decision, the Court rejected the notion that no 16-year-old is "adequately responsible" for his or her actions or "significantly deterred," saying that social science, and even purely scientific evidence, simple cannot prove this fact.

Dissent. Justice Brennan, in writing the dissent (joined by Justices Marshal, Blackmun, and Stevens), began by acknowledging that, while the Court addressed some of the primary determinants of evolving standards of decency, they misinterpreted much of the evidence and ignored others. For instance, the dissent used slightly different mathematical techniques to "add together" the existing state legislation, as follows:

Currently, 12 of the States whose statutes permit capital punishment specifically mandate that offenders under age 18 not be sentenced to death. When one adds to these 12 States the 15 (including the District of Columbia) in which capital punishment is not authorized at all, it appears that the governments in fully 27 of the States have concluded that no one under 18 should face the death penalty. A further three States explicitly refuse to authorize sentences of death for those who committed their offense when under 17, *ante* at 492 U. S. 370, n. 2, making a total of 30 States that would not tolerate the execution of petitioner Wilkins. Congress' most recent enactment of a death penalty statute also excludes those under 18.

The dissent also disagreed with the plurality's decision to discount the opinion of professional organizations, noting that "Where organizations with expertise in a relevant area have given careful consideration to the question of a punishment's appropriateness, there is no reason why that judgment should not be entitled to attention as an indicator of contemporary standards." In general, then, the arguments of the dissent followed the same basic logic as they had when they were the arguments for the plurality just one year earlier.

Comments. In this decision, the Court considered many of the same factors as in the previous *Thompson* decision; however, it viewed them behind a lens with a different focus. Although fifteen of the eighteen states (83%) that set a minimum age for execution prevented the execution of 16-year-olds, they did not feel this represented a national consensus. In the previous case, the Court disregarded the nineteen states that allowed for the death penalty but did not set a minimum age as simply having not addressed the issue. In this case, we see instead the Court interpreted this lack of a minimum age as a statement that, in these nineteen states, the legislature believes it okay to execute youths.

In the *Thompson* case, the Court also relied on the behavior of juries, public opinion, and the position of public-interest groups. Regarding the behavior of juries, the Court had indicated that execution was a cruel and unusual punishment, since it was applied to only five youths in the time period studied. Although the statistics showed still relatively few youths sentenced to death by juries at the ages of 16 and 17, the Court now chose to interpret these statistics differently. Now, the focus was instead on the fact that relatively few juveniles as compared to adults commit murder, which is proposed to explain the discrepancy.

In the *Thompson* case, the Court used the fact that less than 2 percent of all convicted murderers are juveniles, to further purport that the imposition of the death penalty on youths serves no legitimate deterrence purpose. In this case, however, the Court failed to accept this portion of the argument, but it honed in instead on the fact that it couldn't be proven *not* to deter.

The discrepancies between the Court's reasoning in these two decisions, while at first may seem surprising, actually is merely a reflection of the same reasoning applied as the plurality in one case and as a dissent in the other. That is, for the most part, the primary arguments remained the same. Moreover, both cases were decided by a close vote—of 5 to 3 in the *Thompson* decision (Justice Kennedy not participating) and a vote of 5 to 4 in the *Stanford* decision. Clearly, the justices remained divided on this issue.

Roper v. Simmons (2005)

Facts. Christopher Simmons, age 17, along with two juvenile accomplices (ages 15 and 16) plotted to commit a burglary and murder. The night of the murder, the three met at about 2:00 AM; however, one companion changed his mind and left. Simmons and his friend then entered the home of Shirley Crook by reaching through an open window and unlocking the back door to the house. Simmons used duct tape to cover the victim's eyes and mouth, as well as to bind her hands. The two placed Mrs. Crook in her own minivan and drove to a nearby state park. Covering her head with a towel, they walked her to a railroad trestle over the Meramec River. Before throwing her into the river, they further bound her feet and hands with electrical wire and wrapped her entire head in duct tape, and then threw her to her death.

Simmons was arrested several days later, after bragging about the murder. He waived his right to an attorney and agreed to a videotaped reenactment of the crime for police. In Missouri, the juvenile court has original jurisdiction for youths up to age 16, meaning that Simmons, age 17, was automatically tried as an adult. Based on his confession and the videotaped reenactment, he was convicted and sentenced to death. Simmons appealed first on the basis of ineffective counsel, which was denied. After these proceedings, Simmons's attorney filed a new petition for state postconviction relief under the *Atkins v. Virginia* decision (2002), in which the Supreme Court ruled that the Eighth and Fourteenth Amendments prohibit the execution of a mentally retarded person. The Missouri Supreme Court agreed, then dismissed Simmons's death sentence and resentenced him to life imprisonment without eligibility for parole.

Issue. Was the Missouri Supreme Court correct in determining that the execution of a youth who was under the age of 18 at the time of his crime violates the Eighth and Fourteenth Amendments of the United States Constitution?

Decision. The Court affirmed the decision of the Missouri Supreme Court, stating that the "Eighth and Fourteenth Amendments forbid imposition of the death penalty on offenders who were under the age of 18 when their crimes were committed."

Reasons. The Court first returned to the notion of "evolving standards of decency" and searched for evidence of a national consensus against the death penalty for minors under the age of 18. Using similar "calculation" techniques on state law as used in the *Thompson v. Oklahoma* decision, the Court noted that thirty states prohibited the imposition of the death penalty on juveniles, with twelve states specifically rejecting the death penalty altogether and eighteen states prohibiting its application to juveniles. The Court also noted that in the twenty states that did permit the imposition of the death penalty, only three states had actually imposed the death penalty on a juvenile within the past ten years. The Court also pointed to an emerging trend in which, since the time of the *Stanford* decision, five states that had allowed for the execution of 16- and/or 17-year-olds had revised their laws to prohibit its use.

The Court then turned to its previous argument used in the *Thompson* decision, which asserted that the death penalty should be reserved for "a narrow category of the most serious crimes" and for those offenders whose "extreme culpability makes them the most deserving of execution." The Court proposed that there are three scientifically proven differences between juveniles under the age of 18 and adults that "demonstrate that juvenile offenders cannot with reliability be classified among the worst offenders." In summary, these differences are:

1. That lack of maturity and an underdeveloped sense of responsibility are found in youths more often than in adults, and that these qualities lead to impulsive and "ill-considered actions and decisions"[28]
2. That juveniles are more vulnerable or susceptible to negative influences and peer pressure[29]
3. That the character of a juvenile is not as well formed as that of an adult, meaning that personality traits of juveniles are more "transitory"[30]

The Court further maintained that "once the diminished culpability of juveniles is recognized, it is evident that the penological justifications for the death penalty [retribution and deterrence] apply with lesser force than to adults." The petitioner in this case specifically argued that the death penalty should be allowed for juveniles, but that age should serve as a mitigating factor in determining the culpability of the offender and, therefore, the appropriateness of a death sentence. The Court addressed and rejected this argument, stating that:

The differences between juvenile and adult offenders are too marked and well understood to risk allowing a youthful person to receive the death penalty despite insufficient culpability. An unacceptable likelihood exists that the brutality or cold-blooded nature of any particular crime would overpower mitigating arguments based on youth as a matter of course, even where the juvenile offender's objective immaturity, vulnerability, and lack of true depravity should require a sentence less severe than death.

In the final portion of this decision, the Court turned its focus to what it called the "stark reality" that the Unites States is the only country in the world that still supports the death penalty for juveniles in its legal doctrine. Although we are not bound as a nation by the opinions and actions of other nations, the Court placed heavy emphasis on the fact that the United Kingdom, upon which our original laws were modeled, abolished the death penalty for juveniles years before. The Court also used the global rejection of the death penalty for juveniles as an even greater indicator of the universal truth that there are inherent differences between juvenile and adult offenders that rest "in large part on the understanding that the instability and emotional imbalance of young people may often be a factor in the crime."

Dissent. There were two distinct dissents in this opinion—one written by Justice O'Connor and another by Justice Scalia, who was joined in his opinion by Justice Thomas and Chief Justice Rehnquist. The primary argument presented by Justice O'Connor was that there was not compelling evidence that a national consensus against the imposition of the death penalty on any offender under the age of 18 had emerged since the Court handed down its earlier decision in *Stanford*. In her argument, Justice O'Connor acknowledged that while a similar number of states (30) forbade the death penalty for a juvenile under the age of 18, as had forbade the same for a mentally retarded offender at the time the Court handed down its decision in *Atkins*, that this alone was not evidence of a national consensus and that the Court applied additional principles in *Atkins* that simply did not apply in this case. Specifically, she argued that:

> For purposes of proportionality analysis, 16-year-olds as a class are qualitatively and materially different from the mentally retarded. Mentally retarded offenders, as we understood that category in Atkins are defined by precisely the characteristics which render death an excessive punishment. . . . There is no such inherent or accurate fit between an offender's chronological age and the personal limitations which the Court believes make capital punishment excessive for 17-year-old murderers.

The dissent presented by Justice Scalia is more scathing, going beyond merely disagreeing with the ultimate conclusion of the Court but accusing the current Court of proclaiming "itself sole arbiter of our Nation's moral standards." Reverting first to the difference in "counting" schemes used between the *Thompson* and *Stanford* decisions, Justice Scalia argued that those states that ban the death penalty altogether should not be counted as forbidding it specifically for juveniles. The dissent further noted that while four states had banned the death penalty for juveniles since *Stanford*, two states that previously had not set a minimum age, specifically readdressed the question and set that age at 16 (Missouri and Virginia).

The dissent also took offense at the plurality's reliance on opinions outside of the nation's legislatures as relevant to the case. Most strikingly, the dissent argued that the plurality erroneously looked at the opinions of foreign nations, which bode no purpose in interpreting our nation's Constitution. The dissent also accused the Court of handpicking the sociological and scientific studies used to support its own viewpoint on the mitigated culpability of youths, rather than choosing those studies representative of sound research. In support of this notion, Justice Scalia spotlighted the American Psychological Association (APA) as having presented arguments against the death penalty for juveniles that were based on those youths' diminished decision-making capabilities. However, the dissent noted that the APA, when writing earlier in support of allowing juveniles to obtain abortions without parental permission, had presented evidence suggesting that juveniles had decision-making capabilities *similar to* adults.

Comments. The line of reasoning the Court followed in the *Simmons* case is quite similar to the previous arguments; however, it seems to rely more heavily on psychological and developmental evidence regarding the culpability of youths in determining the proportionality of punishment. This decision made two important determinations that we feel may indicate future directions for juvenile justice.

First, it returned the focus to the fact that the offender is a child instead of just a "small" criminal. Here, the Supreme Court said that the juvenile offender is emotionally and cognitively different from the adult offender. But different in what ways? Most simply, he or she is not done developing. The juvenile offender is impulsive by nature, owing to immaturity and lack of judgment. The juvenile offender, as proposed by the original child-savers, is susceptible to negative influences in the environment, over which he or she has no control. And finally, the Court noted that the fact that "juveniles still struggle to define their identity means it is less supportable to conclude that even a heinous crime committed by a juvenile is evidence of irretrievably depraved character." Or in more simple terms, the juvenile is not yet fully developed and can be rehabilitated into a productive adult citizen, if only we remove him or her from the negative influences and provide a nurturing, caring environment.

Second, we suggest that this decision could be extended to propose that since children are so different from adults, adult punishments in general—not merely the death penalty—are an unfitting social response.

Rethinking the Boundary Between Juvenile and Criminal Court

One of our arguments in this book has been that ideas about juvenile justice ultimately are based on ideas about juvenile delinquency and about juvenile delinquents. In this chapter, we see this theme being played out one more time.

Up until the early 1800s, people viewed juveniles as fundamentally similar to adults, so juveniles were processed in the same criminal justice system as adults, although they were given some accommodation because of their age—for example, mitigation of punishments.

The founders of the separate system of juvenile justice took the opposite view. They thought that juvenile delinquents were fundamentally different from adult criminals: delinquents were "malleable" whereas criminals were "hardened." This view of delinquents led to the view that juvenile justice needed to be a separate and quite different system of justice. It was to be a mechanism—first the House of Refuge and later the juvenile court—that would shape these malleable young offenders into law-abiding and productive adult citizens. Similar mechanisms would not work with hardened adult offenders who, in their view, should simply be punished for their offenses.

In the series of decisions on juvenile justice policy handed down in the 1960s and 1970s, the Supreme Court tried to have it both ways. On the one hand, it suggested that juvenile delinquents were fundamentally similar to adult criminals—both were defendants who were presumed innocent until proven guilty and were entitled to the due process protections provided in the Constitution. Certain modifications were made to accommodate juveniles' particular situation—no right to jury trial, a requirement that an "interested adult" be present during interrogations, etc.—but a fundamental similarity remained. On the other hand, the Supreme Court then argued that juvenile justice should be fundamentally different: at the disposition stage, juvenile courts should focus on the juveniles' best interests, rather than simply punishing them for their offenses.

In a practical sense, this idea seemed to make a fair amount of sense at the time, but in fact it tried to merge one idea of juvenile delinquents with a contrasting idea of juvenile justice. It quickly became apparent that this merger simply would not work. Instead, it soon gave way to the "get tough" movement, which transformed the idea of juvenile delinquents as merely physically smaller criminals into a juvenile justice policy that reflected that idea.

With the *Simmons* decision, there is a sense in which the Supreme Court was returning to the view that juveniles are not merely small versions of adults. Research since that time has continued to expose inherent differences between adolescents and adults through more scientific means, such as MRI depictions of brain functions, and advancements in child and adolescent psychology.[31] This new knowledge is leading us back to viewing youths as fundamentally different from adults and, therefore, juvenile delinquents as fundamentally different from adult criminals.

Perhaps, a new definition is that they are not merely needy children who are at risk of becoming paupers or committing minor crimes but, rather, children who, because of their underdeveloped lack of reasoning and susceptibility to negative environmental influences, are capable of committing serious crimes they do not themselves even understand. This means that juvenile delinquents require a fundamentally different system of justice.

This new definition would suggest that even when a youth commits the most serious of crimes, he or she does not fully understand the ramifications, nor is he or she fully culpable for the crime in the sense that an adult offender would be. This is the primary line of reasoning relied upon by the Supreme Court in the *Simmons* decision.

If the Supreme Court's reasoning in this case is indicative of greater public sentiment, then according to our basic premise, policy changes should follow. If the definitions of the juvenile delinquent and juvenile delinquency are indeed shifting, then the focus of juvenile justice should shift as well. In the following chapter, we continue to explore changes in the nation's juvenile justice policy into the twenty-first century, both as these changes fit within the lessons of history and as they suggest future directions.

NOTES

1. Franklin Zimring, *American Youth Violence* (New York: Oxford University Press, 2000).

2. Connecticut had previously lowered the age of maximum juvenile court jurisdiction to 15, but in 2007, the state enacted legislation to again increase the maximum age of juvenile court jurisdiction to 17.

3. *California Welfare and Institutional Code*, div. 2, pt. 1. ch. 2, sec. 707.

4. *Delaware Code*, title 10, secs. 921 and 1010.

5. *42 Pennsylvania Consolidated Statutes*, sec. 6355.

6. Howard Snyder and Melissa Sickmund, *Juvenile Offenders and Victims: A National Report* (Washington, D.C.: Office Juvenile Justice and Delinquency Prevention, U.S. Department of Justice, 2006).

7. *New Hampshire Title XII*, secs. 168:1 and 169-B.

8. *Nevada Revised Statutes*, secs. 62.080 and 62.081.

9. Patrick Griffin, *Different from Adults: An Updated Analysis of Juvenile Transfer and Blended Sentencing Laws, with Recommendations for Reform. Models for Change, Systems Reform in Juvenile Justice* (Pittsburgh: National Center for Juvenile Justice, 2008).

10. *Virginia Code* §16.1–269.1.

11. Snyder and Sickmund, *Juvenile Offenders and Victims*, 112.

12. Ibid., 186.

13. Florida Department of Juvenile Justice, *Trends in the Transfer of Juveniles to Adult Criminal Court* (Tallahassee:, 2002).

14. Snyder and Sickmund, *Juvenile Offenders and Victims*, 113.

15. Ibid.

16. Ibid.

17. Ibid.

18. Ibid., 236, 238.

19. Donna M. Hamparian, Linda K. Estep, Susan Muntean, Ramon R. Priestine, Robert G. Swisher, Paul L. Wallace, and Joseph L. White, *Major Issues in Juvenile Justice Information and Training: Youth in Adult Courts—Between Two Worlds* (Washington, D.C.: Office of Juvenile Justice and Delinquency Prevention, U.S. Department of Justice, 1982); M. A. Bortner, "Traditional Rhetoric, Organizational Realities: Remand of Juveniles to Adult Court," *Crime and Delinquency* 32, no. 1 (1986): 53–73; and Jeffrey Fagan, *The Comparative Impacts of Juvenile and Criminal Court Sanctions on Adolescent Offenders* (Washington, D.C.: Office of Justice Programs, U.S. Department of Justice, 1991).

20. Richard Redding, "Examining Legal Issues: Juvenile Offenders in Criminal Court and Adult Prison," *Corrections Today* 61 (1999): 92–124.

21. Megan Kurlychek and Brian D. Johnson, "The Juvenile Penalty: A Comparison of Juvenile and Young Adult Sentencing Outcomes in Adult Criminal Court," *Criminology* 42, no. 2 (2004): 485–517.

22. Donna Bishop and C. E. Frazier, "Consequences of Transfer," in Jeffrey Fagan and Frank Zimring, eds., *The Changing Boundaries of Juvenile Justice: Transfer of Adolescents to Criminal Court* (Chicago: University of Chicago Press, 2000), 227–276; and L. Winner, L. Lanza-Kaduce, Donna Bishop, and C. E. Frazier, "The Transfer of Juveniles to Criminal Court: Reexamining Recidivism over the Long Term," *Crime and Delinquency* 43, no.4 (1997): 548–563.

23. Michelle Leighton and Connie de la Vega, *Sentencing Our Children to Die in Prison* (San Francisco: University of San Francisco School of Law, 2007); see also Human Rights Watch, *The Rest of Their Lives: Life without Parole for Child Offenders in the United States* (New York, N.Y.: Human Rights Watch/ Amnesty International, 2005).

24. Henry Weinstein, "Focus on Youth Sentences," *Los Angeles Times*, November 9, 2007, B4.

25. Human Rights Watch, *The Rest of Their Lives*.

26. Ibid.

27. Howard Snyder, *Juvenile Arrests 2006* (Washington, D.C.: Office of Juvenile Justice and Delinquency Prevention, U.S. Department of Justice, 2006).

28. In writing the majority decision, Justice Kennedy referenced several psychological and sociological studies, including Jeffrey Arnett, "Reckless Behavior in Adolescence: A Developmental Perspective," *Developmental Review* 12 (1992): 339; Lawrence Steinberg and Elizabeth Scott, "Less Guilty by Reason of Adolescence: Developmental Immaturity, Diminished Responsibility and the Juvenile Death Penalty," *American Psychologist* 58 (2003): 1009–1114; and Erik Erikson, *Identity, Youth and Crisis* (New York: Norton, 1968). Further discussion of differences in adult and adolescent decision making can be found in Lawrence Steinberg and Robert Schwartz. "Developmental Psychology Goes to Court," in Tom Grisso and Robert Schwartz, eds., *Youth on Trial: A Developmental Perspective on Juvenile Justice* (Chicago: University of Chicago Press, 2000).

29. Ibid.

30. Ibid.

31. J. Giedd, J. Blumenthal, N. Jeffries, F. Castellanos, H. Liu, A. Zijdenbos, T. Paus, A. Evans, and J. Rapoport, "Brain Development During Childhood and Adolescence: A Longitudinal MRI Study," *Nature Neuroscience* 2, no.10 (1999), 861–863.

10

Juvenile Justice in the Twenty-first Century

In the *Simmons* decision, the U.S. Supreme Court issued a very narrow verdict based on very broad reasons. The decision applied only to juveniles processed as adults and forbid only the most severe penalty—the death sentence. But the reasons for the decision implied a great deal more. In fact, those reasons form the basis for the differential treatment of juveniles and adults throughout the justice system.

This also was the situation with the *Kent* decision, handed down in 1966. That decision itself was very narrow: it applied only to the District of Columbia and it applied only to a single aspect of juvenile processing that is infrequently used—the judicial waiver. However, the reasons for that decision had enormous implications for the overall practices of the juvenile court, particularly in the Court's suggestion that "studies and critiques in recent years raise serious questions as to whether actual performance measures well enough against theoretical purpose to make tolerable the immunity of the process from the reach of constitutional guaranties applicable to adults." This language suggested that the Court was ready to consider further constitutional guarantees in juvenile court, which it did in the *Gault* and *Winship* decisions. We think there are similarities between these cases, in that the reasoning of the *Simmons* decision has very broad implications for juvenile justice as a whole—much broader than the specific issue of the death penalty, to which it was applied.

First, the Court based its reasoning heavily on recent scientific research that documents the cognitive and emotional differences that distinguish children from adults. These findings show that juveniles are less capable of understanding the consequences of their actions and are more susceptible to outside pressures, than are adults. They also show that juveniles are more amenable to rehabilitation efforts. This scientific research applies to all adolescents, not just adolescents who commit murder; thus, its implications for judicial processing apply to all adolescents, not just those who commit murder. And those implications, if taken seriously, clearly require that all adolescents must be processed differently by the justice system than are adults. We would go as far as to suggest that they imply the need for a separate and different system of juvenile justice.

Second, the Court's reasoning continued to rely on the concept of "evolving standards of decency" in determining what constitutes "cruel and unusual punishment." The nature of this assessment inherently encompasses the broader social consensus incorporating existing law, statements and positions of leading professional organizations, and public opinion. Thus, if the evolving standards of decency suggest that children under the age of 18 are inherently different from adults, the concept of differential treatment for juveniles may then have an impact beyond the mere imposition of the death penalty. Indeed, we believe that there *is* a growing national sentiment that children are different from adults and that the *Simmons* decision may be a beacon alerting us to further change on the horizon.

Finally, we believe that the *Simmons* decision comes at a time when the cycle of juvenile justice, as described in this book, has taken another turn . We have gotten so "tough" on juveniles that we have reached the point of the "forced choice." Because of limited options, juvenile justice officials frequently must choose between harshly punishing juveniles and doing nothing at all, and they see both of these choices as enhancing future criminality. This is when we, as a society, are ready for the large structural changes that mark a return to lenient treatments.

We believe those changes are already under way. In this chapter, we explore recent changes in the juvenile system as they suggest either a continuation of the "get tough" policies of the recent past—indications that officials may be facing a "forced choice"—or the reintroduction of lenient treatments, or both.

The End of "Get Tough" Legislation

After a rash of "get tough" legislation in the 1990s, not much has changed in recent years that would suggest a furthering of this trend. For example, between 1992 and 1997, forty-five states expanded waiver or transfer mechanisms, making it easier to try and sentence juveniles as adults.

Between 2002 and 2004, only four states have altered their transfer provisions, and in only two of these states did the alteration expand them.[1] Between 1992 and 1997, thirty-one states enacted juvenile blended sentencing and enhanced sentencing provisions for juveniles, but since 2000 there have been no further additions. Based on the data, it appears that the climax of the "get tough" movement was reached during the late-1990s, and since that time movement in the direction of further harshness has come to a halt.

The recent absence of "get tough" legislation could have various interpretations. First, it could simply mean that we are happy with the changes that have been made and content with the current state of the juvenile justice system. History would suggest that such contentment is unlikely, however. On the other hand, it could mean that we have reached a point of saturation, at which we feel the current "get tough" policies have provided an oversupply of harsh punishments and have limited other choices for responding to juvenile delinquency.

If we have reached such a point of saturation, then we would expect to find that, in addition to no further movement in the direction of harshness, the current harsh choices would be meeting increasing resistance from those who work in the juvenile justice system. That is, these officials would be facing the "forced choice," in which they have many options for harshly punishing juvenile offenders but few options for providing lenient treatment. In our theory of the cycle of juvenile justice, this is the stage that immediately precedes the reintroduction of lenient treatments.

Avoiding Harsh Punishments

In addition to the lack of further movement in the "get tough" direction, there's another indicator that we have reached a turn in the cycle of juvenile justice: that juvenile justice workers are trying to find ways to avoid implementing penalties they view as too harsh. This could manifest itself in many forms and would vary greatly from jurisdiction to jurisdiction, but we can note several developments that suggest this is happening at the present time.

First, in 2003, Connecticut raised its maximum age of juvenile court jurisdiction. Connecticut had been one of the states that previously set the upper limit at the 16th birthday, so that all 16-year-olds were legally considered adults in regard to justice system processing. Then, this state became the first in recent history to *raise* the age of juvenile court jurisdiction, bringing it back up to the 18th birthday.

More recently, in 2007, the North Carolina Sentencing and Policy Advisory Commission released a report to the state's legislature with five recommendations for improving its justice system. The first recommendation read: "Increase the age of juvenile jurisdiction to persons who, at the time they commit a crime infraction, are under the age of 18."

Although no such legislation has to date been passed, we believe that this sentiment, combined with the Connecticut legislation, provide early indicators that the "get tough" era might be coming to an end.[2]

Second, several states have adopted a mechanism called *reverse waiver*, for sending juveniles in the adult system back to the juvenile justice system.[3] This mechanism provides a pathway out of the adult criminal justice system for youths whom court officials believe were inappropriately transferred, owing to prosecutorial discretion or statutory exclusion. Employed by twenty-two states, this mechanism provides for a *Kent*-like waiver hearing held in criminal court at the request of the defense attorney, intended for juveniles who were transferred to the adult system by a means other than a judicial waiver. At this hearing, the burden of proof is on the defense to prove that the youth is still amenable to treatment and should be returned to the juvenile system for processing. Unfortunately, states are not currently tracking the use of this provision, in either adult or juvenile court data, thus other than knowing that the statutes exist, we cannot assess the popularity of their use.

Third, several states have introduced blended sentencing into the criminal courts.[4] In general, blended sentencing allows a judge in one court to apply sanctions from either or both systems. In the last chapter, we discussed blended sentencing in the juvenile court, which allows the juvenile court judge to sentence juveniles to the more punitive adult correctional system. This was one of the "get tough" measures that helped transform the juvenile court into more of a criminal court. But the opposite is true when blended sentencing is introduced into the criminal courts. In this situation, youths are tried and convicted in criminal court, but the criminal court judge has the option of determining that a sanction or treatment available in the juvenile correctional system is more fitting than one in the adult correctional system. In essence, this change partially transforms the criminal court into something more like the juvenile court. At least seventeen states have adopted this form of blended sentencing.[5]

Fourth, prosecutors in at least some locations are declining to prosecute youths in criminal courts, even when required to do so by law.[6] For example, in South Carolina, statutory exclusion and mandatory waiver provide for the automatic adult processing of youths over 14 who are accused of certain types of crimes, including sexual offenses. However, in a recent review of actions in two of the largest counties, almost every juvenile whose offense would have required a mandatory waiver based on the original charge was allowed to "plead" to a lesser offense that did not require transfer. This was particularly true for sex offenses, which would have the added penalty of placing the youths on the sex-offender registry. In over 90 percent of those charges, offenders were allowed to plead guilty to aggravated assault, which does not involve a mandatory transfer and has no registry requirement.[7] This suggests that prosecutors in these counties regard these legal provisions as too harsh and are simply refusing to implement them.

Fifth, police are handling a slightly larger portion of their juvenile cases themselves and not referring them to the court system at all. Observational research finds that police handle about 85 percent of the juveniles they encounter without arresting them, a figure that has remained stable since the 1970s.[8] Among juveniles whom they do arrest, there has been a modest recent decline in the rate of referrals to the juvenile court. The most recent figures show that police refer 71 percent of all arrested juveniles to juvenile court. This represents a 58 percent increase over the referral rate in 1980, but it is a modest decrease from the 75 percent referral rate reported in 1997.[9] As with the juveniles whom they do not arrest at all, the police handle these cases informally, either by themselves or by referring the youths to voluntary social service agencies. For these youths, the harsher sanctions found in the court system are entirely avoided.

In addition, when police do refer arrested juveniles to the courts, there is at least some indication that they are adjusting the initial charges to avoid some of the harsher sanctions provided by the courts. For example, in 2003, the arrest rate of juveniles for aggravated assault had fallen 38 percent from its peak in 1994, while the arrest rate for simple assault had increased 10 percent over the same time period.[10] One interpretation of this change is that police are charging more juveniles with simple assault and fewer juveniles with aggravated assault. As a result, in 1980, there were twice as many juvenile arrests for simple assault as there were for aggravated assault, but by 2003, there were four times as many of these arrests, with most of the growth occurring after the mid-1990s.[11]

This shift from aggravated to simple assault could reflect true changes in juvenile offending, or it could reflect changes in the initial charging decisions made by police at the time of arrest. In many states, when the police charge a juvenile with aggravated assault, harsh mandatory provisions are triggered that the police would certainly know about but over which they would have no control. In contrast, when police charge juveniles with simple assault, no such mandatory provisions are triggered.

In the 1970s, New York State enacted harsh provisions for juveniles who committed serious violent crimes, including aggravated assault. In response, police in upstate New York largely stopped filing aggravated assault charges against juveniles, and they greatly expanded their filings of simple assault charges.[12] It seems possible that this is now happening at the national level. While this is a speculative suggestion, such actions on the part of police would be consistent with the argument that police themselves think these responses simply are inappropriate for specific juveniles whom they arrest.

Finally, there is some indication that juvenile courts are also moving in a more lenient direction in disposition hearings, although not in adjudication hearings. Recent statistics show that juveniles are more likely to be handled with a formal adjudication hearing than they were in the past, and the overall adjudication rate has remained fairly stable at about two-thirds.[13] However, in disposition hearings, probation as an outcome for the case has continued to increase at a rate that outpaces residential placement as an outcome. Thus, there is at least some indication that juvenile courts are more lenient in the disposition stage as compared to a decade ago.[14] In addition, recent research on public preferences for rehabilitation versus the incarceration of juvenile offenders indicates that respondents would rather have tax dollars spent on rehabilitation and treatment of juvenile offenders than simply having them locked up.[15]

Recreating the Juvenile System within the Adult System

Another indicator that we have reached another spin of the cycle of juvenile justice is that some states are essentially recreating juvenile justice systems *within* their adult criminal justice systems in order to handle all the offenders under the age of 18 who are being processed there. This basically indicates that these offenders are inappropriate for the adult criminal justice system and that the juvenile system is, in fact, the appropriate place for them. Given that fact, one would have to wonder why these offenders are being processed in the adult system in the first place.

First, there is growing evidence that when dealing with youth, the adult criminal courts may actually be recreating the individual, offender focus of the juvenile court, at least at the sentencing stage. Aaron Kupchik observed a criminal court in New York City that was devoted exclusively to processing 13- to 15-year-olds as adults (in New York State, all 16-year-olds are legally adults).[16] He found that the trial phase of the proceeding was formal, adversarial, and offense-focused. As is true in criminal courts generally, the prosecution and defense contested the charges and the judge acted as the neutral referee. However, in the sentencing phase, the adversarial model was discarded and the proceedings became informal, nonadversarial, and offender-focused. All parties seemed to join in a common effort to determine what was best to do with this particular defendant. Most striking was the fact that the defendant often played a central role in the proceedings, typically in direct interactions with the judge. All of this is quite typical of dispositions in juvenile courts, but it would be rare to nonexistent in adult criminal courts.

Kupchik's description of this criminal court almost perfectly reflects the Supreme Court's vision of juvenile justice as the "best of both worlds": the adjudication (trial) phase would be similar to the adult criminal court with due process rights, while the disposition (sentencing) phase would be focused on the best interests of the child. Kupchik concludes that New York State has, at least to some extent, simply recreated the juvenile court within the adult court system in order to try these youth. Thus, his article asks whether this is criminal or juvenile justice.

Second, in response to the "get tough" policies that transferred greater numbers of youths to the adult system, several states have taken action to allow for the housing of youths under the age of 18 who are in the adult correctional system either in the juvenile system itself or in facilities run by the juvenile system. For example, in Delaware, when a youth under the age of 18 is sentenced to prison, the Department of Corrections works with the juvenile system to determine if the youth can be held in a juvenile facility until his or her 18th birthday.[17] In North Dakota, a similar decision is made by a five-person committee designed to review youth cases.[18] Utah has actually built separate facilities on the grounds of adult prisons to house juveniles sentenced as adults, and these facilities are run by the juvenile corrections system.[19]

Third, several states now offer additional programming for youths in the adult correctional system who are under 18, under 21, or even under 24. For example, the Florida Department of Corrections is mandated to separate those under 18 from other adults, and offenders 18 to 24 from older adults. These young offenders are then provided with academic, vocational education, social skills, and substance-abuse treatments not provided in the regular prisons.[20] Other state legislatures have similarly created special categories of offenders that are, using one term or another, generally classified as "youthful offenders," in order to ensure that these offenders are given special treatments. Examples of youthful offender laws and programming are on the books in Colorado, Kentucky, New Mexico, and Wisconsin.

Fourth, professional organization have taken positions on this topic Most notably, the American Bar Association (ABA) calls for the adult system to almost mimic the original intention of the juvenile system.[21] In a 2001 report entitled "Youth in the Criminal Justice System: Guidelines for Policymakers and Practitioners," the ABA set forth the following guiding principles:

1. Youths are developmentally different from adults and these differences should be taken into account.
2. Pretrial release or detention decisions regarding youths awaiting trial should reflect their special characteristics.
3. Detained or incarcerated youths should be housed in an institution or facility separate from adult institutions or facilities at least until they reach the age of 18.
4. Youths detained or incarcerated should be provided programs that address their educational, treatment, health, mental, and vocational needs.
5. Youths should not be permitted to waive the right to counsel without consultation with a lawyer and without a full inquiry into the youths' comprehension of the right and competency to make the choice intelligently, voluntarily, and understandingly.
6. Judges should consider the individual characteristics of the youths during sentencing.
7. Collateral consequences normally attendant to the justice process should not necessarily apply to all youths arrested for crimes committed before age 18.

This separation of housing and programming maintains the original intent of the founders of the juvenile court by separating juveniles from adults and by providing education and treatment rather than punishment, even when the youth is formally processed in the adult criminal justice system. Many of these mechanisms were enacted at the same time as, or immediately following, the "get tough" juvenile reforms that moved these youthful offenders into the adult system in the first place. This indicates that perhaps these reforms were an effort at public relations rather than actual system change. At least to some extent, the reforms were designed to silence the demand for harsh punishments coming from the public while allowing the system to continue doing what it always had been doing—treating juveniles differently from adults.

However, one real difference is that, once processed as adults, these youths can be kept in custody for much longer periods of time than would be provided in the juvenile system, even up to life without parole.

Thus, like blended sentences enacted in juvenile courts, these laws generally provide that the juveniles be transferred into the regular adult correctional system once they pass the specified age.

The Return of Juvenile Justice to a Treatment Philosophy

In addition, to these efforts by the adult system to provide differential treatment for youths, there appears to be growing sentiment that the juvenile system must return to a treatment philosophy. One telling sign is a state that has had enough with the "get tough" legislation. The report of the Blueprint Commission on Juvenile Justice, released by the Florida House of Representatives in February 2008, states that it is time to stop "getting tough" on juvenile crime and time to start "getting smart" about juvenile crime, as follows:

> Since the Department of Juvenile Justice was established in 1994, the State and the Department have taken a "Get Tough" approach to juvenile crime. Today, while overall juvenile crime rates are down, policy makers, experts in juvenile crime, youth advocates and community leaders agree that Florida's juvenile justice system lacks the capacity to provide the spectrum of services needed to significantly impact juvenile crime and public safety for the long term. It is time for Florida to "Get Smart" about juvenile justice.[22]

What exactly is the spectrum of services needed? Well, among other initiatives, the report specifically called for strengthening youth, families, and communities through prevention and intervention activities; the reevaluation and amendment of school zero-tolerance policies to avoid suspension, expulsion, and referral to court for all but the most serious offenses; expansion of home-detention and day and evening reporting centers to reduce the numbers of youths in preadjudicatory detention; provision of adequate health care, mental health care, and substance-abuse treatments to youths; and movement away from large prisonlike residential facilities to smaller, more homelike facilities. The report also called for reinstating the confidentiality of some juvenile records, especially first-time and minor offenders, and for special committees to be convened to explore the yet "unresolved" issues of processing youths as adults and the unfavorable practice of shackling juveniles in transit and in court.

The sentiments of this report clearly reflect the developmental ideal of children under 18 being fundamentally different from adults and in need of different treatment. In addition, it brings into question or calls for the reversal of several of the "get tough" changes, including implementation of zero-tolerance policies, reduced confidentiality of juvenile records, and processing of increasing numbers of juveniles as adults under this state's direct file policy.

Several professional organizations and committees on juvenile justice have begun to speak out on these issues, as well. The Children's Defense Fund, as part of its Cradle to Prison Pipeline campaign, has called for the nation to "stop detaining children and teens in adult jails" and to assign the highest priority to "prevention and early intervention strategies."[23] The National Council of Juvenile and Family Court Judges released a report in 2005 to help states create what it would define as the "model" juvenile court.[24] In this report, it called for juvenile courts to ensure that juvenile dispositions are individualized and provide graduated responses. The report then elaborated the eleven basic services every court should have available as responses, to include probation, restitution, community service, education, mental health, drug and substance abuse, day reporting and treatment centers, sex offender treatment, mental retardation and disability services, wrap-around services, and placement services including foster care, community placements, and nonsecure and secure residential placements. Finally, the Campaign for Youth Justice, a nonprofit organization based in Washington, D.C., is working to universally end "the practice of trying, sentencing, and incarcerating youth under the age of 18 in the adult criminal justice system."[25]

The Lessons of History

It appears that the pieces are in place to mark a turn in the cycle of juvenile justice. The *Simmons* decision by the U.S. Supreme Court concluded that juveniles differ from adults in fundamental ways. That conclusion was applied only to the death penalty, but it has broad implications about the need for an entirely separate and fundamentally different system of justice to process juveniles. In addition, it appears that a consensus is being reached that too many youths are being processed as adults, and that this is not the best approach to solving even very serious delinquency. There also are some indications that states are recreating juvenile justice within their criminal justice systems in order to appropriately handle all the juveniles who are being placed there. Finally, we find that states are moving their juvenile justice systems away from a focus on punishment and accountability, and back toward the individualized treatment approach to justice characterized by traditional juvenile justice.

In order, however, for these initiatives to expand and continue, we must see how well they fit with the lessons of history.

Lesson 1: The Cycle of Juvenile Justice. The widespread perception that juvenile crime rates are unusually high is accompanied by a widespread belief that these rates can be lowered by appropriate juvenile justice policies. This results in a continuous cycle of reform that consists of establishing lenient treatments in a major reform, gradually toughening up those treatments over a long time so that officials end up choosing between harsh punishments and doing nothing at all, and then reestablishing lenient treatments in another major reform.

The public probably still believes that juvenile crime is unusually high today, as compared to the "good old days" of the relatively recent past. But most people connected with juvenile justice are fully aware that juvenile crime is down significantly from its recent peaks. If nothing else, the "superpredator" fiasco established that fact.

With this in mind, many officials have been making attempts within the system to avoid the implication of what may be viewed as overly harsh punishments. The fact that the era of "get tough" legislation has ended and has begun to be replaced not only by rhetoric about leniency but also by actual legislation serves as an indicator that we are on the precipice of a major reform in line with what the cycle predicts.

Lesson 2: Ideas of Juvenile Delinquency. Ideas of delinquency that "sell" (i.e., that succeed in the competition with other possible ideas) propose that delinquents are a subgroup within some larger problem group (e.g., paupers, dependent and neglected children, criminal defendants) with which the public is already familiar. The prevailing idea of delinquency and delinquents thus drives the idea of what juvenile justice should be.

It seems that the new idea of juvenile delinquency being proposed stems from research in the fields of psychology and child development. This research suggests that most delinquents are a subgroup of normal adolescents, and most delinquent behaviors are within the realm of normal adolescent behaviors.

To put it in a simple and intuitive way, research shows that adolescents tend to overvalue immediate costs and benefits, and to be relatively unaware of and largely unconcerned about long-term costs and benefits.[26] Much more than adults, they live in the moment and make decisions about their behavior based on the immediate costs and benefits that the behavior provides.

In addition, adolescents tend to overvalue benefits, especially the immediate social benefits that come from interactions with their peers. In general, adolescents are extremely vulnerable to what other adolescents think about them. The "high drama" that is normal in many high schools is the ongoing saga of who thinks what about whom. Adults may find this behavior bizarre and even obsessive, or they may find it amusing. But most adults also know that it is entirely normal for adolescents to be this way, and so they try to be tolerant and understanding—and at least modestly sympathetic to the sufferings of adolescents who are so buffeted by the hurricane winds of this intense social world. Adults know that, in the long run, adolescents grow up and this kind of behavior fades away. But they also know that, in the short run, adolescent actions are heavily influenced by the immediate social pressures exerted by other adolescents.

Beyond that, adolescents have a strong tendency to underestimate costs of all kinds, especially large costs and long-term costs. They tend to think of themselves as insulated, almost immortal and invulnerable. In some deep-seated and utterly nonrational way, they genuinely believe that "nothing bad can ever happen" to them. They think they can get away with anything, and there never will be any consequences for their actions. As most adults know, many adolescents often are not in the least bit interested in the long-term costs of their present actions. Talking to them about that subject is like talking to a brick wall. It simply does not matter to them.

These characteristics of normal adolescent thinking mean that juveniles' normal decision making often is extremely distorted, at least as compared to what adults see as normal decision making. Their cost-benefit calculus is out of whack. Adolescents, for example, may take enormous risks with their lives and health and well-being, and jeopardize their futures, in order to avoid superficial and fleeting derision from a few discreditable peers. To adolescents, this seems to be not only reasonable but also extremely important, or even virtually mandatory. To adults, this seems so incredibly stupid that it is virtually incomprehensible.

Beyond this large group of essentially normal adolescents engaging in normal adolescent behavior, there is a second, much smaller group. The comparison of the *Simmons* case to the previous *Atkins* case, which dealt with the issue of mental health, may also indicate that at least some juvenile delinquents are a subgroup of persons suffering from mental illness. For these delinquents, their decision making is not only flawed by the normal characteristics of adolescence but also by other impairments of mood or personality. Each definition of a subgroup brings with it a related possible idea of juvenile justice.

Lesson 3: Ideas of Juvenile Justice. Responses to delinquency that "sell" (i.e., that succeed in the competition with other possible responses) are slightly modified versions of responses to the larger problem group of which delinquents are thought to be a subgroup (potential paupers, dependent and neglected children, criminal defendants, etc).

To the extent that delinquents are normal adolescents, and delinquency is normal adolescent behavior, then it is reasonable to expect that juvenile delinquents will simply "grow out of" this behavior as they mature to adulthood. As such, the appropriate idea of juvenile justice is similar to what parents have always thought about their adolescent children. In their treatment of these adolescents, the parents try, as much as possible, to prevent them from harming themselves and others while they are in this stage, and the parents do everything they can to get their adolescents to "grow out of" this stage as quickly as possible.

In the field of juvenile justice, the way to do this is to adapt many of the existing policies and practices of the mental health field. Indeed, many treatment models being proposed and implemented for the juvenile justice system involve individual and group therapy, techniques of behavioral modification, and, psychotropic medication. Many of these policies have been around as cornerstones of juvenile treatment for decades. For example, one of the standard practices in juvenile facilities is behavior modification. Based on fundamental principles of psychology regarding classical and operant conditioning, this approach emphases slowly teaching children the consequences of their actions through a basic punishments-and-rewards system.

This use of techniques from the field of psychology also fits well with the idea that there may be a smaller subgroup of juvenile delinquents who suffer from mental illnesses that lead to their criminal behavior. As suggested in the *Simmons* decision, these youths may have various psychological problems that interfere with and compromise their decision-making ability. In fact, recent estimates are that upwards of 80 percent of children in custody in the juvenile justice system suffer from some type of mental disorder. Often referred to as *comorbidity*, this combination of problems presents a model that assumes the crime or criminal behavior is just one of many possible manifestations of a larger underlying psychological disturbance.

For example, one of the most commonly diagnosed difficulties among these juveniles is attention deficit hyperactivity disorder (ADHD), in which a child is impulsive, has an unusually short attention span, and is hyperactive. According to the American Psychiatric Association's *Diagnostic and Statistical Manual of Mental Health Disorders* (DSM-IV), symptoms of ADHD include an inability to sustain concentration on schoolwork or tasks, inability to pay attention, frequent acting without thinking, being constantly on the go, and being easily distracted.[27] This disorder can lead to delinquency in a variety of ways, including both directly and through interactions with the school system, where ADHD children typically get into trouble and fail.

Other juveniles are diagnosed with even more serious mental conditions, such as bipolar mood disorder or even psychoses such as schizophrenia or paranoia, although these severe conditions are more rare. As these diagnoses continue to be made, we predict that we will see a return to the medical model of treatment for delinquents, relying more and more on treatment techniques from the fields of psychology and psychiatry, such as counseling, group therapy, and psychotropic medications to "reform" offenders.

This idea of juvenile justice, while seemingly new, really is a return to earlier methods employed by the juvenile court. Indeed, Dr. William Healy is credited with introducing the psychiatric approach to the treatment of juvenile delinquents as early as the 1920s.[28] Healy, a medical doctor, was recruited by the same reformers who worked to develop the first juvenile court; they wanted him to direct the Juvenile Psychopathic Institute to investigate the causes of delinquency. Greatly influenced by the work of G. Stanley Hall and Sigmund Freud, Healy argued that juvenile delinquents were primarily normal adolescents who were dealing with internal conflict owing to a variety of eclectic factors. In so doing, he promoted psychotherapy and other emerging psychological techniques as methods for "reforming" delinquents. Thus, while the idea of using a psychological approach to provide treatment and care through the juvenile justice system seems new and exciting, it is really a return to the practices and techniques in place decades ago.

Lesson 4: Economic Interests of the Rich and Powerful. Responses to delinquency that "sell" focus on the behavior of poor and powerless people but ignore the behavior of rich and powerful people. In particular, responses that focus on poor people's behavior do not harm the economic interests of the rich and powerful—that is, they aim to remove delinquents from the streets rather than change conditions on the streets.

Policy responses to delinquency will continue to focus on the delinquents and their families, rather than on the larger social conditions that give rise to the delinquency. As argued in chapter 3, delinquency is a modern phenomenon that originated at the same time as the birth of the modern era, when societies were transformed from rural and agricultural to urban and industrial. America and Western Europe went through this transformation around the year 1800, and other societies have undergone it in waves at various times since then. In virtually all cases, the problem of delinquency has emerged at the same time. The problem of delinquency is linked to the emergence of the concept of adolescence, which describes youths who are physically mature but as yet have no assigned role in society. Prior to this societal transformation, "adolescence" did not exist, as people of this young age in rural and agricultural societies simply assumed the role of adults.

There is no question that the modern problem of delinquency is generated by "the streets." It was possible to address the poor conditions of "the streets" at an earlier time, but no effort was made to do so. Instead, all effort went into trying to help poor youths fit into society as it was at the time. Similarly, today we could address the underlying causes of delinquency in a societal structure that largely excludes adolescents from productive roles, but there is virtually no chance that will be done—and perhaps, one could argue, that it should even be attempted. Instead, the cycle predicts that we will focus our attention yet again on correcting the impulsive and otherwise unacceptable behavior of the delinquents and "help" those with psychological symptoms to adjust to the realities of American society, which includes segregation, economic inequality, and both subjective and institutionalized forms of prejudice.

Lesson 5: Moral and Intellectual Superiority of Reformers. Responses to delinquency that "sell" imply that delinquents and their parents are morally and intellectually inferior, and that the reformers themselves are morally and intellectually superior.

We adults can feel superior to adolescents because we view their risk calculus as distorted, with its enormous overvaluing of immediate social benefits and its massive underestimation of costs, especially large, long-term costs. But that provides very little satisfaction of the kind that moral reformers usually like. Rather, as long as kids have been around, parents have known that one of their main tasks is to get their kids through this stage of life, without their incurring those large and long-term costs that adolescents so greatly underestimate. This, similarly, should be the goal of juvenile justice.

Beyond that, it is easy to see how a definition of the juvenile offender as suffering from a mental impairment maintains the superiority of the reformers. If we were to label the adolescent's impulsive behavior and inability to assess consequences as simply a fact of childhood, then this superiority would be diminished, as we could no longer easily differentiate between the child of a "good" family and one who is "delinquent." Therefore, while some minor offending might be the result of normal immaturity of judgment and self-control, defining more serious delinquency as the outward symptom of internal distress helps to maintain the superiority of the reformer. The reformers are of "sound" mind and can "help" these children by providing the proper treatments to rehabilitate or control their cognitive, intellectual, mood, or other impairments.

Initially, of course, we will have great faith in these proposed new "treatments." After all, they have been scientifically documented and researched. As per the reformers before us, we will have high expectations that these new programs can overcome the ailments of the youths in ways that mere punishment in the criminal justice system could not. The same optimism was held by people over a decade ago, believing that by punishing these young hoodlums they would "get the message" that crime doesn't pay and stop committing crimes. Obviously, their policy did not work, as we are, as always, on the verge or in the middle of a juvenile crime wave.

Lesson 6: The Unfair Comparison. Reformers "sell" their own reforms by an unfair comparison, in which a harsh assessment of actual practices of past policies is compared with an optimistic assessment of reforms, based on good intentions. Because they assume that good intentions directly translate into good practices, reformers promise to solve the problem of juvenile delinquency.

As just noted, we are optimistic that the new policies will work— particularly because they are rooted in sound scientific research. However, as always, to assume and predict the new policies will work better than the previous ones is to implement the unfair comparison. Good research is a "fair comparison"—it compares the actual results of one policy with the actual results of another policy. With research, it almost always turns out that neither policy is a silver bullet that solves the problem of delinquency. But usually one policy works better than the other, and the better policy is the one we should go with.

On a positive note, government funding streams, particularly those administered through the Centers for Disease Control and the National Institute for Justice's Office of Juvenile Justice and Delinquency Prevention, have been supporting and promoting more program evaluation and research initiatives to help conduct "good" research. We are optimistic that policy and practice will, indeed, learn from and build upon such research.

Lesson 7: The Power of the State. Reforms that "sell" increase the power of the state, based on optimistic assessments of how effective the reform will be in solving the problem. The power of the state usually continues to expand regardless of the specific content or nature of the reform.

As in so many earlier attempts at reform, the redefinition of juvenile delinquency as a manifestation of deeper psychological problems gives a way for the state to have power over these children. After all, the state can still provide for the coercive involuntary treatment and confinement of those deemed mentally ill, regardless of age. If juveniles are mentally impaired, we should also see the state taking away certain of their rights to make decisions, as the juveniles would need someone else (interested adults) to make those decisions for them.

It may well be that children under a certain age are incapable of understanding their due process rights and, therefore, are incapable of enacting or waiving them. In fact, several states have already, or are in the process of, taking measures to reduce a juvenile's ability to waive the right to a defense attorney.[29] However, this may prove a double-edged sword. On the one side, this trend could have positive benefits for juveniles. If deemed incapable of waiving their due process rights, then the appearances of defense council in the juvenile court room could expand. However, if juveniles are deemed totally incapable of understanding these rights, then a scenario could also arise in which the defense counsel is more a tool of the court than an advocate for juveniles. That is, instead of providing the most aggressive defense possible, the defense attorney might urge the juvenile to plea to the offense in order to receive "treatment." An alternate scenario is that the defense attorney might more earnestly represent the wishes of the parents and family (or other interested adults deemed to understand the process) than the interests of the juvenile. In this way, the juvenile would be assigned council, but not truly "represented" or protected against the power of the state.

NOTES

1. Howard N. Snyder and Melissa Sickmund, *Juvenile Offenders and Victims: A National Report 2006* (Washington, D.C.: Office of Juvenile Justice and Delinquency Prevention, U.S. Department of Justice, 2006), 113.

2. North Carolina Sentencing and Policy Advisory Committee, *Report on the Study of Youthful offenders Pursuant to Session Law 2006–248, Sections 43.1 and 34.2,* submitted to the North Carolina General Assembly, March 2007.

3. Snyder and Sickmund, *Juvenile Offenders and Victims,* 116.

4. Ibid.

5. Patrick Griffin, *Different from Adults: An Updated Analysis of Juvenile Transfer and Blended Sentencing Laws, with Recommendations for Reform: Models for Change, Systems Reform in Juvenile Justice* (Pittsburg: National Center for Juvenile Justice, 2008).

6. This statistic is based on unpublished research conducted by Megan Kurlychek and John Burrow, in two urban counties of South Carolina. During the research, the head prosecutor (e.g., solicitor) was specifically questioned as to why none of these youths was sent for waiver hearings. The response was simply that the state had already determined who was to be tried in adult court through statutory exclusion laws, so waiver hearings were rarely held anymore. In other words, we had already lost a lot of kids to the adult system without any say; we were simply not going to send anymore over.

7. *S.C. Domestics Relations Code,* title 20, sec. 20-7-6605 and forward.

8. An observational study in the 1990s found that police arrested 13% of juveniles they encountered; see Stephanie M. Myers, "Police Encounters with Juvenile Suspects" (partial), in Thomas J. Bernard, ed., *Serious Delinquency* (Los Angeles: Roxbury, 2006). Two observational studies in the 1970s found approximately the same figure; Donald Black and Albert J. Reiss, "Police Control of Juveniles," *American Sociological Review* 35, no. 1 (1970): 63–77; and Richard Lundman, Richard E. Sykes, and John P. Clark, "Police Control of Juveniles: A Replication," *Journal of Research in Crime and Delinquency* 15, no. 1 (1978): 74–91.

9. Snyder and Sickmund, *Juvenile Offenders and Victims*.

10. Ibid., 127.

11. Ibid., 142.

12. Simon I. Singer, *Recriminalizing Delinquency* (New York: Cambridge University Press, 1996.

13. Snyder and Sickmund, *Juvenile Offenders and Victims*, 173.

14. Ibid., 174.

15. Danial S. Nagin, Alex R. Piquero, Elizabeth S. Scott, and Laurence Steinberg, "Public Preference for Rehabilitation versus Incarceration of Juvenile Offenders: Evidence from a Contingent Valuation Survey," *Criminology and Public Policy* 5, no. 4 (2006): 623–672.

16. Aaron Kupchik, "Prosecuting Adolescents in Criminal Courts: Criminal or Juvenile Justice," *Social Problems* 50 (2003): 439–60, also partially reprinted in Bernard, ed., *Serious Delinquency*.

17. Patricia Torbet, Richard Gable, Hunter Hurst, Imogene Montgomery, Linda Szymanski, and Douglas Thomas, *State Responses to Serious and Violent Juvenile Crime* (Washington, D.C.: Office of Juvenile Justice and Delinquency Prevention, U.S. Department of Justice, 1996).

18. Ibid.

19. Ibid.

20. Ibid.

21. American Bar Association, *Youth in the Criminal Justice System: Guidelines for Policymakers and Practitioners* (2002), http://www.abanet.org/crimjust/juvjus/jjpolicies/YCJSReport.pdf, accessed April 2009.

22. Blue Print Commission, *Getting Smart about Juvenile Justice* (Tallahassee: Florida Department of Juvenile Justice, 2008).

23. Children's Defense Fund, *America's Cradle to Prison Pipeline Report*, www.childrensdefensefund.org/site/PageServer?pagename=c2pp_report2007/#entire, accessed 2007.

24. National Council of Juvenile and Family Court Judges, *Juvenile Delinquency Guidelines: Improving Court Practice in Juvenile Delinquency Cases* (Reno: Author, 2005).

25. The Campaign for Youth Justice is a nonprofit organization based in Washington, D.C., that works with state partnerships to promote research and improve knowledge regarding the sentencing of youth. Its primary mission is to end the prosecution in adult courts of all youths in the United States under the

age of 18. More information about this organization can be found at www. campaign4youth.org.

26. For a detailed collection of articles documenting adolescent decision making, see Thomas Grisso and Robert G. Schwartz, eds., *Youth on Trial: A Developmental Perspective on Juvenile Justice* (Chicago: University of Chicago Press, 2000).

27. American Psychiatric Association, *Diagnostic and Statistical Manual of Mental Disorders*, 4th ed. (Washington, D.C.: Author, 1994).

28. For more on William Healy, see Eric Schneider, *In the Web of Class: Delinquents and Reformers in Boston, 1810s–1930s* (New York: New York University Press, 1992); or Jon Snodgrass, "William Healy (1869–1963): Pioneer Child Psychiatrist and Criminologist," *Journal of the History of the Behavioral Sciences* 20 (1984): 331–339. For more on Healy's own ideas of the delinquent and treating delinquency, see William Healy, *The Individual Delinquent: A Text-Book of Diagnosis and Prognosis for All Concerned in Understanding Offenders* (Boston: Little, Brown, 1915).

29. States that currently limit this right include Arizona, Arkansas, Florida, Louisiana, Maine, Minnesota, Montana, New Jersey, New York, Tennessee, and West Virginia. Also, on May 1, 2008, in case number SC07–1162 (*In Re: Amendment to Florida Rule of Juvenile Procedure 8.165(a)*), the Florida Supreme Court ruled that a juvenile must meet with an attorney before waiving his or her right to an attorney and entering a plea.

11

The Lessons of History Applied Today

Historical and Philosophical Context

In the beginning of this book, we presented the argument that we study history to be able to see ourselves in a historical and philosophical context. In this instance, our historical context is our current place in the cycle of juvenile justice. Only by studying history can we realize where we are in this cycle; otherwise, we see only the present policy and the need to move to the next policy in the cycle. So, as detailed in the preceding chapters, at this point in history we have reached the "forced choice" between two undesirable options and are witnessing a reintroduction of lenient treatments into the juvenile justice system.

Historical context is driven by philosophical context—that is, shared rational and coherent ideas "hang together" to help us make sense of a period in time. This philosophical context for viewing juvenile justice includes the ideas that juvenile crime is exceptionally high, that the problem did not exist in the good old days, and that the cause of the problem lies in current justice policies. It also includes the unfair comparison, in which a harsh assessment of the actual practices of past policies is compared to an optimistic assessment of future policies, based on the good intentions of the reformers.

Only by studying history can we put these ideas into their proper place. In doing so, we realize that many of these ideas about juvenile delinquency and juvenile justice have remained the same for 200 years.

They have been popular whether existing juvenile justice policies are harsh or lenient, whether the proposed policies are harsh or lenient, and whether juvenile delinquency itself is somewhat higher or somewhat lower. Thus, these ideas are like a stopped clock: they say the same thing all the time, so that they are right some of the time and wrong most of the time. It is these ideas that drive the cyclical pattern that characterizes changes in juvenile justice policies.

The Cycle Continues: Repeating the Past

Based on the constancy of these ideas, our prediction is that this cycle of juvenile justice will continue into the future. Juveniles will remain a high crime rate group. As a group, they will continue to receive punishments that are, to some extent, mitigated forms of the punishments provided to adults who commit the same offenses. Adults will continue to believe in the myth of the good old days and that the current juvenile crime wave started in the last thirty to forty years. They will continue to believe that the juvenile system is somehow to blame for that crime wave and that the current policies of the juvenile system must be changed (either from lenient treatment to harsh punishment, or vice versa) in order to end that crime wave and solve the problem of juvenile delinquency. These new policies will expand the power of the state, uphold the moral and intellectual superiority of the reformers, and provide an unfair comparison between existing policies and proposed solutions.

As suggested in the previous chapter, the cycle is currently at the reintroduction of lenient treatments. After over a decade of "get tough" policies and decreasing juvenile crime, the year 2004 saw the first increase in juvenile arrests for violent crime, and this trend continued into 2006, with a 6 percent increase in juvenile arrests over 2005 for violent crimes, particularly homicide and robbery.[1] The overabundance of harsh punishments and lack of lenient treatments will, of course, be blamed for this real (or any imagined) juvenile crime problem. The idea of the juvenile delinquent as a subset of normal adolescents who make poor decisions, or who have a mental illness that further impairs their decision making, will call for juvenile justice policies that emphasize behavior modification, counseling, and other forms of therapy derived primarily from the field of mental health. The reformers can, thus, maintain their superiority in emphasizing what is flawed in the population of delinquents, and the state can continue to maintain and expand its power over those incapable of making decisions for themselves. Finally, these new ideas will benefit from an unfair comparison that focuses on the known negatives of existing practices and magnifies the hypothesized positives of the new reform.

Breaking the Cycle: Learning from the Past

Let us start by emphasizing that the cycle of juvenile justice cannot be broken by any particular juvenile justice policy, since all policies eventually are broken, in turn, by the cycle. The only way to break the cycle is to change the belief that an as-yet undiscovered policy will transform juveniles into a low crime rate group. The public must realize that the juvenile justice system did not create juvenile crime. Juvenile crime is a function of the greater societal ills of a given historical time, and the incidence and nature of juvenile crimes will reflect these ills, not the juvenile justice system itself.

Once we have accepted that our juvenile justice system cannot solve the problem of juvenile delinquency, the next task is to devise a system that deals as effectively as possible with the majority of youths brought before it. On the most basic level, this system must include leniency for some juvenile offenders. A policy that does not include leniency inevitably results in that forced choice between harshly punishing and doing nothing. Given only that choice, the first rule of criminal justice thermodynamics takes over, and many juveniles are let off scot-free, which then results in public pressure to reform the system by introducing leniency. Thus, the cycle continues.

Once we choose the extent to which leniency is available, then we must expect that a certain portion of the juveniles receiving leniency will go on to commit serious offenses. We will then be tempted to lessen the leniency to further reduce juvenile crime. But to do so would be to simply continue the cycle of juvenile justice. The belief that tougher penalties reduce juvenile crime is based on an unfair comparison; in actual practice, a certain portion of juveniles receiving tougher penalties also go on to commit serious crimes. If we go the route of harsher punishment, we ultimately end up with officials having to choose between harsh punishment and doing nothing; then a new reform will follow, again introducing leniency.

In short, the cycle of juvenile justice cannot be broken unless our ideas about juvenile delinquency and the juvenile delinquent change. Those ideas drive the cycle, and they will retire any particular policy that is put into place. Thus, we begin by focusing on changing those ideas about juvenile delinquency and the juvenile delinquent.

Ideas About Juvenile Delinquents and Juvenile Delinquency

To develop a realistic view of juvenile delinquents, we begin by tracing people's views over time, as explained earlier in this text, and drawing out the best and worst aspects of each view and its resulting juvenile justice policy. Because value judgments are involved, people will maintain different ideas about what is best and what is worst. The following are simply our own ideas; they are organized as a discussion of how ideas of juvenile delinquency and the juvenile delinquent relate to the idea of juvenile justice.

No Idea of Juvenile Delinquency

Before the establishment of the first juvenile institution, juvenile delinquency did not exist as an idea. Once children were 6 or 7 years old, they were viewed as people like everyone else, and when they violated the law, they were viewed as criminals like other criminals. The response to juvenile delinquents, therefore, was a modified version of the response to adult criminals: punishments mitigated because of age.

There were two "best" aspects of this policy that are worth retaining. One is the assumption that, under normal circumstances and with few exceptions, juveniles are entitled to receive less punishment than adults for the same offenses. This was not questioned as a policy that benefited both the juvenile and the larger society, since most juveniles took advantage of the reduced punishments and stopped committing crimes. The other is the assumption that juveniles have as many rights in criminal court as do adults. In practice, neither group back then had many rights, but juveniles were not accorded fewer rights than adults.

The "worst" aspect of this policy was that punishment was the only available response. The choice was limited to punishing the juveniles, even if that punishment were mitigated, or doing nothing at all. Given that limited choice, officials often refused to punish at all because they believed that the punishments might increase juvenile crime.

Juvenile Delinquents as Potential Paupers

The term "juvenile delinquent" originated with the idea that some youths were potential paupers. The term itself conveys that meaning, in that pauperism was the subject of much public attention, so that this new idea of juvenile delinquency was easily assimilated. The associated policy response (the idea of juvenile justice) was a modified version of the policy response to paupers: institutionalize the youths to teach them good work habits, and then apprentice them out until they become adults.

The "best" aspect of this policy is suggested by the word *potential*. It implies that children are not "hardened" but, rather, in the process of becoming something else. In this case, it was suggested that they were becoming paupers, which is a more specific version of the idea that children were in the process of becoming adults. Thus, the word *potential* reflected this second concept of childhood as the basis for the idea of juvenile delinquency.

The policy response associated with this notion was to modify the developmental process so that such children could be shaped, molded, and reformed into law-abiding citizens. It is an optimistic attitude that got lost during the later "get tough" movement, as juveniles were redefined as hardened criminals, or worse, and subjected to sentences of life in prison or even death.

The "worst" aspect of this policy was the idea that juvenile delinquents can be reformed by placing them in institutions, and that the problem of juvenile delinquency could be solved without other action. From their very beginnings, the institutions have failed to accomplish this task, and this failure has been exceedingly costly in both human and financial terms.

In 1970, Massachusetts became the first state to officially reject the notion of institutionalization as a solution to juvenile delinquency.[2] Most of those services aimed at reforming juveniles are now purchased from private agencies rather than provided by state employees.[3] All the large juvenile institutions have been closed, and a number of smaller (the largest small facility holding eighteen juveniles) facilities were opened for juveniles too dangerous to be left on the streets. These secure facilities provide extensive treatment services; for example, the eighteen-bed facility has a full-time supervising counselor and three full-time counselors, each with a caseload of six. Many institutions with five hundred juveniles would consider themselves lucky to have such a small counselor to juvenile ratio.

Consequently, Massachusetts maintains relatively low delinquency rates as compared to other states that rely heavily on large institutionalizations, such as California and Florida.[4] Other states, including Utah, Nebraska, and Missouri, have since followed Massachusetts' lead.[5] Additionally, an accumulating body of literature suggests that community corrections is *at least as* effective as institutional corrections as the response to most delinquency.[6] Also, small treatment-oriented secure facilities are proving more effective than large institutions in reforming the few dangerous juvenile offenders who require confinement.[7] Thus, the reliance on large institutions that began with reformers in New York City in 1825 seems to have been a grave mistake.

An even greater mistake was the idea that juvenile justice policy alone can solve the problem of delinquency. While the Massachusetts juvenile justice system might be more effective than Florida's, it still cannot *solve* the problem of delinquency. The solution to the problem requires greater changes—changes to the large social and economic conditions that characterize our society. Earlier socioeconomic conditions such as were in New York City in 1925 and in Chicago in 1899, and those of today in economically stagnant urban ghettos, give rise to juvenile delinquency. The delinquency problem did not arise because of ineffective juvenile justice policies, nor will it disappear solely if adequate and effective policies are instituted.

Juvenile Delinquents as Dependent and Neglected Children

The next idea of the juvenile delinquent was a modified version of the idea of the dependent and neglected child: children who lack proper parental care and support. The expanding child welfare movement shone a spotlight on the problem of dependent and neglected children, so this new idea of juvenile delinquency was easily adopted by the general public. The associated policy response (the idea of juvenile justice) was a modified version of that response to dependent and neglected children. That is, if the natural parents did not provide the proper care and supervision of these children, then the state (as *parens patriae*) would do so.

There are five "best" aspects of this reform. The first is the idea of linking delinquency to parental care and supervision. The founders of the juvenile court believed that dependency is the natural state of all children, and that delinquency is only one of many manifestations of a lack of proper care and supervision. Recent research suggests that there is considerable truth in that view.[8]

Establishment of the juvenile court is the second "best" aspect of this policy. Earlier responses were limited to voluntary treatments in private agencies or coercive punishments in criminal court, so the juvenile court added a third option: coercive treatments. This option is particularly appropriate for children because they are in the process of development (the second idea of childhood) and are not hardened criminals.

The third "best" aspect is the idea that the juvenile court should act in the best interests of the child. The recent "get tough" approach shifted the focus away from helping the child to that of protecting society from the child, even at the cost of harming the child. The founders of the juvenile court would have described this as extraordinarily short-sighted. They saw no conflict between society's interests and those of the child; they believed that society's long-term interests are best served by protecting children. This idea deserves to be part of any future juvenile system.

A fourth "best" aspect is the legal definition that juveniles could not form criminal intent (*mens rea*). Since the court's earliest days, age always has been a factor in the ability to form criminal intent. The juvenile court extended this concept by applying it to all juveniles rather than only to those under the age of 7. This is a legal mechanism that removes juveniles from criminal court jurisdiction and allows them to be processed under a system oriented to serving their best interests rather than awarding punishment. This idea should be retained in any future juvenile justice system.

A fifth "best" aspect is the new language that reflects the structure and function of a social welfare agency rather than a criminal court. To a certain extent, this language masks the true criminal functions of the juvenile court and protects juveniles from stigmatization. It also operates as a symbol that shapes the thinking and behavior of people who work in the juvenile court. In a world full of symbols that push people toward punishment of juveniles, the language of treatment seems worth retaining, even if reality does not always live up to the intention.

The "worst" aspect of this policy was eliminating the juvenile's due process rights. As with the language of social welfare, the theoretical existence of these rights was useful even if reality did not always correspond. The elimination of such rights ignored the fact that the system does not always, if even seldom, live up to its intentions of providing treatment. It also ignored the simple fact that not all youths brought before the system will be rightfully accused or in need of treatment. Even in a system truthfully designed to protect the best interests of the child, mistakes will be made, and children will need and deserve basic legal protections from well-meaning yet ill-advised system officials.

Juvenile Delinquents as Criminal Defendants

In their series of decisions beginning with *Kent* and *Gault*, the U.S. Supreme Court proposed an idea of juvenile delinquency that was a modified version of the criminal defendant. Their idea of juvenile justice, therefore, was a modified version of their policy response to adult criminals: provide juveniles with some (but not all) of the due process rights given to adults.

The "best" aspect of this policy is that it reintroduced due process rights for juvenile defendants. It linked coercive treatment with restrictions on the state's coercive powers, and suggested that juveniles need protection from the state even if the state proposes to act in their best interests.

There are two aspects that we regard, however, as "worsts," in the sense that they should not be included in any future juvenile justice system. Both are related to the fact that the Supreme Court's reform was logical and rational and "made sense" for the juvenile justice system (i.e., it was based on a coherent philosophy), but it did not consider how that system actually performs in its day-to-day activities.

The first "worst" aspect is that, for various reasons, the due process rights of juveniles were not effective in practice. The Supreme Court did not provide to juveniles either jury trial, the right to treatment, or a practical means of appeal. As a result, almost all juveniles are found to have committed the offense for which they are referred (either formally or informally, through adjudication or plea). This means that, in practice, the power of the state is not limited in its relation to juveniles but, rather, expanded. This "worst" aspect effectively nullifies the "best" aspect of the Supreme Court's reform.

The second "worst" aspect is that the Supreme Court failed to ensure that juveniles would actually receive treatment in the disposition phase. The Court correctly observed that juveniles had been punished and not treated in the past, but then based its constitutional argument on the assumption that juveniles would somehow miraculously be treated and not punished in the future. This assumption was unrealistic in light of how things are really done.

Juvenile Delinquents as Hardened Criminals

The "get tough" movement proposed that juvenile delinquents were not merely potential criminals but already hardened criminals or even "superpredators." Such criminals have been the subject of public attention in the last twenty-plus years, but this new idea of the juvenile delinquent and of juvenile delinquency proposed a juvenile justice system that was a modified version of the policy response to dangerous criminals: lock them up for extended periods of time to prevent them from preying on innocent victims.

Some similarity is evident between this recent view and the one that prevailed before the establishment of the first juvenile institution, when there was no concept of juvenile delinquency. In fact, this view is much more severe. Two hundred years ago, it was commonly acknowledged that most juvenile crime was minor and not serious, and that most juvenile criminals were best dealt with by just punishing them less than adults who commit the same offenses. The assumption was that, given a taste of potential consequences, these juveniles would "get out while the getting was good." Thus, mitigation was not questioned as the basic response to juvenile offending.

The view of juveniles as hardened criminals, however, suggested that mitigation is inappropriate and foolish. "Get tough" advocates argued that juveniles use leniency as an opportunity to commit more frequent and serious offenses, without fear of consequences. Thus, this idea of dealing with juvenile delinquency was considerably tougher than the one held two hundred years ago.

The "best" aspect of this idea is that at least some juveniles can form criminal intent and therefore deserve punishment for their offenses. The original juvenile institutions and the original juvenile court were designed to deal with minor offenders; but as the cycle of juvenile justice progressed, both increasingly had to handle more serious offenders and thus ignored the minor offenders they were designed to handle. The "get tough" movement may be correct in arguing that there are some very serious criminals that do not belong under the auspices of the juvenile justice system.

There were, however, several "worst" aspects of this policy as well. First, this reform ignored the growing body of literature that reported that punishment, especially in adult facilities, actually increases criminal activity. Research suggests that recidivism among even the most violent delinquents can be reduced by up to 70 percent in small, secure, treatment-oriented juvenile facilities.[9] In contrast, this same type of juvenile does poorly when punished in large custody-oriented juvenile institutions.[10] The adult system has even less to offer these offenders, and the juveniles themselves cause many problems in it, both as victims and as offenders.[11]

A second "worst" aspect was that "get tough" reformers discarded many of the advances that juvenile justice had made over the last two hundred years. They completely abandoned the developmental conception of childhood and returned to the view that juveniles are simply smaller adults. They eliminated coerced treatment as an appropriate method of dealing with these children, and restricted the court's options to either punish delinquents or do nothing at all. This was an untenable position, and as the cycle of juvenile justice continues, we see this situation leading the way to a major "new" reform that will reestablish lenient treatments.

Ultimately, the "get tough" reformers were designing a juvenile system to deal only with hardened criminals. But these are but a tiny minority of the juveniles handled by the juvenile system. For example, studies indicate that only between 5 to 7 percent of all juveniles who come in contact with the juvenile justice system can be defined as "chronic" offenders.[12] The overwhelming majority are minor and occasional offenders who (sooner or later) use leniency as an opportunity to refrain from further offending. A juvenile justice system should be designed to deal with the overwhelming majority of juvenile offenders, not with a small minority.

Our Idea of Juvenile Delinquency: Naïve Risk Taking

We review these different notions of juvenile delinquency because each can apply to some juveniles coming before the system today. Some juvenile offenders are "potential paupers," but most grow up and settle down and hold jobs and pay taxes, with no or minimal intervention by juvenile justice officials.[13] Many of these same people later demand tough penalties for juvenile offenders. They forget that they received leniency themselves, that they might have been sent to an institution if tough policies had been in effect when they were young. Thus, while some juvenile delinquents are "potential paupers," most are not.

Some juvenile offenders are "dependent and neglected children," but most have imperfect and fallible parents who do their best under difficult circumstances. These parents love their children and try to get them to obey the law, even if they sometimes do so in ways that make the problem worse. It can be helpful to train these parents in more effective parenting techniques,[14] but it is wrong to describe most delinquents as dependent or neglected children.

Some juvenile offenders are presumably innocent "defendants" in need of due process rights, but most are not defendants at all because they never have an adjudication hearing. The police arrest only between 20 and 50 percent of the juveniles they accuse of crimes, and they refer only about half of those they arrest to juvenile court.[15] The juvenile court processes only about half of all accused offenders formally, and many of them plea to the offense rather than having a formal adjudication hearing. In practice, the vast majority of juvenile delinquents are never defendants in the formal sense.

Some juveniles are "hardened criminals," but most are adolescents acting the way adolescents always have: wild and crazy. After years of being children under the total control of adults, they suddenly find they have the freedom to do what they want and adults can't stop them. They celebrate their freedom by doing many of the things they were previously "controlled" from doing, but they have not yet learned that their actions can have hurtful consequences. They believe they can take all kinds of risks and nothing will ever happen to them. Like Superman, they think bullets bounce off their chests. Adults warn them about the consequences of their actions, even yell and scream and threaten, but adolescents laugh it off and ignore it. They are having a good time.

Sooner or later, the consequences happen, either to them or to their friends. Someone flunks out of school and is kicked out of the house, and takes a deadend job or can't get a job at all. Someone overdoses on drugs and suffers permanent brain damage. Someone is seriously injured or killed while driving drunk. Reality rears its ugly head, and the adolescents are overwhelmed. Whereas before they felt confident and joyful, now they feel vulnerable and frightened. We call this "growing up." Thus, some juvenile delinquents are hardened criminals, but most are not.

Finally, some juvenile delinquents suffer from "severe mental illness" such as bipolar disorder or schizophrenia, which renders them less culpable for their actions than a person of sound mind. However, most juveniles who are risk takers, who are impulsive, who lack attention span, can't concentrate on school work, or hate authority, are just normal American kids, like we were. Therefore counseling, therapy, and medication may be useful in responding to some juvenile delinquents, but not for most.

We propose a new idea that would apply to a majority of young offenders. We call this the idea of juvenile delinquents as "naïve risk-takers." This notion is consistent with the position taken by the founders of the juvenile court and that was promoted in the recent *Simmons* decision. The research shows that an adolescent's brain is not yet fully developed; in fact, research shows that full functioning may not be reached until the early twenties. Most specifically, the part of the brain still developing is that which helps us control impulses and reflect on our own behavior.[16] Psychological research complements the biological research, also showing that juveniles do not have the impulse control of an adult, that their temporal focus is more immediate than long term, that they are much more influenced by environmental factors over which they have little control, and most important, that their character is *still developing*.[17]

This research is important to legal doctrine because it relates directly to the previously discussed notion of *mens rea*, or the guilty mind. *Mens rea* is a confusing concept that has been defined in many different ways. Most of those definitions, however, focus on an awareness of the consequences of criminal actions.[18] An offender who lacks this awareness cannot be considered "blameworthy" and therefore cannot be said to have

mens rea. If delinquents are defined as people who do not fully understand the consequences of their actions, then they cannot fully understand the consequences that their criminal actions have for their victims.
For example, in cases where a juvenile has killed another person, the
issue in a waiver hearing usually is whether the juvenile has a sense of
what it is to take a life. At least some younger juveniles have little sense
of death and have only a TV image of cops and robbers shooting everyone in sight. Juveniles who really do not understand death cannot form
criminal intention, in the traditional meaning of the term.

We suggest that there are two different meanings to the statement
that juveniles may not fully understand the consequences of their actions.
First, they may not fully understand the consequences of their criminal
actions for the victims, in terms of physical and psychological injuries
and trauma. Second, they may not fully understand the consequences of
their criminal actions for themselves, in terms of possibly being caught
and punished, with consequences that could affect the remainder of their
lives.

In addition, we draw attention to the final part of the Court's argument in the *Simmons* decision, which places emphasis on the fact that
these youths are still developing their final character. The notion was held
by the original child-savers, as they saw wayward youths as malleable,
being influenced either positively or negatively by their environment.
Therefore, it was the role of the juvenile court as the "parent" to shape
these children into noncriminal adults.

Are There Juvenile Offenders Who Are Rational Calculators?

Despite the above argument, we must acknowledge that some youthful
offenders are not naïve risk takers and are aware of the consequences of
their actions. They do not care about the consequences to their victims of
their criminal actions (i.e., physical or psychological trauma), and they
rationally calculate whether they want to take a chance on the consequences of their actions to themselves (e.g., being sent to prison). As
such, they are capable of forming criminal intention. We describe these
offenders as "rational calculators" because they rationally calculate the
benefits of crime and weigh them against the risks of getting caught.[19]

Such rational calculators, however, owing to their youthful state, may
still be amenable to treatment. For example, a youth who has grown up
in a public housing project surrounded by drug dealers and gangs may
learn early on to carry a gun for protection. Although gun carrying is
illegal, this youth "rationally calculates" the need for protection and
decides that it is better to carry the gun and face potential criminal

justice outcomes than to be caught on the street without one.[20] The same youth may later use this gun to harm or kill another person in a spur-of-the-moment situation. As argued by Franklin Zimring, however, "Young offenders do not become any less young because they pull the trigger."[21] In other words, while such a youth may be "rationally calculating," based on limited life experience and committing a serious act of violence with serious consequences for the victim, he or she is no less a youth with the possibility of amenability to treatment. It is possible that if we remove the youth from this environment and provide effective treatment and care, he or she could still learn to be a productive citizen. In the words of the founders of the juvenile court, perhaps we could still "save" even this child.

However, it is also possible that this youth is truly beyond treatment and would serve only to further corrupt those youths in the juvenile system with whom he or she comes into contact. It is possible that there are some youths whose criminogenic nature is so well formed that they are not suitable for processing and treatment in a juvenile court.

Here is our recommendation: return to the judicial waiver hearing, as defined in the *Kent* decision as the primary, if not sole, mechanism by which juveniles reach adult court. In such a hearing, the juvenile court judge carefully considers all aspects of the youth's individual life circumstance to determine if he or she is amenable to treatment. We recommend this approach owing to our belief that maturity and judgment develop differently across individuals. We also believe that the offense a youth commits may be a greater indicator of local life circumstance and opportunity than it is an indicator of maturity. For this reason, we believe that while there are some youths that belong in the criminal justice system, there are very few such youths and that it is the appropriate role of the juvenile court judge to make such a determination. Thus, we propose that current policies of statutory exclusion and prosecutorial direct file are misguided and are damaging a great portion of our society's youth, and subsequently, the future of our society.

An Idea of Juvenile Justice

If we are to keep the majority of youths within a juvenile justice system, what should such a system look like? If we accept the notion that most of these youths are normal American teenagers who are naïve risk takers, then a primary goal of the system should be to communicate the idea that actions have consequences. Such communication should be child–focused rather than offense-driven. That is, the extent of the consequences should be determined by the need to communicate with the juvenile, not by the nature of the offense.

Initial attempts to communicate ideally should involve diversionary programs that require youths to take some accountability for their actions. Similar to the actions of a good parent, the court should make sure youths understand what they did wrong and why those actions were harmful. If diversionary efforts do not work, the next step would be more formal intervention to better "convince" juveniles that they are headed down the wrong path. If a juvenile still does not respond, then perhaps this particular youth is not in the broad category of juveniles who are merely naïve risk takers, but is a youth suffering from a neglectful or abusive home life, a mental disorder, or other type of problem. The role of the court, then, becomes that of identifying the problem areas and providing coerced treatment. Finally, when the court has exhausted its mechanisms for treatment, a juvenile court judge alone should determine if this particular juvenile should be transferred to adult court for punishment.

In this system, providing punishment and retributive justice would not be a function of the juvenile court; providing accountability and treatment would. The juvenile court would maintain its original rehabilitative ideal, providing myriad lenient treatments to accomplish this goal. In terms of the "criminal justice thermodynamics," the juvenile court would intentionally provide lenient treatments to assure that such responses were broadly applied. Punishment would remain the function of the adult court.

The Current Juvenile System Already Functions This Way

To a considerable extent, the juvenile justice system already functions this way. First-time offenders are often diverted from the system; only upon repeat offending do they penetrate to the adjudication phase. At adjudication, the primary response to deviance remains a period of probation, during which the juvenile is supervised and coerced to perform certain functions such as community service or to attend counseling and treatment. Residential placement is often reserved for the most chronic and repeat offenders.

For example, police officers have their own sequence of escalating threats and coerced treatments that they routinely use when dealing with juvenile offenders.[22] Although they normally do not use the entire sequence with any particular juvenile, they can choose among the various steps in handling a particular case.

For instance, at the lowest level they "counsel and release" the youth— that is, they tell the kid to beat it and not let it happen again. In practice, this involves a type of threat: "If I see you again, then I will take more aggressive action."

At the next level, they may take the juvenile home to his or her parents, without an arrest. Another option is a "station adjust," bringing the juvenile to the police station and having the parents come down. At any of these levels, the police may throw in a "convincer," depending on the police department's policy, such as making the juvenile write an essay or letter of apology.

The next level of the sequence involves an official arrest but no referral to juvenile court. As always this is accompanied by a threat: "If I see you again, then I will make the referral." And finally, the police officer refers the case to juvenile court, at which point the system of escalating threats is taken over by the juvenile probation officer.

In addition to this system of escalating threats, the system maintains a focus on risk and needs assessments to help determine appropriate levels of care. For instance, perhaps it is a police officer's first contact with a youth, but upon returning the youth to his parents or upon conversing with the youth it becomes apparent that this youth needs immediate further intervention. To deal with situations such as this, as well as the progression of chronic offenders, the system has incorporated the notion of "graduated sanctions." This model suggests appropriate levels of intervention with a juvenile given his or her assessed risk and need.[23]

Obviously there are many other successful initiatives ongoing within the juvenile justice systems of the fifty states and Washington, D.C. A discussion of all such programs reaches well beyond the confines of this text; however, these examples demonstrate general practices within the juvenile justice system that lead to its current level of success, as further detailed below.

The Juvenile Justice System Is Already Highly Successful

The juvenile justice system successfully handles a large majority of the youth with whom it deals. This statement is supported by national statistics and various research studies on the distribution of juvenile cases.

Imagine 6,000 different situations in which the police encounter a juvenile who has committed an arrestable offense. On average, this would involve about 2,000 different juveniles, so the average juvenile who encounters the police does so in three different arrest situations.[24] About 1,000 of these juveniles will be arrested, some more than once, so that there will be about 2,000 official arrests in those 6,000 arrest situations.[25] In the situations in which there is no arrest, the juveniles will be counseled and released, taken home to their parents, or "station adjusted."

According to recent estimates, police handle about 20 percent of arrests informally within the police department,[26] meaning that of these 2,000 arrests, 400 would be handled informally and 1,600 would be referred to juvenile court for further action. Approximately 42 percent of these cases would then be handled informally by the probation officer, meaning 672 of these cases would be resolved without a formal court hearing, either with counsel and release, informal supervision, consent decree, and a few outright dismissals.[27]

Of the 928 cases handled formally, about 9 cases will be transferred to criminal court.[28] About 622 of these youth will be adjudicated delinquent (with or without a formal hearing), and the remaining 297 will either have charges dismissed (211) or receive informal diversions (86). Of the 622 youth reaching the disposition hearing, about 386 of the juveniles will be placed on probation, about 143 will be sent to a state or local institution, and the remaining 93 will receive a variety of other dispositions.[29]

Defining success and failure in the juvenile justice system is, to some extent, a matter of opinion. But many people would define the transfers to criminal court as a failure of the juvenile system. Assuming that these "failures" represent 9 different youths, they constitute fewer than .5 percent of the 2,000 youths who originally encountered the system, for a success rate of over 99 percent.

The 143 juveniles sent to an institution could also be considered "failures." They reached the final stages of the system (passing through diversion and coerced outpatient treatments and probation) without changing their ways. Assuming these are 143 different juveniles, they still represent fewer than 7 percent of referred juveniles. Adding these to the 9 transfers, the system would still maintain a success rate of about 92 percent.

Although the argument gets extremely weak, the 386 probation dispositions could also be counted as "failures." This would total 538 failures (9 transfers, 143 institutionalization, and 386 probationers), out of 2,000 different youth. That would still leave the system with a 74 percent success rate. That is, 74 percent of the 2,000 different youths who were identified by police as having committed an average of three arrestable offenses were handled by the system without so much as being placed on formal probation.

The youths who are deemed "successes" apparently drop out of the juvenile justice system. We theoretically deem them successes because if they came back into the system they would advance to the next stage, and thus show up in the statistics. For example, juveniles who received informal probation would be expected to be formally adjudicated if they were arrested again. They would then be expected to receive at least formal probation as a disposition. The fact that there are a relatively small number of formal probation dispositions indicates that the most of those who receive informal probation do not reappear in the system.

Another, perhaps more straightforward measure of failure would be if a youth processed by the juvenile system goes on to become an adult criminal. This is, of course, the outcome the system was designed to avoid. The question of age and persistence in criminality is presently entangled in a complex controversy involving longitudinal studies.[30] The specific issue relevant to this discussion, however, is not contested. There is virtually unanimous agreement that the proportion of all people involved in crime peaks at ages 16 or 17, and then declines rapidly.[31] Given this widespread agreement, we can confidently expect that most juveniles who were involved in the juvenile system do not become further involved in the adult system. Data support this view, showing that fewer than 25 percent of all juveniles involved in the juvenile system at any level go on to commit adult crimes. This statistic, therefore, also suggests a success rate of 75 percent.[32]

Why Does the System Appear to Be a Failure?

If the juvenile justice system has such a remarkable success rate, then why does it have a widespread image of failure? The answer is that most studies of juvenile justice examine only the failures of the system and ignore the successes. Having excluded all the successful cases, the studies conclude that the system is a failure.

In the above figures, there were 143 juveniles who were sent to the institution or waived to criminal court. While these were fewer than 7 percent of the total number of juveniles handled by the system, they were the clearest failures of the system. Many analyses of the juvenile justice system begin with these juveniles who failed and trace their cases backward to the first contacts these youths had with police. That is, they start with the set of juveniles who were institutionalized or waived to criminal court, and then evaluate the entire system solely on the basis of its performance with these selected youths.

In our analysis, we included all cases—successes as well as failures. We then traced their cases *forward* to their outcomes, whether successful or unsuccessful. This is a fairer comparison. Our approach clearly shows that successful cases vastly outnumber failed cases in the juvenile justice system. So, the juvenile justice system as it exists is highly successful. However, while the system has, in essence, "gotten a bum rap," we also realize that there are a significant number of youths whom the system does fail. In the next section, we make recommendations for improving, rather than abandoning, the current system.

The Ideal Juvenile Justice System

If we have convinced the reader of nothing else in this text, perhaps we have convinced you that reality is always far from the ideal. So, although the juvenile system is highly effective for a majority of juveniles, it still suffers from many crucial flaws, and thus there is a portion of youths whom it fails. In addition, there may be many juveniles who would not have gone on to commit more crimes if the system had not become involved; and also, there may be those juveniles who succeed despite of, rather than because of, the system. With the recognition in mind that the juvenile justice system did not create the problem of delinquency and thus can never truly solve it, below we offer our recommendations for improving the practice of juvenile justice for those youths who come within its jurisdiction.

Maintain Leniency

If there is no leniency, then police, probation officers, and court officials will "do nothing" for many juveniles who otherwise could benefit from services. Many juveniles who act out are sending a cry for help. If ignored, the cry will become louder, which in this instance means more serious acts of deviance. By the time the court decides the juvenile is serious enough for the "harsh punishments" available, it may be too late. If we are ever to break free of the cycle of juvenile justice, then we must devise a system that has a broad spectrum of potential responses that include lenient treatments.

Expand Treatment

Based on this argument of maintaining leniency for some, if not most offenders, we suggest that existing treatments be expanded. There is extensive evidence that a wide variety of individual treatment programs can substantially reduce juvenile crime.[33] For example, in the Unified Delinquency Intervention Services project, some moderately well-run rehabilitation programs have all reduced juvenile recidivism by about 50 percent.[34] More recent research documents the effectiveness of restorative justice efforts, mentoring programs such as big brothers and big sisters, and faith-based programming to be well above this level, with some programs reporting success rates of 90 to 95 percent.[35]

It is also evident that any individual treatment program is enhanced when it is embedded in a well-established network of other treatment programs and is expanded to address issues in the youths' environment as well (e.g., family, community, school).[36] Although we have already acknowledged that the juvenile justice system will fall short of addressing the original problems of the street that lead to the modern problem of delinquency, we do suggest, however, that treatment programs must recognize that the juvenile does not live in a vacuum and thus cannot be "treated" in one. Successful approaches such as multisystemic therapy offer direction in this area.[37]

There is also expanding evidence that a vast majority of juvenile delinquents can be handled in a well-developed network of community services, thereby reducing the rate of residential placement.[38] These services are as effective, if not more so, than large juvenile institutions at rehabilitating and reforming delinquents.

Moreover, even for those juveniles who do require placement, there is no place in the modern juvenile justice system for large custody-oriented juvenile institutions. So far as we can tell, the primary function of these institutions is to provide the public with a false sense of security that we are "getting tough" with delinquents. A second function is to provide jobs to state employees.[39] Neither of these functions serves the purposes of an ideal juvenile justice system.

Alternatively, most of the above treatment services can best be delivered through private, rather than public, entities. This allows free-market competition to enter the arena of juvenile corrections, so that better programs will flourish and worse programs will die. In contrast, the inertia that typically accompanies state-run programs usually prevents improvements from being made.

Expand Initial Diagnostic Services

If the role of the juvenile justice system is to communicate the consequences of inappropriate behavior and offer treatment and rehabilitation for youth in need, then the system must ensure that each youth referred to the system receives initial assessments and diagnoses that better inform the probation personnel and the courts of appropriate pathways. While it is most often the intent of the juvenile system to divert first-time offenders from serious consequences, as previously mentioned, the youth may be in need of serious services, even when the offense is deemed relatively minor. This emphasizes the need for the ideal juvenile system to be individual-based, rather than offense-focused.

While a full-blown discussion of specific risk-assessment devices is not warranted here, note that, just as in evaluation research, there have been marked developments in the use of risk assessments, as well as in classifications that take into account differences in needs for treatment.[40] In addition, research such as that by P. W. Harris and colleagues, in a Philadelphia Juvenile Court, have provided groundbreaking evidence that some programs do indeed work better for some types of offenders, and that this knowledge can be used to improve decision making in the juvenile justice system.[41] The myriad effective treatment options suggested here will have little effect if juveniles are not assigned the appropriate treatment. It should always be remembered that the disposition in juvenile court is intended to fit the individual juvenile, and *not* his or her crime.

Continue to Conduct Solid Research

Although great strides have already been made in improving the evaluation of juvenile justice policies and programs, much more work is needed; moreover, officials must look to such research, rather than media hype and public fear, to determine juvenile justice policies. For instance, we now know that some programs work and that others do not.[42] We also know that some programs work better than others. The challenge is to expand and build on those programs that do work or hold promise and to eliminate those—no matter how good they sound or how embedded they are in the system—that have been proven not to work. In sum, policymakers must make fair and informed decisions, based on sound research rather than naïve and optimistic predictions.

Sustain Adequate Funding to Programs

Inadequate funding has always been a thorn in the side of juvenile justice. As a result, juvenile institutions are often overcrowded, probation officers are overworked, and services often are not fully provided. The landmark *Conditions of Confinement* study, published in 1994, reported high levels of overcrowding in juvenile facilities; a problem that leads to a myriad of other difficulties including increased incidence of violence between residents and between residents and staff, lack of service provision, and in some cases even lack of access to such basic services as health care and education.[43] Overworked probation officers with high case loads face difficulties in providing adequate supervision to their probationers.[44] In addition, research on after-care services found that, while many programs were not effective, their failures were most often linked to their never being fully implemented, rather than flaws in the programs.[45] Put simply, even the best program will fail if it does not have sufficient funding to ensure the integrity of implementation. That's all the more reason officials should rely on solid research: the findings will help them avoid wasting scarce resources on programs proven not to work and support their "fair comparisons" in selecting programs with the most promise.

Mandate the Right to Treatment

The final recommendation is that the Supreme Court provide juveniles with a constitutional right to treatment at the disposition stage. This recommendation derives directly from the logic of the Supreme Court's equal protection argument, which demands that juveniles actually receive treatment in the disposition stage in order to offset the loss of due process rights in the adjudication stage.

We previously said that juveniles have almost no due process rights in practice, in part because they have fewer rights to begin with, in part because they fail to exercise the rights they do have (especially the privilege against self-incrimination), and in part because the judge is free to adjudicate when there is reasonable doubt owing to the unavailability of jury trials and appeals. As a result, almost all juveniles are found to have committed an offense for which they can be adjudicated (either the offense for which they were referred or a lesser offense to which they plea).

The absence of full due process in the juvenile system, however, should not necessarily be considered a failure on the part of juvenile justice officials. Rather, at least to some extent, it should be viewed as an inevitable consequence of dealing with juveniles who do not understand that actions have consequences. We have already said that there are two different meanings for this statement: that juveniles may not understand the consequences of criminal actions to victims, and that they do not understand the consequences of criminal actions for themselves. Now, we assert a third meaning: that juveniles may not understand the consequences of their failure to fully exercise their due process rights.[46]

To the extent that the juvenile court deals with naïve risk takers, it should assume that these juveniles will not be able to fully exercise the formal due process rights that they have been granted. This means that denial of the law's equal protection in juvenile court cannot easily be remedied by simply granting full due process rights. Instead, the juvenile court must achieve constitutionality by granting some compensating benefit that juveniles actually receive. The Supreme Court declared that benefit to be "treatment." While several appellate courts have found that, because of the denial of equal protection, juveniles have a constitutional right to treatment in juvenile court, to date the Supreme Court has failed to set the national precedent. We believe it is high time the Court remedy this oversight.

Will Our Ideas Sell?

The lessons of history suggest that breaking the cycle of juvenile justice is not an easy task, and we admit that our ideas of the juvenile delinquent and the juvenile justice system have limited sales appeal based upon the remaining lessons of history. That is, reforms "sell" if they maintain the moral superiority of the reformers, protect the interests of the rich and powerful, expand the power of the state, and provide an overly optimistic assessment of outcomes based on the unfair comparison.

Our definition of a juvenile delinquent as a naïve risk taker suggests that, at some level, the reformers are superior. That is, they make better, more mature decisions than these youths. But this modest degree of superiority is insufficient to give our reform the kind of "sales appeal" that characterized earlier successful reforms, in which delinquents were portrayed as potential paupers, dependent and neglected children, and hardened criminals.

Our ideas do not necessarily protect the interests of the rich and powerful, either. We promote the expansion of services and additional funding to the juvenile justice system to ensure proper implementation of these services. In addition, the right to treatment in the disposition hearings requires that juvenile justice bureaucrats change their behavior. The establishment of a treatment-oriented correctional system requires that state legislators change their behavior, as well. Thus, we fear our ideas have little sales appeal on this front.

Reforms that have "sold" also expanded the power of the state. Here, however, we recommend reducing the power of the state. First, we recommend the elimination of large state-run juvenile institutions and their replacement with small privately run facilities. Moreover, officially granting juveniles the right to treatment in the disposition hearing means that the juvenile court must act in the juvenile's best interests and not in the best interests of the state.

Finally, by suggesting that we not simply "throw the baby out with the bathwater," but retain what is good about the current system and build on these successes through sound research and fair comparison, we also directly defy the sales appeal of the unfair comparison. That is, we do not suggest that the changes will fix the problem of juvenile delinquency, or prevent every juvenile who comes within its auspices from committing another offense; instead, we promote a realistic assessment of the existing system, based on learning from rather than repeating history, with the goal of helping most juveniles with whom it deals.

In conclusion, we admit that our ideas have little sales appeal. They simply do not tell people what they want to hear. Even if they would work in practice, they would not "make sense." Thus, their chances of being implemented are poor.

NOTES

1. Howard Snyder, *Juvenile Arrests 2006* (Washington, D.C.: Office of Juvenile Justice and Delinquency Prevention, U.S. Department of Justice, 2006).

2. See Bruce Bullington et al., "The Politics of Policy: Deinstitutionalization in Massachusetts 1970–1985," *Law and Policy* 8, no. 4 (October 1986): 507–514.

3. Edward M. Murphy, "An alternative Approach to Managing Juvenile Corrections," in Francis X. Hartmann, ed., *The Role of the Juvenile Court* (New York: Springer-Verlag, 1987), 371–383.

4. Thomas J. Bernard and Daniel Katkin, "Introduction," *Law and Policy* 8, no. 4 (October 1986): 391–395.

5. See "Nebraska Legislature Begins to Community Sanctions," *Criminal Justice Newsletter* 21, no. 12 (June 15, 1990): 4–5.

6. Richard J. Lundmand, *Prevention and Control of Delinquency* (New York: Oxford University Press, 1984), chaps. 7, 8, 9; and James C. Howell, *Preventing and Reducing Juvenile Delinquency: A Comprehensive Framework* (Thousand Oaks, Calif.: Sage, 2003), chaps. 9, 10, 11.

7. Donna Hamparian, "Violent Juvenile Offenders," in James C. Howell, *Preventing and Reducing Juvenile Delinquency: A Comprehensive Framework* (Thousand Oaks, Calif.: Sage, 2003), chap. 9; and Jeffrey L. Bleich, "Toward an Effective Policy for Handling Dangerous Juvenile Offenders," in Howell, *Preventing and Reducing Juvenile Delinquency*, chap. 10.

8. For overviews, see Parts I, II, and IV in James Q. Wilson and Glenn C. Loury, eds., *Families, Schools, and Delinquency Preventions* (New York: Springer-Verlag, 1987).

9. Bleich, "Toward an Effective Policy."

10. A frightening account of these offenders can be found in Clemens Bartollas, Stuart J. Miller, and Simon Dinitz, *Juvenile Victimization* (Beverly Hills, Calif.: Sage, 1976).

11. Donna M. Bishop, "Juvenile Offenders in the Adult Criminal Justice System," in M. H. Tonry, ed., *Crime and Justice: A Review of Research* (Chicago: University of Chicago Press, 2000), 81–167. See also F. P. Reddington and A. D.

Sapp, "Juveniles in Adult Prisons: Problems and Prospects," *Journal of Crime and Justice* 20 (1997): 139–152.

12. A. Blumstein, D. Farrington, and S. Moitra, "Delinquency Careers: Innocents, Amateurs, and Persisters," in N. Morris and M. H. Tonry, eds., *Crime and Justice: An Annual Review of Research* 6 (Chicago: University of Chicago Press,1985); D. Elliott, "Serious Violent Offenders: Onset, Developmental Course, and Termination," *Criminology* 32, no. 1 (1994), 1–21; D. Hamparion, R. Schuster, S. Dinity, and J. Conrad, *The Violent Few* (Lexington, Mass.: D.C. Heath, 1978); M. Wolfgang, R. Figlio, and T. Sellin, *Delinquency in a Birth Cohort* (Chicago: University of Chicago Press, 1972); M. Wolfang, T. Thornberry, and R. Figlio, *From Boy to Man, from Delinquency to Crime* (Chicago: University of Chicago Press, 1987).

13. E.g., thirty-five years after the Cambridge-Somerville study, Joan McCord found that 68% of the control group (i.e., those who had received no special treatment) had not died, been convicted of an index offense, or diagnosed as alcoholic, schizophrenic, or manic-depressive; "Consideration of Some Effects of a Counseling Programs," in S. E. Martin, L. B. Sechrest, and R. Redners, eds., *New Directions in the Rehabilitation of Criminal Offenders* (Washington, D.C.: National Academy Press, 1981); see also Wolfgang, Thornberry, and Figlio, *From Boy to Man.*

14. E.g., see Robert G. Wahler, "Contingency Management with Oppositional Children," in Wilson and Loury, eds., *Families, Schools, and Delinquency Preventions*, 112–131.

15. Philip J. Cook and John H. Laub, "Trends in Child Abuse and Juvenile Delinquency," in Hartmann, ed., *The Role of the Juvenile Court*, 110–112.

16. R. W. Thatcher, R. A.Walker, and S. Guidice, "Human Cerebral Hemispheres Develop at Different Rates and Ages," *Science* 236 (1987): 1110–1113.

17. For a discussion of adolescent decision making from a psychological perspective, see Elizabeth S. Scott, "Criminal Responsibility in Adolescence: Lessons from Developmental Psychology," in Thomas Grisso and Robert G. Schwartz, eds., *Youth on Trial* (Chicago: University of Chicago Press, 2000). See also Laurence Steinberg, Laurence and Elizabeth Cauffman, "Maturity of Judgment in Adolescence: Psychosocial Factors in Adolescent Decision Making," *Law and Human Behavior* 20, no. 3 (1996): 249–273; and D. Keating, "Adolescent Thinking," in S. Feldman and G. Elliot, eds., *At the Threshold: The Developing Adolescent* (Cambridge, Mass.: Harvard University Press, 1990).

18. E.g., see Joel Samaha, *Criminal Law* (St. Paul, Minn.: West, 1983), 52–75. In particular, see the *Model Penal Code* reprinted there, which distinguishes among purposely, knowingly, recklessly, and negligently committing crime; each is defined in terms of awareness of consequences.

19. See James Q. Wilson, *Thinking About Crime* (New York: Basic, 1975).

20. These notions are supported by learning theories of crime, as well as subcultural theories of crime. For related discussions of these theories, see

George B. Vold, Thomas J. Bernard, and Jeffrey B. Snipes, *Theoretical Criminology* (New York: Oxford University Press, 2002), particularly chap. 9.

21. Franklin Zimring, *American Youth Violence* (New York: Oxford University Press, 1998), 84.

22. See, e.g., George L. Kelling, "Juveniles and the Police," in Hartmann, ed., *The Role of the Juvenile Court*, 203–218.

23. James C. Howell, "Diffusing Research into Practice using the Comprehensive Strategy for Serious, Violent and Chronic Juvenile Offenders," *Youth Violence and Juvenile Justice* 1, no. 3 (2003): 219–245.

24. E.g., in the Philadelphia birth cohort study, about 3,500 different juveniles accounted for about 10,000 contacts with the police. It is not meaningful to describe the "average" offender, since over half of these youths had only a single contact while other youths had as many as thirty-five. See Thomas J. Bernard and R. Richard Ritti, "The Philadelphia Birth Cohort and Selective Incapacitation," *Journal of Research in Crime and Delinquency* 28 (February 1991): 33–54.

25. In the Philadelphia birth cohort study, about one-third of police contacts resulted in arrest. This is a high figure, however, since only 15% of police contacts resulted in arrest; Donald J. Black and Albert J. Reiss, "Police Control of Juveniles," *American Sociological Review* 35 (1970): 63–67;see also Donald J. Black, "The Social Organization of Arrest," *Stanford Law Review* 23 (1971): 1087–1111. Only 16% of police contacts resulted in arrest; Richard J. Lundmann et al., "Police Control of Juveniles: A Replication," *Journal of Research in Crime and Delinquency* 15 no.1 (1978): 74–91. Taking the lower figure found in these studies would increase the "success rate" that is computed for the juvenile justice system. None of these studies provides clear data on the number of different juveniles involved in these arrests, so we estimated that; see also Robert M. Terry, "Discrimination in the Handling of Juvenile Offenders by Social Control Agencies," *Journal of Research in Crime and Delinquency* 4 (1967): 218–230.

26. This estimate is based on national estimates conducted by the National Center for Juvenile Justice, based on Uniform Crime Report data for the year 2003 and as reported in Howard N. Snyder and Melissa Sickmund, *Juvenile Offenders and Victims: A National Report* (Washington, D.C.: Office of Juvenile Justice and Delinquency Prevention, U.S. Department of Justice, 2006), 152.

27. This estimate is based on national estimates, from research conducted by the National Center for Juvenile Justice and data for the year 2003, as reported in Snyder and Sickmund, *Juvenile Offenders and Victims*, 171.

28. This estimate is based on national estimates by the National Center for Juvenile Justice, revealing that in the year 2002, about 1% of all petitioned cases were waived to adult court; Snyder and Sickmund, *Juvenile Offenders and Victims*, 177.

29. Ibid., 177.

30. See, e.g., the first five articles in *Criminology* 26, no. 1 (February 1988).

31. For a review, see David P. Farrington, Lloyd E. Ohlin, and James Q. Wilson, *Understanding and Controlling Crime* (New York: Springer-Verlag,

1986), chap. 2. The controversy concerns whether the remaining "active" criminals continue to commit crimes at a high rate or whether their rate of offending declines with age.

32. Snyder and Sickmund, *Juvenile Offenders and Victims*.

33. For a review, see Paul Gendreau and Robert R. Ross, "Revivification of Rehabilitation: Evidence from the 1980s," *Justice Quarterly* 4, no. 3 (September 1987), 349–407.

34. Charles A. Murray and Louis A. Cox Jr., *Beyond Probation* (Beverly Hills, Calif.: Sage, 1979). The results of this study often are interpreted to mean that institutional corrections are more effective than community corrections. That interpretation overlooks the major point of the book, which is emphasized by its title: one can achieve major reductions in recidivism once one gets beyond simple probation.

35. Lawrence W. Sherman, Denise Gottfredson, Doris MacKenzie, John Eck, Peter Reuter, and Shawn Bushway, *Preventing Crime: What Works, What Doesn't, What's Promising* (Washington, D.C.: National Institute of Justice, Department of Justice, 1997).

36. Robert B. Coates, Alden D. Miller, and Lloyd E. Ohlin, *Diversity in a Youth Correctional System* (Cambridge, Mass.: Ballinger, 1978).

37. S. W. Henggeler, S. F. Mihalic, L. Rone, C. Thomas, and J. Timmons-Mitchell, *Multisystemic Therapy: Blueprints for Violence Prevention, Book Six*, Blueprints for Violence Prevention Series, series ed. D. S. Elliott (Boulder, Colo.: Center for the Study and Prevention of Violence, Institute of Behavioral Science, University of Colorado, 1998).

38. Lundmann et al., "Police Control."

39. See the response of government employees to the threatened closing of institutions in Illinois; Kenneth Wooden, *Weeping in the Playtime of Others* (New York: McGraw-Hill, 1976).

40. Don Andrews and Jim Bonta, *The Level of Service Inventory*, rev. ed. (Toronto, Ontario: MultiHealth Systems, 1995).

41. P. W. Harris and P. R. Jones, "Differentiating Delinquent Youth for Planning and Evaluation," *Criminal Justice and Behavior* 26 (1999): 403–434.

42. Sherman et al., *Preventing Crime*.

43. Dale G. Parent, Valerie Liter, Stephen Kennedy, Lisa Livens, Daniel Wentworth, and Sarah Wilcox, *Conditions of Confinement: Juvenile Detention and Correctional Facilities* (Washington, D.C.: Office of Juvenile Justice and Delinquency Prevention, U.S. Department of Justice, 1994).

44. Patricia M. Torbet, *Juvenile Probation: The Workhorse of the Juvenile Justice System* (Pittsburgh: National Center for Juvenile Justice, 1994).

45. David Altschuler, Troy Armstrong, and Doris Layton-MacKenzie, *Reintegration, Supervised Release and Intensive Aftercare* (Washington, D.C.: Office of Juvenile Justice and Delinquency Prevention, U.S. Department of Justice, 1999).

46. For a review, see Ted Rubin, *Juvenile Justice*, 2nd ed. (New York: Random House, 1985), chap. 7.

12

The End of Juvenile Delinquency?

Juveniles always have committed more than their share of crime, and the lessons of history suggest that this will not change in the near future. Thus, there is a sense in which the problem of juvenile delinquency cannot be solved because, in one way or another, it is a permanent and unchanging product of human nature.

But the modern problem of delinquency, as a crime against urban property (and more recently violent crime) committed by lower-class youth, appeared in Western Europe and America about two hundred years ago, when the modern, urban industrialized society was born. As other nations have gone through this same modernization process, they have experienced the same modern problem of juvenile delinquency. But because this modern problem appeared at some point in the past, it can also disappear at some point in the future. Thus, there is also a sense that the problem of juvenile delinquency actually could be "solved."

Solving that problem, however, cannot be accomplished merely by introducing a new juvenile justice policy. Rather, it requires changing the larger social conditions that gave rise to the problem. In 1825, New York City did not have a wave of juvenile delinquency because it had an inadequate juvenile justice system; neither did Chicago in 1899. Those waves of delinquency occurred because of the larger social conditions associated with modernization, urbanization, and industrialization. In the language of the time, it was neither the "peculiar weaknesses of the children's moral natures" nor their "weak and criminal parents" but, rather, the "manifold temptations of the streets" that were the source of the problem.

In both New York and Chicago, one possible response to the new problem of juvenile delinquency was to change those social conditions, but the reformers of the time ignored that possibility and focused instead on changing the behavior of juvenile delinquents and their parents. This response was chosen because it would have been very inconvenient to attempt to change the social conditions under which poor people lived.

Today, we continue to attempt to change the behavior of juvenile delinquents and their parents because it is inconvenient to attempt to change the larger social conditions. Yet ultimately it is those conditions that give birth to the problem of delinquency; changing them is the only way to solve the problem.

Traditional societies didn't have a problem of juvenile delinquency because young people were embedded in the larger social context. They were born into a fixed place in society, and they moved from childhood through adolescence and into adulthood with a clear understanding of the roles they would play in society. Such a firm understanding of one's role is not inconsistent with modern, urban, industrialized societies; for example, European countries that have well-developed apprentice programs for their youths have lower delinquency rates.[1] Many middle- and upper-class youths in our own society also sense they are on a clear track that moves them from childhood through adolescence and into an adulthood, and they believe they will have defined roles. Research suggests that such juveniles do not engage in serious acts of juvenile delinquency.[2]

Juveniles who engage in delinquency, however, often lack that sense of having a role and a place in society. This is particularly true for juveniles in the lowest social classes, who are essentially "left out" of meaningful roles. Such youths live in conditions that can generate extreme behavior.[3] Until such conditions change, we should expect to continue to have a serious problem with juvenile delinquency.

Subsequently, we can expect the most serious and chronic "juvenile delinquents" to come from the lowest socioeconomic class in society and from families that suffer from all the ailments of living in poverty and in an impoverished community. In nineteenth-century New York City and Chicago, it was the children of Italian, Irish, and Polish immigrants; in the latter half of the twentieth century, it was the children of African American families; and in the early part of the twenty-first century, it appears to be the newest wave of Hispanic immigrants, as these families struggle to find their social standing and economic footing in American society. Thus, as long as we focus on treating the delinquent and not the social conditions that lead to delinquency, the juvenile justice system will, without fail, reflect the inequalities and segregation of our society. Thus, our juvenile institutions will "play home" to the children of the poorest of today's society.

We doubt that people will choose to bring about the social changes that are required to solve the problem of juvenile delinquency; those changes would be very expensive and would challenge the role of the state, as well as the moral superiority of the reformers. Modern societies evolve in a direction of increasing complexity and structural integration. For instance, witness the changes to our society that have come about as a result of globalization. The face and shape of juvenile delinquency will, likewise, reflect the growing complexities and ailments of our ever-changing society.[4]

Thus, while we do not believe that people will ever solve the problem of juvenile delinquency, we do believe that the problem in its current form will "end." At that point, people will look back on the several hundred years of juvenile delinquency as a historically bound phenomenon, the way we view witchcraft in the Middle Ages[5] or violence in the American Wild West.[6]

In the meantime, we hope that we as a society give up the idea that the problem of juvenile delinquency can be solved simply by making a change in juvenile justice policy. As we have learned, such ideas lead only to another turn of the cycle of juvenile justice. Let us, instead, choose policies on the basis of actual performance, not on good intentions. Let us establish a fair, reasonable, and stable juvenile justice policy that responds to a problem that it has not created and cannot eliminate.

Finally, let us admit that we choose to live with the problem of juvenile delinquency because it is less costly and more convenient than choosing to solve it. That being the case, we hope that we stop describing delinquents and their parents as morally or intellectually inferior. Let us instead respond to delinquents in the spirit of the founders of the first juvenile court: as firm but kindly parents. We cannot ignore delinquent behavior, but we must not forget that, to some extent, it is the result of our own choices. Conscious of our own failings, let us be more gentle with the failings of these juveniles.

NOTES

1. David Greenberg, *Crime and Capitalism* (Palo Alto, Calif.: Mayfield, 1981), 64–66, 118–139. See Greenberg's introductory comments to his article "Delinquency and the Age Structure of Society," *Contemporary Crises* 1 (April 1977): 189–223, now reprinted in his book.

2. In theoretical terms, these juveniles are controlled by "commitment"—the rational investment in conformity and the risks of losing that investment through delinquency. See Travis Hirschi, *Causes of Delinquency* (Berkeley: University of California Press, 1969); and Thomas J. Bernard, "Structure and Control: Reconsidering Hirschi's Concept of Commitment," *Justice Quarterly* 4, no. 3 (September 1987)): 409–424.

3. E.g., Thomas J. Bernard, "Angry Aggression Among the 'Truly Disadvantaged,'" *Criminology* 28, no. 1 (February 1990): 73–96.

4. There are basically two contradictory views on how society might evolve. The first is essentially a Durkheimian view of the evolution of societies, in which people who are currently "left out" are gradually incorporated into meaningful roles; see Emile Durkheim, *The Division of Labor in Society* (New York: Free Press, 1965). Alternatively, a traditional Marxist view suggests that as capitalist societies evolve, more and more people are "left out," ultimately resulting in a violent overthrow of the established order.

5. E.g., Elliott P. Currie, "Crimes Without Criminals," *Law and Society Review* 3, no. 1 (August 1968): 7–32.

6. Eric H. Monkkonen, ed., *Crime and Justice in American History* (Westport, Conn.: Meckler, 1990), vol. 4.

Index

Actual performance. *See* Good
    intentions vs. actual performance
Actus rea, 77
ADHD (Attention Deficit
    Hyperactivity Disorder), 199
Adjudications
    best of both worlds, 122, 140,
        150–151, 193
    certainty of, 129, 192, 213
    compared to criminal trial, 78–79
    discretion in, 123–124
    due process rights in, 102, 108,
        110–112, 114–115, 127–128,
        132, 159
    See also Juvenile court, actual
        practices
Adolescence, 23, 35, 40, 44–45, 200, 233
    decision-making, 180, 184, 187–188
Age
    and criminal behavior, 12–15
    and criminal responsibility, 18–20
    of juvenile court jurisdiction,
        164–165, 189–190
Aid to Families with Dependent
    Children (AFDC), 81
American Bar Association, 128–129,
    194
Appeal
    certainty of adjudication, 226

juvenile's right to, 102, 104, 213
    why there are few appeals, 130–132
Aries, Philippe, 41–42
Atavistic criminal, 73

Balanced Approach
    adaptation in purpose clause,
        145–146
    origin of, 144–145
Best interests of the child
    and "get tough" movement, 140,
        144
    in original juvenile court, 76, 80,
        91, 99
    recommendations for future, 211
    in Supreme Court cases, 124, 130,
        135, 144–146
Best of both worlds, 122, 135, 140,
    150, 154, 193
    See also Worst of both worlds
Beyond a reasonable doubt, 96,
    107–110
Black, Justice Hugo, 112
Blackmun, Justice Harry, 112, 113,
    173
Blackstone, Sir William, 19
Blended sentencing, 152–154, 190
Blueprint Commission on Juvenile
    Justice (Florida), 195

Breaking the cycle, 208–209
Breed v. Jones, case of, 96, 113–116
Brennan, Justice William J., 173, 177
Burger, Chief Justice Warren, 109,
    112–113, 115

Casework agency, juvenile court as
    coercive treatment, 80–83, 91
Chancery Court, 59–60, 76, 80, 88,
    118, 133
Childhood, ideas of, 40–44, 210–211,
    214, 233
Children's Aid Society, 55–56
Coerced treatment, 80–83, 91
Compensating benefit, 139
Competency development, 151, 163,
    194
Colden, Cadwallader, 51–52
Concurrent jurisdiction, 166–167
    See also Prosecutorial waiver
Confidentiality of proceedings, 148
Confront and cross-examine
    witnesses, right to, 102, 127
Counsel
    at adjudication, 102, 127
    at disposition, 149–151
    lack of, 127–130
    at waiver, 98
Criminal defendants, delinquents as,
    117–118, 132–133, 141, 155,
    212
Criminal justice thermodynamics, 28,
    208, 219
Criminal (nonstatus) offenses, 35, 58,
    77, 83, 87, 95
    See also Juvenile crime
Crouse, Mary Ann, case of, 57–59
    expansion of state power, 67–68
    and the Fisher case, 83–85
    and founding of the juvenile court,
        76, 83
    and the Gault case, 105–106, 109
    and the O'Connell case, 59–62, 67
    unfair comparison, 66–67, 90
Cycle of juvenile justice, 3–4, 155,
    and "get tough" movement, 155–159
    and House of Refuge, 86–87
    ideas that drive, 4–6
    predictions about the future,
        207–208

return to leniency 188–189, 192,
    195–197
Supreme Court decisions, 116, 132

Darwin, Charles, 72
Death penalty, Supreme Court cases
    involving juveniles
    Roper v. Simmons, 178–183
    Stanford v. Kentucky, 175–178
    Thompson v. Oklahoma, 172–175
Decriminalization, of status offenses,
    16–18
Defendants, criminal, delinquents as,
    117–119, 133, 141, 155,
    212–215
Deinstitutionalization, of status
    offenses, 16–18
Dependent and neglected children,
    81–82, 85–87, 211, 215
Dispositions
    in actual practice, 152–154,
    in best of both worlds, 122, 135,
        140, 150
    compared to criminal trial, 80
    and "get tough" movement,
        122–130, 139–146, 151–154
    return to leniency, 195–197
    See also Punishments
Donovan, Frank R., 20
Double jeopardy, 114
    See also *Breed v. Jones*, case of
Douglas, Justice William O., 112–113
Due process
    in actual practice, 125, 127, 129,
        132–135, 139–141, 143, 150,
        153–154, 159, 167, 183, 193
    in blended sentencing, 153
    discretion vs. due process, 123
    economic interests of the right and
        powerful, 134
    expansion of power of state, 67, 91,
        135
    recommendations for future,
        212–213, 215, 226
    right to, 59, 61–62, 83–85, 212
    Supreme Court decisions, 95–96,
        98–99, 102–106, 108–109,
        111–113, 115, 118–119, 140
    waiving rights, 203
    See also Equal protection

Economic interests of the rich and
    powerful, 64–66, 88, 92, 118,
    133–134, 141, 156–157, 200
Eddy, Thomas, 50–51, 59, 71
Equal protection, 99, 101, 103–104,
    139, 226–227
    See also Due process
Evolving standards of decency, 173,
    176–177, 179, 188

Ferdinand, Theodore N., 35, 39
Fisher, Frank, case of, 83–85
    and earlier court decisions, 85
    and Supreme Court decisions 96,
    105–106, 109
Florida Department of Corrections,
    193
Forced choice
    and the cycle of juvenile justice,
    3–4, 116, 170, 188
    and first juvenile court, 87
    in the future, 206, 208
    and "get tough" movement, 155
    and return to lenient treatment, 189
    and Supreme Court decisions 116,
    188
Fortas, Justice Abe, 112–113, 124
Freud, Sigmund, 200

Gault, Gerald, case of, 96, 101–107,
    212
    and actual practice, 124–131, 148,
    150–151
    and earlier court decisions, 106
    and future court decisions, 187
    and other Supreme Court decisions,
    109, 111–115, 119, 139
"Get tough" movement, 8, 134, 136,
    210–214
    and the criminalized juvenile court,
    143–154
    the end of, 188–190, 193–197, 207
    and the idea of delinquent,
    140–143
    and the lessons of history, 154–159
    and youth in adult court, 163–165,
    168–169, 171, 184, 188
Good intentions vs. actual
    performance, 66, 67, 90–92, 119,
    134, 158, 202

earlier court decisions, 58, 60, 61,
    84, 85
House of Refuge, 58, 60, 61, 67
    in juvenile court, 135, 139, 151
    recommendations for the future,
    234,
Supreme Court decisions, 100, 103,
    105–106, 113, 117
    See also Unfair comparison
Green, Harvey, 20
Griscom, John, 50

Habeus corpus, 60, 62, 83,
Hall, G. Stanley, 200
Hardened criminals, delinquents as,
    210–211, 213–216, 227
    See also "Get tough" movement;
    Rational calculators
Harris, P. W., 225
Harsh punishments, 3–4, 27–29, 63,
    86–87, 92, 116, 118, 132, 155,
    194, 197, 207
    avoiding, 189–192, 197, 223
    See also Criminal justice
    thermodynamics; Forced choice
Healy, Dr. William, 200
Help vs. punishment, 58, 60–62, 74,
    76, 78, 84–85, 100, 103, 106, 112
Historical context, 10, 45, 49, 72, 87,
    117, 140, 206
Hoover, J. Edgar, 24, 26
House of Refuge, 39, 52–55, 76, 117,
    139, 163, 171, 183
    and economic interests of rich and
    powerful, 67–68, 88, 133
    as idea of juvenile justice, 64–65
    legal issues, 57–63, 83–86
    and unfair comparison, 66–67, 90
    See also Institutions

Ideas
    and cycle of juvenile justice, 3–4
    in history philosophy and law, 6
Ideas of childhood and adolescence,
    41–44
Ideas of juvenile delinquency, 5–6
    criminal defendants, 117–118,
    132–133, 141, 155, 212–213
    dependent and neglected children,
    81–82, 85–87, 211, 215

Ideas of juvenile delinquency
(*Continued*)
in earlier times, 33, 38–40, 209
hardened criminals, 210–211,
213–216, 227
mental illness, 198–199, 207, 216
naïve risk-takers, 215–219, 226
potential paupers, 50–57, 64, 74–
78, 81, 87, 209–211
predictions for the future, 223–228
small criminals, 117, 140–141, 155
that stay the same, 11, 15, 18, 20,
25, 28
Ideas of juvenile justice, 5–6
communication, 199, 218–219
due process protections, 118, 133
House of Refuge, 64
juvenile court, 88
predictions for the future, 223–228
tough punishment, 143, 155–156
treatment, 198–200
Immigration, 35, 38–39, 49, 54,
72–73, 233
Industrialization, 34, 36–37
Institutions, 39, 45, 48, 52, 58–59, 62,
106, 110, 210–211
See also House of Refuge
Intent, criminal, 77, 212, 214, 217

Jones, Gary. See *Breed v. Jones*, case of
Jury trial, 110–113, 130, 134, 135,
139, 183, 213, 226
Juveniles
in adult correctional facilities,
170–172
in adult court, 169–170
ideas of, 41–44
and proportion of crime, 11–15
and the death penalty, 172–183
Juvenile court
actual practices, 124–132
compared to criminal court, 78–80
changes to, get tough movement,
141–142, 146–154
jurisdiction of, 164–169
legal challenge to original court,
83–85
original juvenile court, 74–83
recommendations for the future,
223–228

Supreme Court decisions, 95–116
See also Adjudications; Dispositions
Juvenile crime
actual statistics, 12–15
belief in crime wave, 3–4, 11,
20–25, 29, 63, 86–87, 155
"get tough" movement, 141–142
Juvenile delinquency
end of, 232–235
origin of, 6, 8, 33–45
See also Ideas of juvenile
delinquency; Juvenile crime
Juvenile justice system court
actual practices, 124–132,
219–222
as cause of delinquency, 33, 38–39
changes to process of, 146–151
future of, 223–228
purpose of, 143–146
recreating in the adult system,
192–195
success of, 219–223
See also Cycle of juvenile justice;
Institutions; Judges; Police;
Probation

Kent, Morris, case of, 96–101, 212
and other Supreme Court cases,
103, 112–113, 125, 139, 187
recommendations for future, 218
as related to other measures of
transfer to adult court, 166–169,
190
Kupchik, Aaron, 192–193

Lathrop, Julia, 74–75, 86
Lawyer
representation by, 95, 97–100,
102–107
lack of representation by, 127–129
Lenient treatments
as cause of delinquency, 4, 25–27
mitigation of punishments, 18–20,
150, 183, 214
return to, 195–196
See also Criminal justice
thermodynamics; Forced choice
Lessons of history
cycle of juvenile justice, 63, 86–87,
91, 116–117, 132, 155, 197

economic interests of rich and powerful, 64–65, 88–89, 92, 118, 133–134, 156–157, 200–201
expansion of state power, 67–68, 91, 92, 120, 135, 158–159, 202–203
idea of juvenile delinquency, 64, 87–88, 92, 117, 132–133, 155, 197–198
idea of juvenile justice, 64, 88, 92, 118, 133, 155–156, 198–200
moral and intellectual superiority of reformers, 65–66, 89–90, 92, 118–119, 134, 157, 201–202
unfair comparison, 66–67, 90, 92, 119, 134–135, 157–158, 202
Lombroso, Cesare, 72

Mandatory waiver, 168–169
See also Waiver
Manifold temptations of the street, 54, 64, 72, 74, 88, 233
Marshall, Justice Thurgood, 112–113, 173
McKeiver, Joseph, case of, 96, 110–113
and certainty of adjudication, 130
Mens rea, 77, 174, 212, 216
Mitigation of punishments, 18–20, 150, 183, 214
See also Harsh punishments; Lenient treatments
Moral and intellectual superiority of reformers, 65–66, 89–90, 92, 118–119, 134, 157, 201–202
Morgan, Ted, 26
Murphy, Patrick, 131
Myth, of good old days, 12, 20, 29, 207

Naïve risk-takers, 215–218
Newsweek, 23, 24
Nixon, President Richard M., 109, 112, 116
North Carolina Sentencing and Policy Advisory Commission, 190
Notice of charge, 102, 127

O'Connell, Daniel, case of
and future court decisions, 85, 88, 95, 96, 103, 119, 139
and original juvenile court, 59–62, 67–68, 71, 74, 76, 78, 83, 85, 87, 88, 106, 133
and other court cases, 61–62, 83, 85, 90, 95, 96, 106
O'Connor, Justice Sandra Day, 181

Parens patriae, 58, 59, 60, 61, 62, 76, 78, 82, 84, 85, 88, 100, 101, 103, 104, 141, 143, 211
Parents
aspects that stay the same, 15, 20–22, 65, 144
and early court cases, 51, 58–59, 60–62, 67, 118
and early roles in delinquency definition, 15, 16, 17, 35, 64–65, 66, 89
and House of Refuge, 54, 56, 65
and ideas of childhood, 16, 20–22, 41–44
and original juvenile court, 17, 71, 72, 74, 76, 77, 80, 81, 82, 84, 87, 89–90, 92, 118, 124, 134, 157, 201
See also Parens patriae
Parole, life without, 166, 171–172, 175, 179, 194
Paupers, 50, 75, 76, 81, 87
delinquents as potential, 39, 50–55, 57, 60, 64, 65, 117, 118, 132, 133, 141, 155, 156, 184, 197, 198, 209–211, 215, 227
and the new juvenile court, 77, 78, 92
poor as potential, 71, 74, 77, 81, 92, 118, 184
prison and jail as solution for, 53, 54, 55, 64
prison and jail as source of, 27
vs. delinquents, 56–57
Philosophical context, 45, 64, 117, 206–207
Platt, Anthony, 73
Police
changes in behavior as a cause for delinquency, 12, 15
role in juvenile cases, 126, 147, 167, 191–192, 204, 215, 219–221, 223, 230
as a solution, 74

Poorhouses, 28, 52–54, 55, 57, 74, 86
Poor laws, 57, 64, 78, 88, 117
Power of the state, 61, 67–68, 89, 91, 92, 107, 120, 123, 133, 135, 141, 158–159, 202, 203, 207, 213, 227
Predictions about the future, 3, 8, 10, 11, 15, 18, 20, 29, 41, 66, 67, 207, 208, 223–228
Preponderance of the evidence, 107–109, 110, 123
Presumptive waiver, 168
Probation, 16, 17, 18
  and a balanced approach model, 144–145
  as a disposition, 81, 110, 111, 131, 152, 192, 196, 219, 221
  as a fact in early court cases, 97, 101, 110
  informal, 126, 127
  officer, role of, 80, 124, 126, 130, 146, 148–149, 151, 220, 221, 223, 224, 225
  successes and failures of, 221–222
Prosecutor, role of in juvenile court, 26, 130, 144, 148–152, 154, 156, 165, 168, 169, 190, 191, 203, 218
Prosecutorial discretion, 166–167, 169–170, 190
Prosecutorial waiver, 166–167, 169, 190–191.
  See also Concurrent jurisdiction
Punishments
  capital, 18, 36, 176–177, 181
  as "convincer," 220
  cruel and unusual, 173, 176, 178, 188
  harsh, 3, 4, 8, 25, 27, 28, 29, 63, 86, 87, 92, 116, 118, 132, 155, 189–192, 194, 197, 207, 208, 223
  mitigation of, 18–20, 33, 150, 166, 175, 180, 182, 183, 207, 209, 214
  as new purpose of juvenile justice, 117, 122, 125, 135, 145–146, 154, 158, 159, 166
  proportionality to offense, 80, 84, 151, 182
  threat of, 219–220

Rational calculators, 217–218
  See also Hardened criminals, delinquents as
Rehnquist, Justice William, 174, 181
Rendlelman, Douglas, 53
Reverse waiver, 190
Right to treatment, 140, 213, 226–227
Roper v. Simmons, case of, 178–183, 217

Scalia, Justice Antonin, 174, 176, 181–182
Self-Incrimination
  failure to exercise, 126–127, 226
  privilege against, 96, 102, 105
Simmons, Christopher. See Roper v. Simmons, case of
Small criminals, delinquents as, 140–143
Social history report, 78, 80, 114, 130, 150
Social work movement, 80–83, 87–89, 117
Society for the Prevention of Pauperism, 50–52, 55
Society for the Reformation of Juvenile Delinquents, 33
Socrates, 21
Solutions to problem of delinquency
  "get tough" movement, 139–154, 163–172
  House of Refuge, 39, 52–55, 76, 117, 139, 163, 171, 183
  juvenile court, 74–83
  recommendations for future, 223–228
  return to treatment, 195–196
  Supreme Court Cases, 96–116
  See also Good intentions vs. actual performance; Unfair comparison
Stanford v. Kentucky, case of, 175–178
State power. See Power of the state
Statutory exclusion, 165–166
Status offenses, 15–18, 79, 83, 87, 95, 108, 128
Stevens, Justice John Paul, 173, 175, 177
Stewart, Justice Potter, 105, 109, 113
Superiority of reformers, moral and intellectual, 65–66, 89–90, 92, 118–119, 134, 157, 201–202

Thermodynamics, criminal justice, 28,
    208, 219
Thompson v. Oklahoma, case of,
    172–175
Threat, 216, 219–221,
Time magazine, 23, 24, 25
Traditional mechanisms, for
    responding to youth, 34–37
Transcript, right to, 102–104, 131
Transfer to criminal court, 143,
    164–169
Treatment. See Coerced treatment;
    Dispositions; Help vs.
    punishment; Lenient treatments;
    Mitigation of punishments;
    Right to treatment; Solutions to
    problem of delinquency
Tuthill, Richard, 74

Undeserving poor. *See* Paupers
Unfair comparison, 66–67, 90, 92,
    119, 134–135, 157–158, 202
    See also Good intentions vs. actual
    performance
Urbanization, 7, 34, 37–39, 40, 44,
    65, 232

Victims
    and the balanced approach, 146
    inclusion in juvenile court, 149–150

Waiver
    discretionary, 176–168
    mandatory, 168–169
    presumptive, 168
    recommendations for future,
        218
    in regards to Kent decision, 96–101
    reverse, 190
Walker, Samuel, 28
Warren, Chief Justice Earl, 96,
    112–113, 116, 156
Wines, Frederick, 75
Winship, Samuel case of, 96, 107–110,
    123
    and certainty of adjudication, 125,
        127
    and other Supreme Court cases,
        111–115, 187
Women, and the first juvenile court,
    73–74
Worst of both worlds, 100, 113
    See also Best of both worlds

Youth
    in adult correctional facilities,
        170–171
    in criminal court, 169–170
    in population, 12–15

Zimring, Franklin, 218